SKIMMED

SKIMMED

BREASTFEEDING, RACE, AND INJUSTICE

ANDREA FREEMAN

STANFORD UNIVERSITY PRESS
Stanford, California

STANFORD UNIVERSITY PRESS
Stanford, California

Some of the research featured in this book was previously published in the *Fordham Law Review* and *Hastings Law Journal*.

Printed in the United States of America on acid-free, archival-quality paper

Library of Congress Cataloging-in-Publication Data is available upon request.

ISBN 978-1-5036-0112-3 (cloth)
ISBN 978-1-5036-1081-1 (electronic)

Cover design: Rob Ehle
Cover photo: The quadruplet daughters of Annie Mae and James "Pete" Fultz sit up for a birthday picture in the nursery of their home near Madison, N.C., May 19, 1947. Seated in the order in which they were born, the girls are, left to right, Mary Ann, Mary Louise, Mary Alice, and Mary Catherine. They will be a year old on May 23. (AP Photo)
Text design: Kevin Barrett Kane
Typeset by Motto Publishing Services in 10/14 ITC Galliard Std

To Alia and Serafino,
who are everything

CONTENTS

PROLOGUE

I never expected to fall in love with Pet Milk's poster children, "the famous Fultz Quads," or to feel such a deep affinity with their mother, Annie Mae Fultz. At first glance, Annie Mae and I appear to have little in common. Born Annie Mae Troxler on May 14, 1909, in Rockingham County, North Carolina, Annie Mae faced obstacles growing up Black and Cherokee in the rural South that I can only imagine. When meningitis robbed her of the ability to hear and speak as a child, she had to learn how to navigate a frequently hostile world without words. Despite these challenges, she met and married James "Pete" Fultz and gave birth to six healthy children before she became pregnant in 1945 with, according to her doctor, triplets.

In 2008, I learned that I was pregnant with triplets. I reacted with a mixture of joy and fear. Until that moment, I had firmly believed that my body was incapable of carrying children. With little to lose, I had taken advantage of my insurance policy's coverage of one treatment of in vitro fertilization. If my doctors had known that I would suffer the worst side effect of this process, ovarian hyperstimulation, they never would have let me try it. But, as luck had it, by the time they figured it out, the procedure had already worked. After my first ultrasound, only a few days into the pregnancy, I went straight home from the doctor's office to start indefinite bed rest.

When my next ultrasound detected three tiny heartbeats, my doctor immediately recommended selective reduction. This is a euphemism for sticking a large needle through my stomach to eliminate one of those heartbeats. Theoretically, the procedure would have increased the chances of survival for the other two. But after years of trying to have kids, I could not see my way to deliberately endangering any of those three potential lives. I went back home to bed and cried through the night. In the end, the universe made the decision for me. At my next visit, the ultrasound picked up only two heartbeats.

Two months before my due date, I went in for a routine checkup and learned that my cervix was almost fully dilated. The doctor sent me straight to the hospital. For the next week, the hospital staff tried desperately to keep the babies inside me long enough to inject their lungs with steroids. If it worked, it would increase their chances of breathing on their own when they came out. The hospital put me on magnesium sulfate, inducing what I can only describe as the worst feeling in the world. One morning, while I lay quietly suffering in my cot, alarms suddenly went off. A dozen hospital employees burst through the door on an urgent mission to revive one of the babies, whose heart appeared to have stopped. After throwing me around the bed and barking instructions, they determined that there was no danger. A machine had malfunctioned.

The next day, I decided that, regardless of the consequences, I could not stand another minute on the drip. Miraculously, the hospital staff agreed, took out the IV, and sent me home prepared for seven weeks of complete bed rest. The next morning, at 5:00 a.m., my water broke. Back at the hospital, the staff threatened to try to stop the babies from coming for another few days. My impatient children had other ideas. They were born an hour later and immediately whisked off to the NICU. Refusing pain medication and rest, I got out of my hospital bed and followed them there. The next few weeks were a sleepless blur. Every day, NICU doctors warned me that my babies, despite their progress, could die at any time. Every few hours, an alarm went off signaling that one of them had forgotten to breathe. I had to shake them to remind them to start again.

One consequence of their premature birth was that I never got around to reading any pregnancy or parenting books. I had no plan. I knew only one thing: I wanted to breastfeed. I quickly understood that this seemingly simple goal would be anything but. First, I learned that nursing a baby takes eleven hours a day. I did the math—nursing two babies takes twenty-two hours a day. Second, I discovered that my body did not want to cooperate with my mind. On such short notice, it simply could not produce enough milk for two infants who desperately needed to grow.

In a NICU, you have to weigh babies after every time they nurse. Any increase in weight is the measure of the amount of milk consumed. If the numbers fail to meet hospital standards, you have to supplement with formula. While my NICU neighbor cried as she filled shelf after shelf of the communal fridge with bottles of milk that her baby could not digest, I struggled to squeeze out even a few drops. A relentless routine took over my life. Pump for thirty minutes; try to breastfeed one baby for thirty minutes; weigh the baby; try to breastfeed the other baby for thirty minutes; weigh the baby; give the first baby half of the pumped milk; give the second baby the other half of the pumped milk; feed the first baby formula; then feed the second baby formula. Repeat all day and all night. I laughed and refused when the nurses encouraged me to take a night off, go home, and sleep. That would have been giving up.

The hospital released my babies a month later, when they stopped forgetting to breathe and gained enough weight. At home, the grueling regimen continued. Through it all, I tried to keep up with my job as a clerk for a federal judge. I worked on my laptop every time I pumped. I could not leave the house for more than a few minutes at a time or I would miss a crucial step in the sequence. Eventually, one child decided to give up nursing. The other persisted until she was four years old and there was simply no milk left. Even then, she threatened to continue until she was a teenager, because it comforted her. Although I never did get around to reading any parenting books, these early experiences laid the foundation for our close relationships. I knew what it felt like to face, day after day, the possibility of losing them, and I never forgot. I also had no illusions about the painful realities of pregnancy and childbirth.

My heart hurts at the thought of Annie Mae, stuck for weeks in the isolated and underequipped basement of Annie Penn Hospital, waiting for her babies to come. I doubt that anyone expected her to breastfeed, or would have, even if, in the end, she had given birth to only three, or two, or one baby. When her daughters arrived, a team of nurses immediately fed them formula through medicine droppers.

There is no record of what made Annie Mae's doctor, Fred Klenner, decide to auction off her lovely, thriving girls to a formula company. Did he approach the corporations, or did they approach him? Either way, it happened so quickly that the only thing Annie Mae likely knew for sure when they finally went home was that whatever her girls' fates might be, she would have little control over them.

I have devoted many years to researching, writing, and thinking about the complex and often hidden relationships between racism and food. The Fultz family's story touched me in a way that no other has. But, it is not my story. I am wary of White people telling Black people's stories. I wish that I had been able to interview the Fultz sisters and their families. All four sisters are gone now, and the relatives that run their Facebook page preferred to maintain their privacy when I reached out to them to talk. Because the Fultz sisters never documented their lives and I did not want to speak for them, I pieced together this narrative by relying on news items and magazine features. Poring over these words and pictures, I grew to love these girls and their mother and to feel the heartbreak of their losses. I wanted to share their story and connect it to the racism that continues to shape food law and policy. Their legacy of strength, beauty, and joy opens a window of defiance against the exploitation and commodification of Black girls' bodies that must end.

SKIMMED

A FORMULA FOR DISCRIMINATION

On May 23, 1946, in the rural southern town of Reidsville, North Carolina, a small miracle occurred. The woman responsible for this miracle was Annie Mae Fultz. Annie Mae was a tall, beautiful, Black-Cherokee mother of six children. She had lost her ability to speak and hear during a childhood illness.[1] Beginning at 1:13 a.m., Annie Mae gave birth, in short intervals, to the world's first recorded identical quadruplets.[2] Against the odds, each of these four tiny girls survived their first few hours and began to grow steadily. Word of their birth spread quickly throughout the country. Annie Mae's joy at her perfect new daughters was irrepressible, expressed in exuberant debates with friends and relatives at her hospital bedside about possible names for the girls. But this overwhelming happiness was far too short-lived.

Fred Klenner was the White doctor who delivered the girls in Annie Penn Hospital, in the basement wing reserved for Black patients.[3] Dr. Klenner quickly realized how his new patients' instant celebrity could benefit him. He began testing his controversial theories about vitamin C on the girls on the day of their birth, injecting them with fifty milligrams each.[4] He did not stop there. Dr. Klenner snatched the privilege of naming the girls from Annie Mae and their father, Pete, a tenant farmer on a nearby tobacco farm. Dr. Klenner gave all the sisters the first name Mary; then middle names belonging to his wife, sister, aunt, and great-aunt: Ann, Louise, Alice, and Catherine.[5]

Dr. Klenner was still not done. He began negotiating with formula

Trading on the popularity of the Fultz sisters and, later, the horror of Tyler's death, the formula industry sold Black families lies about formula. It invited Black women to believe that their formula purchases proved they were good mothers. Modern marketing continues to associate successful Black parenting with formula use. At the same time, popular images equate ideal parenting with White breastfeeding. The message is clear: because bad Black mothers use formula, good White mothers can raise themselves above them by breastfeeding. A Black woman, like Tabitha, who pursues the breastfeeding ideal but falls short of it is a criminal. A White woman who tries but fails is a saint.

Formula is a seventy-billion-dollar industry.[16] First designed to help infants without access to breast milk survive, formula now serves as a common replacement for human milk. The product allows many women to participate fully in the workforce, absent the structural support necessary to make both working and breastfeeding possible. Formula's transformation from emergency supplement to common food item arose from employment demands combined with pervasive marketing touting its near equivalency to breast milk. Medical professionals' and government programs' promotion and purchase of formula in exchange for contributions and support from the industry also create high demand for the product.

Black mothers use formula much more than White mothers. Black women and children suffer from conditions and diseases linked to formula feeding at significantly higher rates.[17] These disparities usually do not arise from lack of education or cultural or personal preferences about infant feeding. Instead, for the most part, they reflect the absence of choice created by government policies and unaccommodating social structures.[18]

An Unhealthy Alliance

The federal government, through the US Department of Agriculture (USDA), is the single largest purchaser of formula in the United States.[19] The USDA receives generous rebates on these purchases, paying only about 80 percent of the regular price of formula.[20] The rebates go directly into the budget of the federal nutrition program for Women, Infants, and Children (WIC), allowing it to provide services to a wider cross section of communities. WIC, in turn, distributes formula free to women in its program, significantly increasing the likelihood that these women will choose not to breastfeed their children.[21] The proportion of WIC participants who choose formula over breastfeeding is higher than in the general population.[22] Families that have received formula free through WIC go on to purchase it later. These sales compensate for the hit the companies take from the rebates, allowing them to come out ahead even with the discounts.[23]

The USDA also benefits from distributing free formula to poor families because most of the ingredients in formula are subsidized commodities that the agency is responsible for. Formula contains primarily corn (in the form of corn syrup) and either milk or soy.[24] Through the Farm Bill, corn, dairy, and soy receive significant subsidies, which incentivize farmers to produce more of these foods than consumers want.[25] The USDA, under its institutional mandate, must purchase and resell or distribute the resulting surpluses. The agency has found creative ways to do so. Its strategies include grocery store giveaways and collaborations with fast food companies to develop and promote products, such as Domino's seven-cheese American Legends pizza, that contain obscene amounts of milk.[26] The USDA also distributes foods made from subsidized commodities, such as chicken nuggets, cold cuts, and pizza, to low-income public school students through its National School Lunch Commodities Program.[27]

Using its WIC and School Lunch nutritional programs to redistribute the food that consumers do not want to buy is a particularly elegant, if suspect, solution. Women and children in need of government assistance cannot afford to refuse free food, regardless of its harmful effects on their health. Exploiting this vulnerability in the context of children's first food seems particularly egregious and has enduring consequences. The taste preferences that infants develop can last a lifetime. When high-sugar processed formula is their first food, they are likely to crave this type of food into adulthood.[28] This diet creates a high risk of obesity, type 2 diabetes, and other preventable conditions.[29]

Breastfeeding Facts
The health advantages of breastfeeding over formula feeding are numerous and virtually undisputed. The most esteemed global health entities, the World Health Organization and UNICEF, recommend breastfeeding for at least two years.[30] The American Academy of Pediatrics and the American College of Obstetricians and Gynecologists advise breastfeed-

ing for at least one year.[31] The US government, through multiple agencies, including the Centers for Disease Control and Prevention, the Surgeon General, and the Department of Health and Human Services, urges mothers to breastfeed for as long as possible to avoid a host of harms, from ear infections to premature death.[32] A UNICEF statement lays out exactly how high the stakes are: "Breastfeeding is the closest thing the world has to a magic bullet for child survival."[33] Globally, multiple studies link low breastfeeding rates to high infant mortality.[34] Of the twenty-six largest industrialized and twenty wealthiest nations, the United States has the highest rate of infant mortality.[35] This rate is twice as high for Black infants as for White ones.[36]

The factors that contribute to Black women's low breastfeeding rates are manifold, complex, and interconnected. They include race-targeted marketing, unequal distribution of resources for new mothers, and historical and present discrimination. Underlying these factors is the symbiotic relationship between the US government and formula corporations that gives the government a stake in the formula industry. This partnership harms women and infants in all communities but has a disproportionately negative impact on Black women and children.

Black women are overrepresented in the government assistance programs that distribute free formula.[37] Too often, Black women live in *"first food" deserts*, a term for neighborhoods bereft of government services for new mothers.[38] The hospitals in their communities dispense more free formula than hospitals in White neighborhoods do and discharge new mothers before they can receive guidance and support for nursing their newborns.[39] Laws designed to protect breastfeeding mothers at work do not apply to part-time jobs or the small businesses that employ many Black women. Under 1996 welfare-to-work reform, many Black women, who make up a disproportionate number of welfare recipients, must return to work before their infants are ready to stop nursing, under conditions that make breastfeeding impossible.[40]

Long-standing false narratives about Black mothers obscure the structural causes of their low breastfeeding rates. Collective belief in the existence of the Bad Black Mother leads to low or no investment in resources for breastfeeding Black mothers. It also underlies health care professionals' assumptions that Black women do not require nursing support or education. The Bad Black Mother stereotype has its roots in slavery.[41]

Southern slave-owning society created this trope to justify the inhumane practice of separating Black mothers from their children when slave owners sought out enslaved mothers as nurses and caregivers or sold or gave away their children.[42] The Bad Black Mother myth and its corollary of the self-sufficient Black child have persisted throughout history, evolving into the myth of the Welfare Queen.

In the modern age, the Welfare Queen is the most prevalent representation of a Black mother.[43] This fabled figure either cunningly reproduces for the sole purpose of acquiring government benefits or is too stupid to use birth control or exercise self-control. The money she extorts from taxpayers goes straight into her own pockets for designer clothes and high-end cars, with nothing left over to meet her children's needs.[44] In contrast, White mothers are perceived as kind, generous, and self-sacrificing. They spend all their time and money to ensure that their children have the best of everything. They are natural, beatific breastfeeders, willing to set aside their own happiness and physical comfort for their children's well-being, without question or complaint.

Stereotypes of Black mothers help formula companies sell their products. Bombarded by false images from the media and popular culture, Black women and their families often internalize these tropes. Many Black women seek to distance themselves from the historical indignity of breastfeeding White infants as slaves or wet nurses.[45] Black women may also resist breastfeeding, particularly in public, because of other stereotypes that hypersexualize them or cast them as angry and frightening, making it difficult for them to elicit empathy and support for the simple, nurturing act of breastfeeding.

Thanks to omnipresent images sexualizing Black women's bodies, the possibility of exposing a breast while nursing in public may bring on feelings of shame or of jealousy and possessiveness in male partners.[46] A fear of or aversion to breastfeeding can also stem from a lack of role models. The grandmothers who experienced and witnessed the legally enforced consequences of being Black women in a White supremacist society sometimes put up the greatest opposition to breastfeeding.[47]

Ubiquitous images of luminous White women breastfeeding their children creates a culturally collective belief that nursing is only for them. Acceptance of this false premise, created by companies for marketing purposes, does more than sell formula. It also justifies a lack of in-

tages, formula can harm infants while providing none of the substantial benefits of breastfeeding. Breastfeeding reduces the risk of suffering from sixty-eight different conditions, including ear, respiratory, and blood infections; sudden infant death syndrome; cancer; asthma; diabetes; diarrhea; and impaired speech, language, motor, and brain development.[61] In short, from a purely health-focused perspective, formula is unequivocally inferior to breast milk. When it is needed, formula is a lifesaver. But when it isn't, all infants should have equal access to the benefits of breastfeeding. All parents should have a real choice about how to feed their infants.

Breastfeeding Ideals

In a perfect world, to maximize physical and psychological benefits, infants would breastfeed exclusively for six months.[62] They would then continue to breastfeed while eating complementary foods until the age of two, and beyond then for as long as they desire.[63] To make this happen, a nursing parent must stay with their baby twenty-four hours a day to breastfeed on demand, bring the child to work with them, or pump milk into bottles that other caregivers can give to the infant. To maintain an adequate milk supply, a nursing parent must pump at regular intervals that generally coincide with the baby's individual feeding schedule and demands.

Although it is possible to pump by hand, the most efficient method is through use of an electric pump. Pumping, or expressing milk, requires a sink to wash hands, an electric outlet to plug in the pump, a private space, and a cool, clean place to store the bottles of expressed breast milk.[64] A pumping session can last up to thirty minutes. To breastfeed a baby outside the home, there must be a comfortable, private place to do so, free of disruptions and harassment. Without these basic elements in place, successful breastfeeding is unlikely. Parents with the time and desire to breastfeed often feel confined to their home to avoid public shaming. Attempts to intimidate women out of breastfeeding have taken place in locations as varied as a courtroom, a Victoria's Secret store, a homeless shelter, a church, a concert venue, and a restaurant, among others.[65]

Approximately 83 percent of White mothers and 82.4 percent of Latinx mothers report ever attempting to breastfeed, while 66.4 percent of Black mothers report ever trying.[66] Only 37 percent of low-income

Black women initiate breastfeeding.[67] At six months, 35.3 percent of Black women still breastfeed, compared to 56 percent of White mothers and 51 percent of Latinx mothers.[68] These disparities reflect the fact that Black mothers often have little or no choice about infant feeding. Many Black babies grow up in "first food" deserts that mimic and accompany the food deserts that are home to many low-income Black families. Kimberly Seals Allers coined the phrase *"first food" desert* to describe "communities with minimal to nonexistent breastfeeding resources and support mechanisms."[69] But the problem is even deeper.

In the food deserts typical of low-income, urban neighborhoods of color, there is a lack of fresh, healthy food. In contrast, in a "first food" desert, there is an ample supply of breast milk, but laws and policies cut it off, making it inaccessible. Processed food, in the form of formula, replaces fresh food (breast milk), even when both are available. It might be more accurate to call this a *"first food" swamp* instead of a "first food" desert. A food swamp is an area rampant with establishments selling high-calorie junk food and fast food.[70] A "first food" swamp inundates Black women with formula through WIC, prominent placement in drugstores, and other marketing tactics. Because the Bad Black Mother myth crosses class lines, the "first food" swamp is not limited to low-income communities. It is everywhere and carries serious health consequences.

Black infants suffer more from these consequences than White, Latinx, American Indian/Native Alaskan, and Asian/Pacific Islander infants do.[71] In 2011, out of 100,000 Black infants, 1,051 died, in comparison to 523 White infants, 458 Latinx infants, 445 American Indian/Alaskan Native infants, and 378 Asian/Pacific Islander infants.[72] Black women and children also experience higher rates of diseases and conditions related to formula feeding, including eczema, diabetes, cancer, blood infections, and asthma.[73]

Black women may also derive unique benefits from breastfeeding. An epidemiological study found that breastfeeding could counteract a specific form of breast cancer to which Black women are particularly susceptible after multiple childbirths.[74] Although race-based medical studies are problematic on many levels,[75] this type of research has the potential to lay medical and scientific foundations for programs designed specifically to increase breastfeeding in the Black community. To date, Black women have been the primary engineers of these efforts. This type of grassroots organizing, although powerful, can go only so far without the funding and support of government entities.

Critical Race Theory and Intersectionality

The argument that low breastfeeding rates among Black women is a systemic and not a personal problem, caused and perpetuated by seemingly neutral laws and policies, embodies a Critical Race Theory (CRT) perspective. CRT encompasses diverse and evolving views but rests on a few fundamental principles. One is that racism is built into our social, legal, and political systems. This often makes it invisible. It is not dependent on bad actors or blatantly racist rhetoric, although these things confirm the persistence of White supremacy. Even in the absence of forthright declarations of racial superiority, racism thrives in the replication of White privilege in every important social sector: housing, employment, education, criminal justice, police violence, consumer credit, social services, property, and health. Racism is permanent.[76] Recognizing that law and policy play an important role in maintaining racial disparities in all these areas, CRT scholars focus on how to use these powerful tools to shift social power and eliminate racial subordination.

Critical race theorists believe that stories matter.[77] The language of law often puts itself forth as objective, unattached to human experience or suffering. In the face of this purported neutrality, personal narratives bring forth the realities of lives shaped by law and policy. These stories can affirm the dignity of all human beings and unite people across social boundaries. And although statistics often overshadow stories, data is not the sole preserve of those who claim objectivity and advocate for color-blindness. Statistics overwhelmingly support the existence of structural racism in all sectors of society. They bring to light racial disparities in breastfeeding that call for an explanation more complex than simple cultural preferences. Critical Race Theory and Empirical Methodology, or eCRT, is an important new field that has paved the way for this examination of breastfeeding and health disparities.[78]

Intersectionality, one of the greatest insights of CRT, is particularly relevant to this issue. Intersectionality recognizes that it is misleading and harmful to divide identities such as race, gender, and class into discrete categories.[79] In people's lived experiences, these social markers are so intertwined as to be inextricable. Even more importantly, possessing multiple identities subject to oppression and marginalization results not just in compounded experiences of discrimination but in entirely novel ones. The law has lagged in recognizing and seeking to remedy these unique harms.

Attempts to equate Black and White women's experiences with breastfeeding ignore the realities of intersectionality. Even this analysis, which compares the two, excludes the experiences of many other women, making the problem appear to exist solely in the Black/White binary. That is not the case. All women of color have unique challenges to breastfeeding and confront specific forms of racism and other oppression. In this book, I focus primarily on the disparities between Black and White breastfeeding rates. In doing so, I do not intend to erase the experiences of other women. Instead, I hope to increase access to breastfeeding for all women.

Almost every book on breastfeeding, whether based in history, politics, or parenting philosophy, ignores or glosses over the profound differences in the circumstances that shape how Black and White mothers decide to feed their infants. This book fills that gap, exposing the cultural assumptions and prejudices that disguise White women's privilege. It challenges the accepted wisdom that White mothers represent a gold standard of parenting that most Black mothers fail to achieve. It illuminates Black women's resistance and resilience by uplifting their stories.

Road Map

The following chapters weave together the story of the Fultz sisters with a legal, political, cultural, and social analysis of low breastfeeding rates in the Black community. Chapter 1 begins in the hospital with Annie Mae awaiting the birth of her soon-to-be celebrity daughters. It follows the life of the Fultz family until the girls turn six and begin attending school. Chapter 2 presents a history of infant feeding in the United States from a racial perspective. It explores the lasting impact of slavery on Black mothers, documenting changes in infant feeding practices associated with Emancipation, Reconstruction, and the Great Migration of Blacks from the South to the North between 1915 and 1970. It traces evolving attitudes toward women's and physician's roles in infant feeding from the emergence of the field of pediatrics at the beginning of the twentieth century to the present.

Chapter 3 examines the evolution of formula marketing to Black women. It begins with a brief history of race-based marketing to Blacks in the United States. It describes formula marketing to Black women from its origins in the late 1940s to its shift to social media platforms in the present. It returns to the story of the Fultz girls during their school-age years. Chapter 4 explores the stereotype of the Bad Black Mother. It surveys portrayals of Black motherhood from slavery-era publications through film history to modern news items. This historical journey demonstrates the link between perspectives and stereotypes popularized during slavery and myths and misperceptions about Black mothers today.

Chapter 5 describes the laws, policies, and practices that create obstacles to Black women breastfeeding. The US government has a complicated relationship to breastfeeding. On one hand, its agencies have unequivocally and unwaveringly recommended it, reflecting decades of medical and scientific research revealing its benefits. On the other hand, the government provides enormous support to the formula industry, primarily as its best customer. Chapter 6 engages in an analysis of potential solutions to racial disparities in breastfeeding rooted in constitutional principles, innovative international approaches, and milk commodification. Finally, chapter 7 follows the Fultz sisters' lives after the end of the Pet Milk contract.

When possible, I use gender-neutral language to recognize that not every breastfeeding woman is a mother and that not every person who breastfeeds is a woman. Nonetheless, the words *mother* and *woman* dominate these pages. I do not intend these words to exclude nonparent and nonfemale breastfeeders. Individuals who breastfeed include fathers, nonbiological mothers, caregivers unrelated by blood, and gender-nonconforming parents. By focusing primarily on the experiences of Black mothers here, I hope to inspire reforms that will benefit everyone.

This book may appear to promote the idea that breast is best. This concept is troubling to some feminists who perceive this slogan as an oversimplification of medical research. This assertion, stated or implied, may also seem to degrade the choices of parents who use formula to maintain their employment or their personal autonomy or for any other reason. That is not my intention. This book's urgent call for structural reform is rooted in the imperative to create genuine, universal choices about infant feeding. Its advocacy and analysis come with no judgments.

Chapter 1

THE FAMOUS FULTZ QUADS

Annie Mae Fultz could not afford to let anything go wrong with her pregnancy. Her doctor, Fred Klenner, had detected three tiny heartbeats inside her. It was 1946. Annie Mae was a tall, strong, thirty-seven-year-old half-Black, half-Cherokee woman from Tennessee.[1] Dr. Klenner, although originally from Pennsylvania, happily adhered to southern racial norms.[2] He had separate waiting rooms for Blacks and Whites in his downtown Reidsville, North Carolina, office. The old-fashioned decor of his practice matched his dated views. His segregated waiting rooms gave way to treatment rooms full of ancient furniture and unusual medical instruments.[3] His walls displayed White supremacist literature and, later, a "Vote for George Wallace" poster.[4] He vigorously defended Hitler as misunderstood to anyone who would listen.[5] The local hospital where he delivered babies, Annie Penn Memorial, relegated Black mothers to the basement.[6] Despite his unapologetic racism, Annie Mae had faith in Dr. Klenner's medical abilities.

Annie Mae had plenty of challenges to overcome in the face of the growing lives inside her. A childhood battle with spinal meningitis had robbed her of the ability to hear or speak, rendering the possibility of a medical emergency, when urgent communication would be essential, even more frightening.[7] On the tobacco farm where Annie Mae's husband, James, a fifty-nine-year-old Black man known to all as Pete,[8] toiled as a tenant farmer, there was no electricity.[9] The family had no car, and the road leading out to the farm was rutted, long, and lonely. On Dr. Klenner's advice, Annie Mae left her six children in their father's care and moved into Annie Penn's basement to wait out her delivery.[10] To pass the long hours that followed on her hospital cot, Annie Mae conversed with her nurse, Margaret Ware, through gestures and lip-reading.[11]

The odds that all three of Annie Mae's triplets would survive were slim. Although any mother expecting triplets must come to terms with multiples' low survival rate, Annie Mae confronted more obstacles than most. Advances in modern medicine that could have eased the birth process had yet to reach the basement. The neglected ward housed Annie Penn's least valued patients and its oldest, shabbiest equipment. Annie Mae's meager bedside boasted only bare-bones paraphernalia: a single-unit hot plate and a ten-quart kettle.[12]

At 1:20 a.m. on the morning of Thursday, May 23, 1946, Annie Mae let Margaret know that the babies were on their way.[13] Dr. Klenner came quickly to supervise Annie Mae's labor, which was surprisingly fast and easy. Three babies arrived like clockwork, at three-minute intervals.[14] Annie Mae, Margaret, and Dr. Klenner then received a shock when a fourth baby, hiding behind her sister, suddenly appeared. Margaret ran upstairs to commandeer help from other doctors and nurses. Under Dr. Klenner's instruction, they filled hot-water bottles, wrapped the four tiny babies in cotton gauze, and laid them next to each other for warmth while feeding them formula through medicine droppers.[15] Miraculously, all four girls survived their first few hours, becoming the first living identical quadruplets on record in the United States.[16]

Back on the tobacco farm, Pete received a late-night visit from his breathless brother-in-law, Bill Troxler, who exclaimed, "Man, you better get up to the hospital quick. You got a whole bunch of babies. They's so many of them, they laying 'em cross-wise of the bed."[17] Pete's reaction was no less dramatic. He fell back on the bed, letting out a cry of "Good God!" and declared, "I never heard of so many babies at one time."[18] But Pete was no stranger to large families. Each of his two brothers had fifteen kids, with four sets of twins among them.[19] Both Annie Mae and Pete were also twins.[20]

Perhaps this shared experience formed part of their unlikely attraction. The couple, twenty years apart in age, married in Guilford County,

North Carolina, in 1930 after a three-month courtship.[21] Their first child, Doretha, was sixteen when her sisters arrived. She had married three years earlier at age thirteen.[22] The girls' other siblings were George, who was fourteen; Charles, who was nine; twins Bernard and Frances Lee, who were also nine; and James Jr., who was one.[23] Longevity ran in the family in addition to multiples. Pete's mother, who lived with them, was still going strong at the ripe old age of 104.[24]

Pete visited Annie Mae and the babies at Annie Penn the next morning, but he could not stay long. He had never made more than five hundred dollars a year in his life,[25] and he now had ten children, a wife, himself, and his mother to feed. Nonetheless, he left the hospital feeling hopeful. Dr. Klenner predicted that, if the girls lived through their first ten days, they would have a normal life expectancy.[26] Neither Pete nor Annie Mae could foresee that the actions Dr. Klenner took on the girls' first day of life and in the following weeks would undermine his optimistic declaration and their happiness.

In a radical departure from standard medical practice, as the Fultz sisters teetered on the edge of life and death, Dr. Klenner unnecessarily injected each of them with fifty milligrams of ascorbic acid.[27] Dr. Klenner had arrived at the conclusion, after curing his wife of gum disease many years back, that vitamin C had special healing powers. He devoted his life's work to proving this theory, firmly believing that vitamin C could cure polio and twenty-nine other diseases.[28] Although his peers ridiculed him, patients traveled from all over the country to avail themselves of this miracle remedy.[29]

Dr. Klenner was determined to show the experts they were wrong about him.[30] He grew up in a small White Pennsylvania community, where he inherited his father's fondness for Adolf Hitler. He was the first member of his family to attend college. At Duke, he was a perpetual outsider. While there, he fell in love with Annie Hill, valedictorian of her nursing class, a basketball guard, and the second woman ever to receive a bachelor's degree in science from the university.[31] Her high-society family was less than thrilled about her choice of a suitor. Fred was a Yankee and a Catholic. His ultraconservative political views upset Annie's parents. He openly supported the Nazis and joined the White supremacist John Birch Society, the White Citizens' Council, and the Christian Crusade.[32] He vocally opposed integration, public education, communism, feminism, President Franklin D. Roosevelt, and Dr. Martin Luther King Jr. He was determined to earn his in-laws' acceptance in any way possible.

Dr. Klenner interpreted the unexpected appearance of the Fultz sisters as a sign that, with these subjects at his disposal, he would soon prove his worth. He never sought consent from Annie Mae or Pete for the experiments he performed on their girls. The babies could not object to the shots they received and were unlikely to live to tell the tale if anything went wrong. But the sisters defied everyone's expectations by growing steadily. Emboldened by their increasing strength, Dr. Klenner continued their daily injections, incrementally raising their dosage and carefully documenting their reactions for a research paper.[33]

Outside Annie Penn's basement, the world got word of the miraculous birth. Media representatives from around the country flocked to the hospital. Its switchboard flashed all day and night as exhausted operators fielded calls from every time zone. Universal Studios sent a representative to record footage of the girls. Even the *New York Times* reported on the "Girl Quadruplets Born" in small-town North Carolina.[34] Bodyguards stood watch outside Annie Penn's doors to detect and deter potential kidnappers.

The Fultz Quads were instant celebrities. Everybody wanted a piece of them. The residents of Reidsville, a town of thirteen thousand near the Virginia border, basked in the sudden, unexpected glow of the national spotlight.[35] Before the Fultz sisters came along, Reidsville's only claim to fame was being home to Lucky Strikes cigarettes. Still, while the rest of the country avidly consumed the news of these miniature VIPs, the local *Greensboro Daily News* relegated the story of their birth to page nine, with no picture.[36] The paper staunchly reserved its coveted front pages for White news.

Inside the hospital, Annie Mae's recovery went well.[37] She was a private person, unimpressed by the splash that she and her babies had made and unwilling to make a statement to the press. With an ever-watchful eye on the girls' progress, Annie Mae simply smiled and shook her head no every time her nurse Margaret playfully told her that someone else had asked to keep one of her adorable babies.[38] But while the women joyfully teased each other, Dr. Klenner was setting in motion a series of events that would lead Annie Mae to lose not just one but all four of her precious new daughters.

As soon as Annie Mae was well enough to entertain visitors, she began the happy task of selecting baby names. No sooner did she settle on Betty, Clara, Billie, and Anne than a group of friends talked her into Laurinda, Belinda, Lucinda, and Magenda.[39] After she committed to those names, an aunt persuaded her to change them again, and Annie Mae decided definitively on Rosetta, Loretta, Margretta, and Henrietta.[40] In the end, none of her choices stuck. Instead, Dr. Klenner stepped in and named the girls himself, after members of his own family. He gave each girl the first name Mary and then assigned them the names of his wife, Ann; daughter, Louise; aunt Alice; and great-aunt Catherine. None of the sisters ever went by Mary.

Observing this theft of Annie Mae's right to name her own daughters, Margaret Ware chalked it up to just one more indignity that rich White folks had the privilege of inflicting on poor Black folks. As she explained, "At that time, you know, it was before integration, they did us how they wanted. And these were very poor people. He was a sharecropper, Pete was, and she couldn't read or write."[41] Outside Annie Penn, most people never knew of Dr. Klenner's betrayal. Newspapers around the country reported the couple's fondness for the "grand old name" Mary, some speculating that they all received the same name because of their likeness. Others assumed that Annie Mae had chosen to honor her doctor by naming her girls after his relatives.[42]

Five days after the sisters' birth, a newsreel photographer first captured them on film with their parents.[43] The sweet girls, distinguishable only by their identification bracelets, continued to sleep together in one bed.[44] When the sisters were eleven days old, Dr. Angus McBryde, the head of obstetrics at Duke medical school, Dr. Klenner's alma mater, examined them. He gave them a greater than 50 percent chance to live.[45] At six weeks old, each of them weighed almost five pounds, kicked vigorously, and could lift themselves up to reach their bottles.[46] Reporters praised both their skills and their beauty, emphasizing their White features. One reporter rapturously described them as having "light brown complexions, silky, straight, half-inch long black hair, high cheek bones, and beautifully molded features."[47] With each passing day, it became clearer that the sisters would not just survive but grow into healthy, lovely, and highly photogenic girls.

While Annie Mae looked forward to bringing her girls home to the farm where they could play with their father, sisters, and brothers, Dr. Klenner made other plans. Without consulting Annie Mae and Pete, he entered into negotiations with three formula (then evaporated milk) manufacturers: Carnation, Borden, and Pet Milk.[48] The corporations vied for the right to sponsor the nation's and possibly the world's first identical quadruplets and to use the light-skinned girls as the poster children for their first foray into marketing targeted at Black mothers.

Dr. Klenner got the most favorable terms from the St. Louis–based Pet Milk and selected the company for the opportunity.[49] He commandeered his sister-in-law, Susie Sharp, an attorney who would go on to become the first woman ever elected chief justice of a state supreme court, to oversee the contract.[50] Under its terms, Susie become the girls' trustee. This was only one of the many perks that Dr. Klenner and his family got out of the deal. Pet Milk agreed to purchase land for the Fultz family from Dr. Klenner's father-in-law for $6,000 (the equivalent of over $77,000 in 2019).[51] The land was high on a hilltop and consisted of rugged terrain unsuited to any type of farming. The purchase was a steal for Dr. Klenner's in-laws. Most importantly, through the contract, Dr. Klenner found a way to keep himself active in the girls' lives. The deal meant that he could continue his experiments on them uninterrupted. He could also take credit for their good health, should they continue to thrive.

In exchange for exclusive rights to the sisters for its marketing purposes, Pet Milk offered to support the girls until they turned ten years old. By the terms of the agreement, Pet Milk would provide the family with formula, food, medical care, a nurse, and a small, regular income.[52] It would also construct a four-room house on the land it purchased from Dr. Klenner's father-in-law. The home would come complete with a faucet, electricity, a gas hot plate, and a nursery, designed according to Dr. Klenner's specifications.[53] Pete could work the surrounding land himself, freeing his family from the yoke of tenant farming. Pet Milk even threw a mule into the deal. When the girls turned twenty-one, the farm would belong to them. Pet Milk also persuaded Bennett College, a private, historically Black liberal arts college, to offer scholarships to the sisters upon their high school graduation.

On paper, the agreement looked like an offer that Annie Mae and Pete could not afford to refuse. They had never had their own land to farm. Their children's education had always been sporadic, dictated by the demands of household chores. They had never dreamed that any of their children would get a college education. That White people would offer these opportunities to a poor Black family seemed surprising, if not too good to be true. Many of their friends and family could not believe Annie Mae and Pete's luck. They encouraged the couple to seize the opportunity quickly, before it disappeared, as so many "gifts" from White people tended to do.

Some of their more cautious family members tried to warn Pete about the poor value of the land before he signed the papers. His brother-in-law Bill enlisted a farm agent to show Pete the incurable defects of the 147 acres. The infertile, hilly terrain would be impossible to reach by road whenever it rained.[54] The land was not suited to tobacco farming, which was the only type of work that Pete knew. Pete listened but was undeterred. Bill's wife, Audrey, bemoaned Pete's stubbornness, lamenting that "he wanted to do it his way."[55] Pete's recalcitrance was understandable. For a man on the verge of sixty, with many mouths to feed and few, if any, other prospects to advance beyond tenant farming, independence would be irresistible.

Annie Mae would do anything that she believed would help or protect her babies. Despite her kind and quiet demeanor, when confronted with a threat to her children, she became fierce. Once, when a group of boys played too roughly with her sons, she came at them with a double-barreled shotgun. Another time, when she witnessed Pete punishing the kids too severely, she threw him against the wall.[56] With the lives of her daughters still in Dr. Klenner's hands, she may not have dared question his wishes and authority. On August 3, 1946, just over two months after the girls' birth, Annie Mae and Pete signed the agreement. One of Annie Mae's nurses at Annie Penn, Elma Saylor, viewed the transaction as one of pure exploitation. In her eyes, Dr. Klenner, an upper-class White man, was taking advantage of poor Black folks, who Elma herself held in low esteem as "backwoods people."[57]

Black tenant farmers in the South, although considered slightly better off than sharecroppers, lived in perpetual poverty and squalor. Their small log or clapboard houses had no windows or screens, and their bathrooms were outdoor privies only a few yards from the house. Their diets consisted almost exclusively of cornbread, corn mush, fatback pork, and molasses. The poor state of the roads leading up to their farms kept them socially isolated and vulnerable to sudden, unanticipated economic ruin. As a nurse, Elma enjoyed greater stability and an elevated social status.[58]

With the contract in place, Dr. Klenner released the girls from Annie Penn Hospital on October 20, 1946, almost five full months after their birth. Despite their celebrity status, they could not travel home in a dignified fashion. They rode to the new farm in two McLaurin Funeral Home ambulances, the vehicles designated by the hospital for "colored" transport. Their two nurses, Margaret and Elma, went with them. They helped the girls settle in and ensured that Dr. Klenner's prescribed daily injections of vitamin C would continue. Pet Milk paid for the hours that the nurses worked on the farm.

Despite the girls' departure from his direct care, Dr. Klenner checked on them regularly to chart their progress. He ordered a glass window for the girls' new nursery, then took out an advertisement in the *Reidsville Review* announcing daily public viewings from 2:00 to 4:00 p.m.[59] These actions furthered a long tradition of putting Black folks on display for White folks to observe. Human zoos exhibited Africans, Native Americans, Filipinx, and other people of color beginning in Europe in the 1800s and continuing into the 1900s in North America at venues including the St. Louis World's Fair, the Cincinnati Zoo, and the Bronx Zoo.[60]

The most infamous example of this type of exploitation began in 1910 when an exotic animal dealer lured twenty-year-old Saartjie Bartman from her home in Cape Town, South Africa, to London, England.[61] After she arrived, exhibitors put Saartjie, known as Sarah, in cages as a sideshow act. She then moved to Paris, where racial anthropologists claimed and then abused her. After only four years in Europe, she turned to prostitution and drinking.[62] After her death, Paris's Museum of Mankind exhibited her skeleton, brain, and sexual organs until 1974, twenty-eight years after Dr. Klenner put Alice, Catherine, Louise, and Ann on display in Reidsville.[63]

North Carolina was no stranger to dehumanizing displays. In 1931, fifteen years before the Fultz sisters' birth in the hospital named after his mother, Annie Penn,[64] tobacco magnate Charles Penn constructed a model of an antebellum plantation home complete with slave quarters in Leaksville, a town a half hour's distance from Reidsville.[65] Penn commandeered a former slave of his family, whom he called Uncle Buck, to live in the cabin with his wife, "Aunt Fanny," to give the plantation an aura of authenticity. Not content with their mere presence on the grounds, Penn compelled the couple to dress and cook as though it were still the 1850s and they were still his family's slaves.

The roads leading out to the Fultz farm were dangerous and unpredictable. When it rained, the winding road connecting the farm to the highway became so muddy that it was impossible to use. Visitors who came to view the girls left their cars on the main road and hiked the two to three miles in to the farm. Despite these formidable obstacles, journalists reported that between eight and nine hundred visitors had braved their way out to the farm to see the girls before they turned one year old. They marveled at the beauty and strength of the Fultz sisters, who, at seven months old in December 1946, each weighed almost eighteen pounds.[66] Reporters willingly attributed their excellent health to their steady diet of Pet Milk.[67]

As the family adjusted to their new life and the stream of strangers coming through their home, Margaret continued to assist them occasionally as a part-time nurse.[68] Elma, who had lost her two-year-old daughter to polio, resigned from Annie Penn Hospital to become the girls' full-time nanny. Pet Milk paid her salary.[69] The farmhouse was very small, with fourteen people crowded into its four modest rooms. Confronted with these close quarters, Elma chose to sleep in a bed in the closed-in front porch. She shared the bed with Margaret whenever Margaret spent the night.[70]

A rare opportunity to photograph the famous sisters came on their first birthday. On this occasion, journalists began noticing and reporting on the girls' distinct personalities.[71] One photographer allowed to enter the inner sanctuary of their home observed that Catherine, the surprise baby who had hidden behind her sisters, sucked on her fingers until the camera's flashbulb popped. At that point, the entire nursery erupted into chaos, with strollers circling the room and Louise emitting a sound like a fire truck.[72]

Although Annie Mae and Pete did not give statements to the press, Elma had no qualms about communicating with journalists. Perhaps ungenerously, Elma told a reporter that Louise was "the meanest of the four. She wants to fight all the time."[73] Clearly resenting the influence that Dr. Klenner continued to have over the girls' lives, Elma then blamed this bad behavior on his insistence that the girls remain isolated from other children.[74] Compelled to spend every day on the farm, they lacked opportunities to build social skills.

On the weekends after their first birthday, the onslaught of visitors continued, creating a long line of cars on the obscure part of the road closest to the farmhouse. The girls wore identification bracelets, even as they grew into toddlers, sometimes confounding even Annie Mae and Elma with their near identical appearances. They also had name tags on their cribs. During the long summer days on the farm, Elma strove to amuse the girls with their meager collection of toys, while Annie Mae engaged in the more arduous tasks of cooking, cleaning, and washing their cloth diapers and clothes.[75] Pete, now sixty, focused on trying to force the farm's stubborn terrain to yield a valuable crop.

In November 1947, with the girls just past one and a half years old, Annie Mae discovered that she was pregnant again. Pete did not take the news well. He confessed his apprehension to Alex Rivera, a reporter for the *Pittsburgh Courier* who documented the sisters' early lives. Sitting outside with Alex, whittling on a stick while Annie Mae and Margaret dressed the girls for a photo shoot, Pete confided: "[S]he's gone and got pregnant again. I sure wish to God she hadn't got that way."[76] Margaret told Alex that Pet Milk had paid for X-rays and that the film revealed three distinct spines.[77] This would have upset Pete even more. In the end, though, it turned out that Annie Mae would not give birth to multiples this time. Three weeks later, Alex reported that Annie Mae was expecting only one child.

Alex's coverage of the Fultz family throughout the girls' childhood represented much more than a celebrity beat. Born in Greensboro, North Carolina, to the son of a member of the NAACP, Alex was a natural activist in the struggle for racial equality.[78] After attending Howard University, he began his career as a journalist at the *Washington Tribune*.[79] During World War II, he served in navy intelligence.[80] After the war, he took a position at the *Pittsburgh Courier*, a prominent African American newspaper that published from 1907 to 1966.[81] As a photojournalist, Alex toured the South advocating for integration and carefully documenting many of the defining moments of the civil rights movement. He covered the infamous trial for the murder of Emmett Till, the cases leading up to *Brown v. Board of Education*, and the last reported incidents of lynching in the South.[82]

When it came to reporting on the Fultz family, Alex had his work cut out for him. On the eve of the girls' second birthday, Annie Mae first promised to pose for him but then locked herself inside to avoid his camera's gaze.[83] The girls characteristically refused to sit still, engaging in wild acrobatics. This prompted Pete, who Alex called "one of the most famous fathers of modern times," to label them his most mischievous children, proclaiming his single-birth children to be "more normal."[84] It seemed as though only James Jr. wanted to cooperate with Alex, sitting down beside him and explaining how his brothers and sisters frequently stayed home from school to do the washing. This information prompted Alex to call James Jr. "an exceptionally alert youngster who impressed reporters as worldly far beyond his years."[85]

Watching the girls perform exuberantly for the camera, Alex noted their distinct personalities. Catherine inquisitively peered through his camera and showered her sister Louise with affection. This time Louise did not fight with the others, but Alex noted that Catherine, who loudly banged on her drum set, tore her hair out in moments of frustration. This alarming gesture was clearly a habit, one that had left a bald patch on her otherwise lovely head.[86]

At his next annual visit, with the sisters on the precipice of three years old, Alex reported that the "little queens are hale, hearty, happy, and normal."[87] Immediately following this pronouncement, he qualified his use of the word *normal*: "Normal, so the child psychologists say, for children of their ages who do not have contact with other children outside their own little world."[88] Although physically healthy, the girls lagged behind other children their age in behavioral and developmental markers.

Undaunted by this fact, Elma took it upon herself to defend the girls' aptitude to Alex, bragging about their accomplishments. Elma declared that all four had made a start on the alphabet and counting. They shared a fervent enthusiasm for Mother Goose, particularly the tale of Lucy Locket. ("Lucy Locket lost her pocket, Kitty Fisher found it. Not a penny was there in it, only ribbon round it.") To prove their ardor for these rhymes, the girls read aloud from their book in unison, in languages of their own invention.[89]

The girls' true passion, though, was music. Elma boasted a collection of bebop records that joyously inspired them.[90] Louise sang longest and strongest. At thirty-one pounds and twenty-seven inches, she weighed the most and stood an inch taller than the others, likely because she had the best appetite. Catherine fell in the middle. Ann was the smallest, and Alice was the most outspoken.[91] The girls fought constantly over their small collection of belongings, which included a few picture books, sand buckets, and shovels. Their favorite possessions were the tricycle and double swing they received as gifts from a group of college students at the Agricultural and Technical College in Greensboro, North Carolina.[92] The girls all tried to use these at once, leading to many showdowns and more than a few bruises.

As their third birthday approached, Elma expressed her concerns about their ability to get a good education. She found it unfair that Pet Milk had arranged for them to attend Bennett College as young adults but had neglected to provide for the expenses that would enable them to go to good public schools to prepare for college.[93] Frustrated that Pet Milk left the public with the false impression that it provided for all the girls' needs, Elma revealed that this was far from the truth. Urging Alex to set the record straight, Elma predicted that, if the public knew the reality of its beloved girls' situation, readers would be willing to send them gifts to improve their quality of life. Using the *Pittsburgh Courier* as a platform, Elma made a plea for toys, especially educational ones, to advance the girls' learning and keep them occupied.[94]

At home, Dr. Klenner wanted the girls separated from their brothers and sisters as a precaution to maintain their good health, which had become invaluable to him and to Pet Milk. Still, ever cognizant of the girls' responsibilities to the company, Dr. Klenner allowed them to perform in public just after they turned three. Their first major performance took place at Reidsville's municipal auditorium. As guest stars in the annual Program of the Year, they sang nursery rhymes and then stole the show by breaking out into unrehearsed interpretive dance.[95] The audience howled with laughter, but Annie Mae collapsed in a faint.[96] Her reaction may have been due to the chaos and uncertainty of what was only the girls' second outing since they had moved to the farm two and a half years before. Possibly, witnessing strangers delight in her girls' antics overwhelmed her with a feeling that she had little control over their lives.

Despite Annie Mae's alarming episode, Dr. Klenner considered the venture a success and agreed to a second performance in Virginia in June.[97]

Shortly after the *Pittsburgh Courier* published Elma's plea for educational gifts, Dr. Charlotte Hawkins Brown, the president and founder of the Palmer Memorial Institute of Sedalia, North Carolina, started a scholarship fund for their secondary education.[98] Palmer began as an institute for Black teenagers in a converted blacksmith shop in 1902.[99] Hawkins strove to expand the campus, which eventually spanned 350 acres and included a working farm that produced food for its students and teachers.[100] Initially an agricultural- and manual-training facility, the school's curriculum evolved to focus on academics and culture. By the time of its sudden closure in 1971 after a destructive fire, it had received national accreditation as a prep school.[101] Nearby Bennett College purchased the school's property and created the Charlotte Hawkins Brown Museum, which still stands in that space today.[102] It was an honor for such a prestigious Black institution to invest in the Fultz sisters' futures.

As the girls' prospects grew, so did their comfort with performing. Reviewing their June show, the *Courier* celebrated the girls' natural talent and the patience they demonstrated by waiting in the back of a car for their turn on stage.[103] By the time they turned three and a half in November 1949, they had perfected their poise, causing Alex to describe them, in contrast with his earlier consternation at their wild behavior, as "model children."[104]

At almost four years old, the sisters caught a lucky break. *Ebony*, a magazine that has been documenting African American life and culture since 1945, took the girls to Washington, DC, to do a photo shoot for a feature story on their lives. The cameraperson and writer who accompanied them tried in vain for three days to find a notable politician to pose with the girls. This was not an easy task for a Black magazine in 1950. The final stop on their tour was Blair House, one of the four buildings on the grounds of the White House that make up the president's guest quarters.[105]

Fortuitously, as the girls and their chaperones approached the building at 11:00 a.m. on April 16, 1950, President Truman and his guards were leaving it. President Truman spotted the girls and remarked, "My, aren't they pretty?" Then he stopped to pose for a picture with them.[106] The photograph catapulted the sisters back into the national spotlight, to

Pet Milk's delight. One newspaper speculated that the photo would advance the cause of civil rights in a post-war nation still struggling to conform its own laws and attitudes concerning race to the standards it had claimed to fight for overseas in World War II.[107]

Back on the farm, preparations for the girls' fourth birthday party were underway. This year, tired of sharing, the girls insisted on having their own cakes, with four candles each.[108] Annie Mae and Pete invited all their neighbors to join in the festivities.[109] It was a happy, low-key celebration, followed by a relatively peaceful year.

On May 27, 1951, Pet Milk hosted a celebration of the girls' fifth birthday.[110] It was the biggest event that had ever taken place in Rockingham County. The day of the party was extraordinarily hot. The guests rejoiced when Pet Milk sent three trucks full of ice cream up the hill and let them take as much as they wanted. Lacking modern amenities such as refrigerators or iceboxes in their homes, neighbors filled their arms with ice cream that they scrambled to eat before it melted. Seeking a broad audience for this grand promotional event, Pet Milk wired the party for television and radio broadcasts that aired in Greensboro and Charlotte in North Carolina, and in Norfolk and Richmond in Virginia. Southern radio and TV personality Grady Cois was the master of ceremonies.[111]

It was quite a spectacle to see Pet Milk executives trudging up the back roads to the farm to attend the party. Dr. Klenner brought his wife, Annie, and Susie Sharp, now North Carolina's first female superior court judge. Pet Milk's general manager, Major L. A. Bellew, flew in from Johnson City, Tennessee, and made himself useful by reading a Pet Milk–produced volume of fairy tales to the girls. The party's most celebrated guest, invited to attract radio and television audiences, was North Carolina governor William Kerr Scott.[112]

North Carolina has never had a Black governor. In 1951, Scott was its most racially progressive governor to date. Although his efforts toward racial reconciliation fell short of explicitly advocating for integration, he quietly sought to promote Blacks to prominent positions and to appoint others to powerful roles who would do the same.[113] For example, Scott selected the University of North Carolina's notoriously racially progressive president, Frank Porter Graham, for a vacant Senate seat, leading to a vicious battle for the seat in the following election year, when conservatives sought to oust him.[114]

In keeping with the occasion of the girls' birthday, Governor Scott delivered a message about race. After complimenting the Fultz sisters, he proclaimed that "both races are proud of them and have taken an interest and contributed to their welfare."[115] He heralded this as a welcome sign of racial cooperation and declared his concern for the well-being of North Carolinians of all races. To many, his photograph with the girls signaled the promise of integration in the South's future. The sisters symbolized this hope for many Black southerners, with their universal appeal and ability to attract the attention of White politicians, including Governor Scott, President Truman, and Reidsville mayor George Hunt. The mayor had previously posed with Pete and two of the girls on the courthouse steps.[116]

In response to Governor Scott's praise, the Fultz sisters were dutifully charming. After his speech, they sang renditions of "The Lord's Prayer," "Jesus Loves Me," and "If I Knew You Were Coming, I'd A-Baked a Cake."[117] Wearing blue jumper dresses and white blouses, they quelled their excitement over their cake and ice cream until they were away from the cameras' watchful eyes. Overall, it was almost a perfect day, marred only by the notable absence of Annie Mae, who was famously camera shy and did not enjoy crowds.[118] Her disabilities made large gatherings with strangers challenging. The local paper explained her reticence, commenting that "her language is not universal."[119]

In conjunction with their fifth birthday, the girls made a visit to Bennett College, "the Vassar of the South,"[120] upon invitation of its president, Dr. David D. Jones. Alex Rivera went with them to document the event. He reported that "from the instant of their arrival on the serene campus until their departure several hours later all normal activities were disrupted and near bedlam reigned."[121] According to Alex, the sisters "invaded [President Jones's] office and literally undressed him as they searched for watches, pens, pencils, tie clasps and other personal effects."[122]

Bennett College began in 1873 as a "normal school," a teacher's training college specifically designed for freed slaves, both women and men. Its first class had seventy students, who assembled daily in the basement of Warnersville Methodist Episcopal Church in Greensboro, North Carolina.[123] In 1926, the Women's Home Missionary Church transformed the school into a historically Black women's liberal arts college, with its

Mae and Pete could. Dr. Klenner pointed to the Fultz family's perpetual poverty, Pete's old age, which he described as approaching retirement, and the couple's seven other children. Persuaded, the court drew up the papers, and Pete signed them.[136]

Doretha explained, "Daddy signed the papers, but he didn't read the papers."[137] It is doubtful that Pete, who had worked on farms all his life, could read or understand the legal documents. Annie Mae was heartbroken. Doretha told reporters that "Mama cried like I don't know what, they thought my mother wasn't able to take care of them, and Pet Milk took over and switched everything around."[138] As part of the new arrangement, Pet Milk allowed Pete to keep the farm. The company also agreed to extend their contract until 1960, when the girls would be fourteen years old.[139]

Elma and Charles welcomed the prospect of becoming the girls' official guardians. The couple had wanted children since their daughter's untimely death, and the court order allowed them to live under one roof again, with an instant family. The financial burden of taking on four children seemed manageable because of Pet Milk's support. The company would continue to pay Elma's salary and provide food and clothing for the girls. The only change was that now all that money would go directly to the Saylors, and none of it would go to the Fultz family.

Musing on this turn of events in the *Courier*, Alex lamented that "what always seems to be better for the quads inevitably widens the separation between them and their family."[140] Nonetheless, he observed that the girls often referred to Elma as their mother and that they looked more like Elma than like Annie Mae.[141] Surprisingly, Elma emerged as the hero of the story. The *Courier* described her as the girls' "guardian angel," who rescued them from poverty and isolation.[142] In words echoing stereotypes of poor Black people as savages in need of salvation, an article written by Alex's wife, Hazel, described Elma's influence over the girls as almost a taming one. Hazel praised Elma for taking the girls into her home and proclaimed that "with the advice and assistance of the Pet Milk Company she was instrumental in developing their personalities into fully integrated young women who are completely normal and Americanized to the core."[143]

Pet Milk bought a modest brick house for the Saylors and the Fultz girls in Milton, a town thirty miles away from the farm.[144] This distance made regular family visits impossible, especially in light of Annie Mae's overwhelming responsibilities. The girls enrolled in the all-Black, K–12 Caswell County Training School in nearby Yanceyville in September 1952.[145] Annie Mae and Pete stayed on the farm, but it quickly went to ruin. It became so overgrown that it was impossible to see the little house until you were standing in front of it. Pet Milk blamed Pete for the land's unproductivity, claiming that there was timber on it when the company bought it but that Pete left his equipment out to rust and sold off his mule after drinking too much.[146] Friends and family insisted that Pete had never had a chance to make a living from the hilly, infertile acres.[147]

The move to Milton set the girls along an irreversible path of separation from their family. At the same time, Dr. Klenner managed to keep his hand in the girls' upbringing. The doctor's desire to use the girls to bolster his reputation and serve as subjects in his discredited medical experiments converged with Pet Milk's corporate interest in expanding the market for its product to Black families. It is unlikely that Dr. Klenner or Pet Milk executives ever took the interests of the girls or their family into account.

Ultimately, the harm that Dr. Klenner and Pet Milk unleashed on the Fultz family reached far beyond what any of them could have imagined at the time. Pet Milk's strategy was highly successful from the company's perspective. It opened the door to racially-targeted marketing of formula to Black mothers that remains unregulated today. The exploitation of the Fultz family, whose story continues in chapter 3, was, on one hand, simply another case of racial injustice. On the other hand, it contributed significantly to persistent racial disparities in breastfeeding. Looking at the history of infant feeding in the United States from a racial perspective sheds light on how these disparities began and why they persist.

Chapter 2

BLACK BREASTFEEDING IN AMERICA

Annie Mae Fultz probably did not object to Dr. Klenner's decision to give her babies formula at birth and throughout their infancy. Any mother of quadruplets would struggle to produce enough milk to feed all four of her newborns. She also would not want to take any risks in the crucial first days and hours of their lives. Even once the girls were out of danger, nursing probably did not seem like a viable option to Annie Mae. For a Black woman in the 1940s, formula was the norm. The potential for negative effects from formula feeding on Black infants was either unknown or considered unimportant by health professionals. No one would have informed Annie Mae of potential health risks associated with its use or encouraged her to try breastfeeding.

A Racial History of Infant Feeding in the United States

The efforts of slave owners to appropriate Black women's reproductive capacities for economic gain led to the disruption of the mother-child relationship at its most physical level.[1] The intimacy of breastfeeding, the literal giving of one's body to sustain the life of another body, is a pain and a privilege often upheld as the ultimate sacrifice and symbol of motherhood. Characterizing the act in this way can serve to glorify White motherhood. Throughout history, it has been primarily White, well-off mothers who have had the time, resources, and support to facilitate successful breastfeeding, particularly for an extended period. Reverence of breastfeeding can appear to demean Black mothers who do not nurse, framing their reliance on formula as the product of unfortunate choices instead of circumstances.

Historical accounts of breastfeeding in the United States inevitably focus on the experiences of White women, sometimes with a cursory nod to wet nursing by enslaved women. These narratives usually fail to account for racial disparities in breastfeeding rates. This ahistorical approach to these disparities can lead to the false conclusion that they represent cultural preferences easily eliminated through education. Instead, the disparities reflect long-standing, deep-rooted, institutionalized practices and policies that ignore or devalue the needs of Black women and children.

Attitudes to and adoption of breastfeeding have fluctuated dramatically over time in White communities. Perhaps the only consistent feature of popular breastfeeding philosophies and practices has been the deliberate exclusion of Black women.[2] Low rates of breastfeeding among Black women have served various White interests throughout history. During slavery, they made breast milk, an invaluable food often referred to as liquid gold, available to White infants while denying its significant benefits to Black babies.[3] When Black mothers did not breastfeed their children, they became available to perform exploitative labor for Whites, both during and after slavery.

In the twentieth century, promoting formula to Black women while simultaneously restricting resources for Black mothers who wanted to breastfeed resulted in large profits for the formula industry at the expense of the health of Black mothers and babies.[4] This chapter draws a line from slavery to the present to demonstrate that today's breastfeeding disparities emerge directly from slavery's brutal practices. The persistence of these disparities represents reluctance to implement changes that would redress past harms and reverse current practices that benefit the formula industry.

Breastfeeding in Early Colonized America

The history of breastfeeding and race in the United States begins with the arrival of the English and their quest to establish stolen land as their own. These settlers sought to create a sustainable economy without the resources, knowledge, and labor required to replicate their previous way of life. Their audacity included the ambition to impose their culture on others, forcibly if necessary. These colonizers brought with them the widespread English belief that breastfeeding provides ideal nutrition for babies.[5] Who should perform this breastfeeding, however, was a complex question.

Colonizers who belonged to social groups that had employed wet nurses in England continued this tradition in America.[6] These settlers included doctors, clergypeople, merchants, and other members of the upper and noble classes. Members of the lower and artisan English classes who prospered in their new home sought to imitate the habits of the upper classes by hiring wet nurses.[7] But many of the religious male settlers encouraged their wives to breastfeed as part of their Christian duty.

Puritan minister Cotton Mather embodied this approach, condemning mothers who did not nurse their children as lazy and irreverent.[8] In *Ornaments for the Daughters of Zion*, his influential 1692 treatise dictating the proper conduct of colonial women, he wrote, "You can suckle your infant your self if you can; be not such an ostrich as to decline it merely because you would be one of the careless women, living at ease. Of such we read, they are dead while they live."[9] Puritans also thought that many women chose to stop breastfeeding so they could engage in sexual intercourse, an act commonly viewed at the time as incompatible with nursing.[10] Seventeenth-century English physicians believed that breast milk was menstrual blood of a different color and that sex would trigger menstruation, turning the milk back into blood and thus rendering it unsuitable for infant feeding.[11]

Poor diets in colonized America made breastfeeding a challenge for White mothers of all social classes. A woman who is breastfeeding requires a substantial daily intake of calories from nutritious foods to sustain herself and her child. Nursing infants deplete their mothers of nutrients, which can lead to dramatic weight loss and other health problems if the mother cannot replace what the baby takes. Satisfying a nursing baby's demands became increasingly difficult as colonists struggled to feed themselves from a succession of meager harvests. By the early 1600s, most families with the means to do so hired wet nurses, to maintain the strength of mothers and babies.[12]

Alternative feeding methods, including both wet nursing and "dry nursing" with food and milk, also became necessary when mothers died, fell ill, or otherwise became separated from their children. Settlers believed that women transmitted their temperament to babies through breast milk, leading them to select their wet nurses carefully.[13] This caution reflected both classism and racism. The traits defined as undesirable in wet nurses generally consisted of those attributed to the lower classes and included physical attributes such as dark skin and other non-White features.[14]

The Wet Nurse's Tale, a 2010 novel set in the Victorian era, describes its heroine, a White wet nurse, in the following terms: "She's promiscuous, lovable, plump, and scheming. Luckily for Susan, her big heart is covered by an equally big bosom, and her bosom is her fortune—for Susan becomes a professional wet nurse, like her mother before her, and she makes it her business to know all the intrigues and scandals that the upper crust would prefer to keep to themselves."[15] This racy description of a wet nurse in high demand illustrates English society's ideal of the women they sought to welcome into their homes and intimate lives. Until the profession fell out of favor in the early twentieth century, White wet nurses were in high demand and low supply, allowing them their pick of employers.[16]

Most often, paid wet nurses were lower-class White women who had lost a baby, which was a common occurrence from the time of colonization all the way through the 1900s.[17] Women could work as wet nurses for eight to nine years after giving birth, as long as they maintained their milk supply by nursing continuously.[18] By the end of the seventeenth century, rising infant mortality rates in the middle and upper classes caused many parents to blame their children's deaths on wet nurses' negligence. Most deaths were actually a result of the colonizers' exposure to diseases, including smallpox, yellow fever, malaria, and diphtheria, that their bodies were poorly equipped to fight off.[19] Good medical care was not available to save them. But frightened families turned away from wet nurses, feeding their infants cow's milk, tea, or pap, a mixture of flour, sugar, water, and milk, instead.[20] Babies often fared no better under this feeding regime due to the often fatal consequences of ingesting unpasteurized milk or spoiled food.[21]

Breastfeeding and Slavery

Different concerns animated the history of infant feeding on slave plantations. Enslaved women breastfed for far shorter lengths of time than mothers in Africa did. Black women in the United States generally nursed, when circumstances allowed it, for only one year instead of the two or three years common in their home countries.[22] Several factors contributed to this significant difference. Slave owners often prevented women under their control from breastfeeding longer than a year because they believed that nursing was a form of contraception. Impatient to produce more slaves, slave owners would often rape mothers, even ones with young children.[23]

Slave owners also wanted new mothers to continue to work, taking as little time off as possible to care for their infants.[24] Breastfeeding on demand, which was necessary without the technology of breast pumps, bottles, and refrigeration, interrupted the steady flow of labor. To avoid retribution for missed work, enslaved mothers commonly shared breastfeeding duties by cross-nursing—taking turns nursing their own and others' infants.[25] This communal approach to feeding helped ensure that babies received breast milk in the first days and months of their lives, fortifying them against a number of potential health problems.

One of the many duties that removed enslaved mothers from their infants was the directive to act as a wet nurse for children of White slave owners.[26] Some plantation owners favored the use of their slaves for wet nursing over their wives' breastfeeding because they believed that slaves were immune to malaria. In the 1600s, malaria viciously claimed the lives of many settlers and Native Americans. Because many Africans were immune to malaria, they died of the disease at lower rates than White settlers did.[27] Slave owners believed that African mothers could transmit this immunity to White babies through breast milk.[28] Although it was true that Black mothers could pass the immunity on to their own children through their placenta, they could not transmit it to White infants through nursing.[29] Plantation owners also sought to maximize their number of heirs by avoiding the contraceptive effects of breastfeeding on their wives.[30]

The task of wet nursing wrenched Black mothers away, sometimes permanently, from their babies when they needed their mothers' care the most. Even after White infants stopped breastfeeding, their wet nurses often continued to care for them until they became old enough for schooling from tutors or grew to adulthood.[31] In some cases, the nurses of slave owners' daughters accompanied them when they married and moved away. Separation of Black mothers and their children also occurred in response to a demand for wet nurses from distant plantations. If there were no women on a plantation to serve as a wet nurse when needed, slave owners with new babies sometimes hired or purchased new mothers from other plantations, forcing them to leave their infants behind.[32]

Forced wet nursing involved multiple, complex layers of displacement of maternal care. It led some enslaved mothers to transfer some of their nurturing and affection from their own infants to the children of slave owners, creating anguish and guilt for Black mothers and distress for their babies.[33] It sometimes created resentment in White women of the affection their children lavished on the Black nurses that cared for them.[34] White women may also have felt empathy for enslaved women's pain at separation from their newborns. At the same time, racist views inspired fear that the milk Black women gave to White babies might be tainted by racial inferiority.[35]

The ambivalence of the relationship between Black wet nurses and the White infants under their care created a discomfort in White observers that often registered as shock. White English traveler J. Davis described the closeness between White children and Black wet nurses as a unique American phenomenon. He wrote, "Each child has its Momma, whose gestures and accent it will necessarily copy, for children, we all know, are imitative beings. It is not unusual to hear an elegant lady say, Richard always grieves when Quasheehaw is whipped, because she suckled him."[36]

As thoughtlessly evidenced in this letter, nursing and raising slave owners' children did not protect Black women from cruelty. Slave owners often gave the children of wet nurses to other mothers or sold them to other plantations.[37] Occasionally, wet nurses could keep their babies and feed them simultaneously with their White charges.[38] Some wet nurses also benefited, relative to other enslaved women, by escaping field labor to live in houses, as recounted by Mattie Logan, whose mother worked on an Oklahoma plantation.

> My mother belonged to Mistress Jennie who thought a heap of here, and why shouldn't she? Mother nursed all Miss Jennie's children because all of her young ones and my mammy's was born so close together it wasn't no trouble at all for mammy to raise the whole kaboodle of them. I was born about the same time as baby Jennie. They say I nursed on one breast

while that child, Jennie, pulled away at the other! That was a pretty good idea for Mistress, for it didn't keep her tied to the place and she could visit around with her friends most any time she wanted 'thout having to worry if the babies would be fed or not. Mammy was the house girl and account of that and because her family was so large, the Mistress fixed up a two room cabin right back of the Big House and that's where we lived. My brother and sisters were allowed to play with the Master's children, but not with the children who belonged to the field Negroes.[39]

Even in the best of circumstances, wet nursing, like all slave labor, was difficult and debilitating.[40] Ellen Betts, a wet nurse on a Texas plantation, describes the deprivation that resulted from a life devoted to wet nursing.

Miss Sidney was Marse's first wife and he had six boys by her. Den he marry de widow Cornelius and she gave him three boys. With ten chillen springin' up quick like dat and de cullud chillen comin' long fast as pig litters. I don't do nothin' all my days, but nuss, nuss, nuss. I nuss so many chillen it done went and stunted my growth and dat's why I ain't nothin' but bones to dis day.[41]

In cases like hers, wet nursing could create physical challenges approaching or equivalent to the harsh demands of work in the fields.

Some of the harmful effects of forced wet nursing during slavery persist today. Blogger LaSha of Kinfolk Kollective, a website dedicated to exploring issues of racial justice through Black perspectives, eloquently recounts the practice's destructive legacy.

During my teen years, I read and learned a lot about slavery in America. One of the images that stuck with me was of a black woman nursing a white baby. Of all the customary violations of black bodies during that time, this one haunted me most. That a black woman's breasts, organs meant to grow and sustain the life of her own children, would be used as tools to grow the babies of white enslavers—babies who'd one day grow to be the enslavers of the same black women who had used their breasts to nourish them—was inconceivable to me.[42]

LaSha further explains that because of this legacy, refusing to breastfeed initially felt like a way to reject an act that signified reenslavement and to take back Black women's power and control over their bodies. Later, she transformed her thinking and came to view breastfeeding not as a reenactment of slavery practices but instead as a joyful symbol of emancipation. She describes this revelation:

> The real revolutionary act would have been to go against the racist capitalist conditioning I'd been consuming for decades and feed my baby at my breast, bonding and nurturing him. I would have been the warrior I wanted to be had I sat and learned from that nurse all about breastfeeding. A real revolution would have been declaring my breasts not as objects solely meant for sexual pleasure, but as instruments of nourishment for the most important person in my world. I was not revolting, I was conforming.[43]

LaSha's initial response to the complex relationship between breastfeeding and slavery is a common one that often informs the advice of grandmothers and other family members.[44]

Other aspects of slavery, including violence, sexual assault, and forced mating, had the effect of disrupting not only the attachment between mother and child but also the relationship between women and their bodies. In acclaimed writer Toni Morrison's novel *Beloved*, she harrowingly portrays a traumatizing rupture in an enslaved mother's control over her maternal functions.[45] Morrison's depiction highlights the lasting impact of breastfeeding practices during slavery. It also provides insight into experiences that were difficult, if not impossible, for women to document at the time.

In this incident, two nephews of the plantation's schoolteacher hold protagonist Sethe down and steal the milk from her breasts.[46] This theft provokes greater outrage and sadness in Sethe than the beating she receives for reporting it, which left a lasting, complicated scar that she likens to a tree on her back.[47] Describing the attack, Sethe first relates how important it was for her to reach her child quickly so that she, and only she, could nurse her: "All I knew was I had to get my milk to my baby girl. Nobody was going to nurse her like me. Nobody was going to get it to her fast enough, or take it away when she had enough and didn't know it. Nobody knew that she couldn't pass her air if you held her up on your shoulder, only if she was lying on my knees. Nobody knew that but me and nobody had her milk but me."[48]

Next, Sethe recounts the events that prevented her from getting to her baby on time.

> "After I left you, those boys came in there and took my milk. That's what they came in there for. Held me down and took it. I told Mrs. Garner on 'em. She had that lump and couldn't speak but her eyes rolled out tears. Them boys found out I told on 'em. Schoolteacher made one open up my back, and when it closed it made a tree. It grows there still."
> "They used cowhide on you?"
> "And they took my milk."
> "They beat you and you was pregnant?"
> "And they took my milk!"[49]

In the novel, Sethe's ability to breastfeed her children is the one thing she possesses that no White person can take away, until the boys assault her. Morrison's moving depiction of this indignity effectively conveys the high value that enslaved women placed on breastfeeding and the unique vulnerability they experienced because of it.

The Great Migration

Although some freed Black women found jobs in packinghouses, steam laundries, and garment factories after slavery, they most commonly held the position of domestic worker. In this role, many Black women continued to act as nurses and wet nurses for White children.[50] In 1912, a Black nurse living in Georgia described her duties.

> I frequently work from fourteen to sixteen hours a day. I am compelled to by my contract, which is oral only, to sleep in the house. I am allowed to go home to my own children, the oldest of whom is a girl of 18 years, only once in two weeks, every other Sunday afternoon—even then I'm not permitted to stay all night. I not only have to nurse a little white child, now eleven months old, but I have to act as playmate, or "handy-andy," not to say governess, to three other children in the house, the oldest of whom is only nine years of age. I wash and dress the baby two or three times each day; I give it its meals, mainly from a bottle; I have to put it to bed each night; and, in addition, I have to get up and attend to its every call between midnight and morning. If the baby falls to sleep during the day, as it has been trained to do every day about eleven

o'clock, I am not permitted to rest. . . I live a treadmill life; and I see my own children only when they happen to see me on the streets when I am out with the children, or when my children come to the "yard" to see me, which isn't often, because my white folks don't like to see their servants' children hanging around their premises.[51]

Although formerly enslaved women were legally free at this time, many Black mothers felt that there was little distinction between the onerous duties that severely restricted their abilities to nurse and care for their children, and those of slavery.

The nurse continued: "Perhaps a million of us are introduced daily to the privacy of a million chambers thruout the South, and hold in our arms a million white children, thousands of whom, as infants, are suckled at our breasts—during my lifetime I myself have served as 'wet nurse' to more than a dozen white children." She implored southern White women to ally themselves with their Black nurses.

If none others will help us, it would seem that the Southern white women themselves might do so in their own defense, because we are rearing their children—we feed them, we bathe them, we teach them to speak the English language, and in numberless instances we sleep with them—and it is inevitable that the lives of their children will in some measure be pure or impure according as they are affected by contact with their colored nurses.

But the racial divide between Blacks and Whites was simply too wide to allow White women to agitate for the rights of Black nurses.

White women experienced sexism that might have given them insight into the oppression of the Black women in their households. But their empathy went only so far. Easing the burdens on Black nurses might have created more work for White women, further decreasing their social status. Even love for their children, who would have benefited from improvements in their caretakers' well-being, was not enough to overcome the need of White women to maintain an elevated position over Black women.

During this period, many Black women continued to live in close-knit communities where cross-nursing was possible. Children received nurturing, sustenance, and affection from community members beyond their blood relatives.[52] But in 1916, the Great Migration began to disrupt this communal caring.

Economic instability in the South after the Civil War led to extreme poverty for Black southerners, who suffered under harsh laws designed to keep them in a state of near slavery.[53] The Black Codes were enacted directly after the abolition of slavery to facilitate ongoing White exploitation of Black labor. These laws took advantage of the Thirteenth Amendment's exception for "punishment for crime." Section 1 of the Thirteenth Amendment states, "Neither slavery nor involuntary servitude, except as a punishment for crime whereof the party shall have been duly convicted, shall exist within the United States, or any place subject to their jurisdiction."[54]

The Black Codes, relying on this loophole, expanded the definition of crime to include many common or unavoidable activities.[55] For example, the Mississippi Black Code criminalized

> all rogues and vagabonds, idle and dissipated persons, beggars, jugglers, or persons practicing unlawful games or plays, runaways, common drunkards, common night-walkers, pilferers, lewd, wanton, or lascivious persons, in speech or behavior, common railers and brawlers, persons who neglect their calling or employment, misspend what they earn, or do not provide for the support of themselves or their families, or dependents, and all other idle and disorderly persons, including all who neglect all lawful business, habitually misspend their time by frequenting houses of ill-fame, gaming-houses, or tippling shops.[56]

Law enforcement officers used this statute and others like it to apprehend Black men, throw them in jail, and force them to work without compensation.[57] By transforming innocent free Blacks into criminals, the Black Codes enabled Whites to continue the economic model established in slavery. The Black Codes served as precursors to the operation and conditions of modern mass incarceration and policing.

In 1866, the Republican Congress enacted the Civil Rights Act, formally abolishing the Black Codes.[58] In the subsequent brief Reconstruction period, during which Republicans controlled Congress and enjoyed popular support, Black people's fortunes rose.[59] But soon after, following a recession in the 1870s, the federal presence retreated from the South. Southerners seized this opportunity to reinstate White supremacy.[60] The ensuing southern Redemption undid the political and economic gains of Reconstruction. This era saw the emergence of the sharecropping system[61] alongside notoriously harsh prison farms such as Parchman Farm, the oldest prison in the United States and the only maximum-security prison in Mississippi.[62]

Jim Crow laws, upheld by the Supreme Court in *Plessy v. Ferguson* in 1896, legalized segregation.[63] These laws made it nearly impossible for Blacks to prosper economically by severely restricting their freedom to participate in White commerce. Segregation encompassed all aspects of society, from schools to the military.[64] A 1917 North Carolina law exemplifying this type of statute declared that "any instructor who shall teach in any school, college or institution where members of the white and colored race are received and enrolled as pupils for instruction shall be deemed guilty of a misdemeanor, and upon conviction thereof, shall be fined in any sum not less than ten dollars nor more than fifty dollars for each offense."[65]

A comparable Louisiana parish ordinance prohibited freed slaves from engaging in entrepreneurial activities, providing that "no negro shall sell, barter, or exchange any articles of merchandise or traffic within said parish without the special written permission of his employer, specifying the articles of sale, barter or traffic. Any one thus offending shall pay a fine of one dollar for each offence, and suffer the forfeiture of said articles, or in default of the payment of said fine shall work one day on the public road, or suffer corporeal punishment as hereinafter provided."[66]

In the face of relentless oppression and economic exclusion, over six million Blacks left the South for urban centers in the North. Many northern jobs opened up to Blacks and women in the wake of the massive military mobilizations required to fight two world wars in the first half of the twentieth century.[67] Migration necessarily entailed the breakup of communities, leaving most Black mothers isolated from friends and family members who had previously provided essential assistance as cross-nurses and babysitters.

In their new urban environments, Black women had to work outside the home to support their families.[68] This work consisted primarily of menial labor in the domestic and manufacturing spheres.[69] For most Black women, breastfeeding became impossible. For White women, it had become unfashionable. Breastfeeding rates declined in industrial cities for all communities.[70] This change inspired scientific research proving that breastfeeding led to greater infant survival[71] and public health campaigns designed to persuade new mothers of its benefits.[72] At the same time, researchers set out to prove a connection between skin color and breast-milk quality. Racial theorists posited that the whiter the mother, the less nutritious her milk,[73] a belief that originated in the 1600s.[74] Even medical textbooks, from the late 1800s up to 1947, asserted that Black women had more and better milk than White women.[75]

In the late 1800s and into the early 1900s, public health advocates targeted White women with the message that breast is best, eventually leading to a transformation in their attitudes toward infant care and feeding. For White mothers who could afford not to work, employing wet nurses fell out of favor. A new vision of the priceless child emerged.[76] Mothers became solely responsible for safeguarding the health and character of their children. Breastfeeding became a symbol of the value a mother attached to her child. It represented an ideal that even mothers who could not afford the luxury of staying home to nurse strove to attain.

This new perspective on parenting marked the beginning of the valorization and glorification of breastfeeding in the White community. A cultural belief equating nursing with good mothering masked the social and financial realities that drove many Black mothers to alternative feeding methods. Wealthy White women's opportunities to breastfeed looked like reflections of good choices, not good fortune.[77]

Medicalized Motherhood

In 1867, the first attempt to replicate breast milk resulted in a strange concoction of wheat and malt flour, cow's milk, and potash (salt containing the mineral potassium).[78] In 1910, a Boston doctor created the first human milk bank.[79] This innovation treated infant food as something measurable and medical. In the following decades, formula manufacturers strove to perfect their product using pasteurization techniques to render cow's milk safe to drink. Similar technologies allowed women who might previously have served as wet nurses to bottle and sell their breast milk. Evaporated milk initially served as baby formula.[80] Ultimately, pasteurization and the medicalization of milk distribution combined to make artificial bottled milk an acceptable substitute for breast milk.

At the beginning of the twentieth century, most wet nurses worked either in orphanages or in wealthy homes.[81] The demand for private wet nurses declined significantly over the next two decades. The few remaining jobs entailed working in hospitals with premature infants or temporarily taking in abandoned babies.[82] The developing commodification of breast milk as "therapeutic merchandise" eventually put even these women out of a job.[83] When pasteurization rendered bottle-feeding cow's milk relatively safe, the wet-nurse profession became virtually obsolete.[84]

As wet-nursing waned, pediatrics emerged as a new and somewhat suspect field of medicine. Its practitioners worked hard to establish themselves as legitimate physicians.[85] To do so, pediatricians sought to displace mothers as the experts on child-rearing and infant feeding. With support from the emerging formula industry, they waged an information campaign to convince mothers that their instincts when it came to infant feeding were unreliable at best. Pediatricians insisted that babies require medical, scientific management of their first food, absent which they are likely to die or fall desperately ill.[86]

Pediatricians' claims to expertise preyed on mothers' natural anxieties about breastfeeding.[87] It is impossible for mothers to measure how much milk infants consume while nursing without putting them on a scale before and after feedings. The mechanics of breastfeeding, from latching on to the nipple to staying on it, and the pain that often accompanies the process can be frustrating for both mother and child. Many women are shocked at how burdensome nursing is because new mothers typically do not share their breastfeeding troubles with expectant mothers. Their reticence may arise from feelings of isolation or shame or reflect a fear of discouraging or frightening others. This lack of communication can lead mothers to experience self-doubt when nursing proves to be more difficult than anticipated. But providing women with accurate information about the challenges of breastfeeding might not solve the problem. It might deter them from trying it at all. Amidst this uncertainty, handing the task of ensuring adequate feeding over to an individual cloaked in the authority of the medical profession is appealing to many new mothers.[88]

Instead of guiding new mothers through best breastfeeding practices, pediatricians took advantage of women's insecurities. They succeeded in persuading a new generation of mothers to defer to them in all maternal matters. A wealth of letters published in White women's magazines demonstrate the eagerness of some mothers to do this. The letters directed a broad range of questions about child-rearing and feeding to pediatric experts.[89] One mother of a two-week-old baby asked, "Will you kindly tell me whether a patent food or cow's milk will be best to give him and how to prepare it?"[90]

The medicalization of motherhood occurred swiftly, over the course of a few decades. By the 1940s, it was firmly established. Parenting became a journey carefully punctuated by visits to the pediatrician's office for annual or biannual checkups and for any minor or major affliction.[91] This ascendancy of male doctors over the once female domain of motherhood took place alongside popular reverence for technology and Darwinism.[92] Both embraced a vision of masculinity as essential to humankind's survival and progress. Male supervision was necessary to control, civilize, and modernize infant feeding practices in a way that females, dominated by instinct and emotion, could not. The unpredictability of breastfeeding called for medical intervention to tame the natural forces at work in women's bodily functions.

Immediately upon birth, pediatricians took charge of infants' nutrition. They prescribed and individually mixed doses of formula and insisted on regular visits to monitor adequate growth.[93] The formula companies, recognizing a unique opportunity to expand their market, provided a steady supply of free products to pediatricians for them to distribute to new mothers.[94] This gamble proved to be highly successful. It created years-long dependence on products by mothers who would otherwise have transitioned from breastfeeding to solid food without ever purchasing formula. This strategy also resulted in a far wider customer base than traditional advertising could. Most women did not even recognize that it was a marketing ploy. They received the product directly from doctors, who did not reveal to their patients the mutually profitable relationships they had with the formula corporations.[95]

In exchange for pediatricians' covert promotion of their product, formula companies portrayed these physicians as experts in their advertising campaigns. Carnation Milk declared its formula to be "The milk all doctors know" and praised it as "Doctor recommended."[96] One of Pet Milk's 1950s ad campaigns clearly delineated the division of labor between mothers and pediatricians: "Your baby. Yours to love, protect, care for. To be sure he gets the best of milk, ask your doctor about PET evaporated milk."[97] After several decades of steady growth, the field of pediatrics officially arrived in 1948 with the publication of the first issue of the American Academy of Pediatrics' (AAP) journal, *Pediatrics*.[98] The AAP has consistently recommended breastfeeding as the optimal source of infant nutrition[99] while simultaneously promoting and distributing formula.

Successful marketing through pediatricians' offices and women's magazines in addition to rising numbers of women working outside the home led to the increased popularity of formula in the first half of the twentieth century. By the 1950s, only 5 percent of women reported breastfeeding their babies for an extended period of a few months, and only 24 percent of mothers in hospitals breastfed at all.[100] Alarmed at this unprecedented low rate of breastfeeding, groups of women organized to challenge the medical model of motherhood and bring attention to the profit-driven motivations of the formula companies.

This movement led to the birth in 1956 of La Leche League. A group of White women formed the organization, which promoted breastfeeding by providing lactation support to new mothers, primarily in White communities.[101] La Leche and like-minded groups also led the boycott of Nestlé in the 1970s. At least one million babies in African countries died in the 1960s after caregivers mixed or diluted Nestlé's formula with contaminated water.[102] In the responding campaign against the company, predominantly White activists used the suffering of Black mothers and babies abroad to transform attitudes toward breastfeeding at home. The subsequent shift in the United States from formula use to breastfeeding and the accompanying health benefits primarily benefited the White community.

In response to La Leche's advocacy, the AAP officially reasserted in 1978 that breastfeeding provides greater health benefits than formula.[103] By that time, the field of pediatrics was in no danger of disappearing, and neither was its alliance with the formula industry. Despite their professional association's official stance, pediatricians have never stopped distributing formula to new mothers, regardless of need. Even so, breastfeeding rates have continued to rise steadily since La Leche's successful 1970s campaigns.

As breastfeeding rates rose generally, Black women's breastfeeding rates continued to lag behind those of Whites and Latinx, even though Latinx and Black women have similar poverty rates.[104] This disparity demonstrates that low socioeconomic status does not always lead to formula use. Race, rather than class alone, accounts for disparities in breastfeeding.

From 1986 to 1991, breastfeeding rates among Whites and Latinx were 58% and 56%, while Black women's rates stayed flat at 22%.[105] From 1992 to 2001, White women's breastfeeding rates rose to 68%, and those of Latinx surpassed them at 76%. Throughout this period, Black women made good strides, despite their smaller percentages, jumping from 26% in 1994 to 45% in 2001. By 2002, White women had achieved breastfeeding rates of 79%, while Black women fell slightly to 44%. To date, Black breastfeeding rates have never even approached those of Whites or Latinx.[106] In 2008, approximately 75% of White mothers and 80% of Latinx mothers initiated breastfeeding, while only 59% of Black mothers ever tried it, with only 12% still breastfeeding at one year. In contrast, 26.3% of Latinx and 24.3% of White women still breastfed at one year.[107]

The most recent study, published in *Pediatrics* in 2016, reports that 61% of Black mothers initiate breastfeeding, compared with 90% of English-speaking Latinx mothers, 91% of Spanish-speaking Latinx mothers, and 78% of White women.[108] After successful initiation, Whites and Latinx continue to breastfeed for 17 weeks.[109] Black women average only an additional 6.4 weeks.[110] By six months, only 35.3% of Black women still breastfeed, compared with 56% of White mothers and 51% of Latinx mothers.[111]

Race and class exclusion permeated the historical arc of the medicalization and displacement of motherhood by pediatricians. Throughout the twentieth century, White mothers dominated the popular dialogue on best parenting practices.[112] Only middle- and upper-class White women had the time and resources to make regular pediatric visits. Economically privileged White mothers and pediatricians created notions of ideal parenting that excluded Black and poor mothers. This narrow construction of motherhood continues. Ideal White, upper-middle-class parenting now demands great amounts of time and money.[113] This creates a standard that many working-class families neither can nor desire to emulate. Race magnifies the stigma of bad motherhood that this standard imprints on poor mothers.

Contemporary Infant Feeding

For some, breastfeeding now signals status in a way that the consumption of material goods such as expensive handbags and electronics no longer does.[114] Anyone can flaunt designer things, but time is money. Social structures make working and nursing fundamentally incompatible. Breastfeeding symbolizes the luxury of time born of the lack of the need to work. Where wealthy women once relegated the "dirty work" of breastfeeding to the lower classes, they now embrace it as a status symbol.

Low breastfeeding rates feed the formula industry, contributing to billions of dollars in yearly profits.[115] Formula companies benefit directly from the laws, policies, and social conditions that create and perpetuate low breastfeeding rates in the Black community. These corporations actively attempt to discourage breastfeeding through advertising, falsely equating the health benefits of their products with those transmitted through breast milk. They manipulate consumers' emotions by using images of breastfeeding mothers in their promotional materials. They work to prevent the dissemination of information about the potential harms of formula feeding. These strategies are particularly harmful in communities that lack clinics and organizations that support new mothers.

The Formula Industry

The infant formula industry has three or four major players. Mead Johnson (Mead), which manufactures Enfamil products; Abbott Laboratories-Ross (Abbott), the producer of Similac products; Nestlé, which makes Gerber products; and, more recently, Danone.[116] Shares in the formula market fluctuate frequently.[117] In 2016, Mead and Abbott together had approximately 80 percent of the market. Nestlé had 16 percent.[118] Formula prices are generally high relative to production costs.[119] Enfamil and Similac cost more than other formula brands.[120] A can of Enfamil or Similac that lasts approximately three to five days for one average-size baby costs about twenty dollars.[121]

Nestlé traditionally operated primarily in the international market but sought to gain a foothold in the domestic market after La Leche successfully organized the international boycott of its products in the 1970s.[122] Perhaps when Nestlé sought to take hold in the United States it relied on the prevailing White indifference to Black deaths, whether they result from poor nutrition, lead and water poisoning, or police violence.[123] Or maybe it assumed that world events would not affect the purchasing decisions of Americans, who typically take an inward-looking, myopic approach to the news.

In 1978, Nestlé began efforts to compensate for its international losses by gaining a larger share of the US market. This threatened Abbott's and Mead's dominance.[124] The companies responded by trying to block Nestlé's entry. They lobbied for domestic restrictions on infant-formula advertising—a set of laws that they would ordinarily zealously resist. At the same time, seeking to fill the gap in the international market created by the Nestlé boycott, Abbott and Mead vigorously opposed similar restrictions on international formula advertising. This morally suspect strategy sought to replace the small share of the White market that they might lose through limits on advertising in the United States with a new market of Black and Brown women abroad.

Both Mead and Abbott could afford the risk of decreasing their profits from domestic advertising because they relied primarily on formula distribution through hospitals, doctors, and health workers to promote their products.[125] The companies petitioned the American Academy of Pediatrics for support to implement their plan.[126] To sweeten the deal, they made significant contributions to the professional association. They paid about one-third of the construction costs of its new headquarters, provided it with grants, underwrote pediatric conferences, and offered loans to medical students and pediatricians.[127] In total, as part of this joint effort, Abbott and Mead donated a million dollars a year to the AAP for nearly a decade.[128]

In 1986, the AAP executive committee confirmed its dependency on this funding from the formula companies in a memo regarding the request to join their efforts against Nestlé. The memo asserted, "There is a need to make this statement reaffirming the AAP's position on marketing, breast milk, lay advertising, etc. If there is a marketing war, there may be a shift in industry's distribution of funds and the AAP may have to cut back on anticipated income from industry."[129] Although the AAP already officially opposed formula advertising, the organization unethically vocalized and heightened these objections in response to industry pressure. The formula corporations, in turn, used the AAP to attempt to obscure their anticompetitive goals. Although the corporations' goals and the AAP's mission were compatible in this case, the companies' ability to use the AAP to further their profit-driven agenda set a dangerous precedent.

In 1993, Nestlé sued the AAP, Abbott, and Mead under the Sherman Act, claiming that they had conspired to prevent Nestlé's entry into the American formula market by jointly developing opposition to direct-to-consumer advertising.[130] The jury found for the defendant formula companies and AAP. The Ninth Circuit Court of Appeals upheld the decision.[131] After Nestlé's defeat in court, the efforts to restrict domestic formula advertising succeeded, albeit temporarily. In response, Abbott and Mead raised formula prices to six times the original prices.[132] This increase harmed all formula consumers, with a disproportionate negative effect on Black families, who earned less on average than White families and were more dependent on formula.[133]

The advertising restrictions and inflated prices came to an abrupt halt thanks to an antitrust suit that prosecutors filed against Mead and Johnson.[134] The complaint alleged that the companies had engaged in price collusion, bid rigging, and conspiracy to prevent advertising.[135] The suit culminated in a $230 million settlement, one of the largest antitrust settlements in history.[136] This opened the door to Nestlé's entry into the US formula market, where many consumers appeared to have forgiven or forgotten the company's past transgressions.[137]

The conclusion of the Nestlé saga did not mark the end of the formula industry's influence over the medical profession.[138] In 2003, Alabama physician Carden Johnston became AAP president. Soon after, he took a meeting with formula company executives about an imminent national government campaign to promote breastfeeding.[139] The Department of Health and Human Services' (DHHS) Office on Women's Health developed the campaign in response to the publication of over one thousand research papers in four years that revealed significantly better health outcomes for breastfed children.[140]

The campaign sought to impress the importance of breastfeeding on the public by equating it with stopping smoking, car seat use, childhood vaccinations, and SIDS prevention.[141] After Johnston's meeting with the formula representatives, he sent a letter to DHHS raising objections to the campaign on behalf of the AAP.[142] The letter did not include any medical or scientific support for his position, likely because none existed.[143]

Formula companies employ many marketing techniques that reach disproportionately more Black mothers than White ones. Typically, women receive their first can or sample of formula from a benevolent and trusted emissary—their doctor, nurse, or WIC benefits worker—who looks nothing like a salesperson.[144] The implementation in many hospitals of baby-friendly practices, designed to facilitate breastfeeding, has done some work to mitigate the harm of giving free formula to new mothers who don't need or request it.[145] But there are fewer baby-friendly programs in hospitals that serve Black neighborhoods. Black women in all hospitals disproportionately receive free formula from doctors and nurses, who often rely on stereotypes and assume that Black women will choose not to breastfeed.[146] These stereotypes lead some hospital employees to assume that all Black mothers are single or on welfare, regardless of their actual income and marital status.

A 2001 experiment at Boston Medical Center established that increasing breastfeeding immediately after birth, the most important period for infant health, depends on policies and support, not individual preferences.[147] After the hospital prohibited the distribution of free formula to new mothers except in the event of an emergency, 90 percent of the new Black mothers in its care initiated breastfeeding with their newborns. That number exceeded the percentage of White women who initiated breastfeeding in hospitals with baby-friendly policies. The national average at the time was only 59 percent.[148] The experiment demonstrated that by choosing not to engage in formula marketing, hospitals can significantly increase the breastfeeding rates of Black women and help eliminate racial disparities.[149]

The formula industry's sway over government policy complicates the ability to put these findings to good use. Abbott, Mead, and Nestlé maintain their influence through generous campaign contributions, aggressive lobbying, and a revolving door of employees who successively hold key positions in their corporations and in government administrations.[150] Over a twenty-five-year period, Abbott donated over $18 million to political campaigns.[151] In 2008, Abbott gave the greatest percentage of its contributions to Barack Obama's presidential campaign, although it otherwise supported only Republican candidates.[152] Several lobbyists employed by Abbott previously or subsequently held important positions in government administration.[153] For example, Austin Burnes went from being the director of the Office of Legislative Operations as House minority whip to being an Abbott lobbyist.[154]

Similarly, seven out of Mead's nine lobbyists in 2014 had previously held positions with the government.[155] Their main lobbying efforts concerned the reauthorization of WIC,[156] the nutrition program for women and children and the largest purchaser of formula in the United States.[157] Nestlé employed similar tactics. In 2013, fourteen out of Nestlé's twenty-two lobbyists had previously held government positions.[158] Nestlé spent nearly $5 million dollars on lobbying that year, with a focus on nutrition labeling, food safety, and the reauthorization of the Supplemental Nutrition Assistance Program (SNAP, formerly known as the Food Stamp Program).[159] SNAP allows its participants to use their benefits to purchase formula.[160]

Government support for the formula industry also comes from the agricultural subsidies mandated in the Farm Bill.[161] Dairy and soy subsidies significantly lower the cost of producing formula, and in turn the formula industry purchases a significant percentage of these commodities. The USDA has a stake in the formula industry's continued success because of the agency's mandate to support soy and dairy. It also relies on formula rebates to maintain the WIC program.[162]

Before WIC came into existence in the 1970s, with strong support from the formula industry, formula companies relied primarily on the medical detailing model to market their product.[163] This method, traditionally used to sell pharmaceutical products, built a customer base by persuading hospitals, physicians, and health workers to give formula to their patients and clients. Its success required extensive legwork, time, and expense. Replacing it with distribution through WIC meant significant savings for the formula manufacturers.

Black women are disproportionately represented in WIC.[164] Because WIC participants use more formula than nonparticipants do, scaling down or eliminating WIC's free distribution of formula might increase Black women's breastfeeding rates. But reversing this policy is complicated, because removing or restricting formula giveaways would likely harm poor women.[165] Some mothers might try breastfeeding in the absence of free formula and increase the health benefits to some infants, particularly in their first few days or weeks. But unless there are also changes in workplace conditions, the impact of stopping the program would be narrowly circumscribed. Women who work would simply have to buy formula and likely forfeit other necessities. Without formula rebates, WIC would have to reduce its services, including breastfeeding promotion, which reaches a significant number of mothers.

The US government also supports the formula industry by not signing on to the World Health Organization's *International Code of Marketing of Breast-Milk Substitutes* (the WHO Code).[166] The WHO Code restricts formula advertising[167] to prevent harm to women and children.[168] Because the WHO Code does not apply to the United States, formula companies are free to market to even the most vulnerable mothers without limits.[169] The formula companies spend $480 million a year on marketing. The government spends only $68 million a year on breastfeeding support and promotion.[170]

By expending considerable resources to support politicians and pediatricians, corporations exert extensive influence over decisions and practices that encourage, facilitate, and promote the use of formula over breastfeeding. The resulting laws, policies, and actions disproportionately increase Black women's use of formula. The formula companies gain from the relatively low breastfeeding rates of Black women. They can increase their profits by exploiting existing racial inequalities and misperceptions about Black mothers that make Black women more vulnerable to industry sales tactics. Formula corporations appear indifferent to the harmful consequences of their actions for the health of Black women and children. The next chapter shows how the formula industry fine-tuned methods to target Black consumers after it got over its reluctance to court them.

Chapter 3

RACE-TARGETED FORMULA MARKETING

Before Pet Milk "adopted" the Fultz girls in 1946, formula companies had never marketed their product directly to Black women.[1] Common wisdom among marketing experts in the early twentieth century held that advertising aimed at White consumers would trickle down naturally to Black consumers, who would seek to emulate White tastes and habits.[2] Research conducted into Black spending power and shopping habits beginning in the 1920s told a different story.[3] Black consumer advocates argued that to capture a Black market, companies should appeal to unique Black aspirations. Successful campaigns would need to use Black models depicting Black families that had achieved social equality and financial prosperity.[4] Black consumers did not want to be White consumers. They simply wanted to be wealthier, more comfortable versions of themselves.

Marketing Formula to Black Mothers

Pet Milk's decision to adopt the Fultz sisters represented a significant step in the history of advertising to Black consumers and in formula marketing. Before formula became widely available in stores, pediatricians created formula mixes in their offices, customized to each baby's individual and constantly changing needs.[5] Formula companies directed their first advertising campaigns at pediatricians. But as the field of pediatrics grew and pediatricians' offices became busier, the time-consuming practice of mixing formula became unsustainable. In the 1920s, Dextri-Maltose,

Mead Johnson's marketer, produced a film showing new mothers how to mix formula at home.[6] Soon after, all formula companies switched to a one-size-fits-all version of their product, freeing pediatricians and mothers alike from the burdensome task of carefully measuring and dispensing distinctive mixes of milk, water, and carbohydrates.[7]

Throughout the 1930s and 1940s, formula marketing narrowly pursued an elite White consumer base. The companies branded their product as emblematic of sophistication and leisure.[8] This advertising was highly misleading, because it relied on the message that formula not only was convenient but also provided nutritional benefits equal to or greater than breast milk.[9] This simply was not true, particularly in the early stages of formula development. These campaigns belied the medical research that breast milk, with its ability to respond to infants' unique needs and provide important immunities to health hazards, is best. They preyed on women's insecurities about the quality and quantity of their breast milk.[10] By sowing seeds of doubt in mothers who were often already overwhelmed, formula companies sought to displace maternal instinct and replace it with commercial and medical expertise.

At the same time that formula advertisements began to target White mothers with these predatory strategies, select Black trade journals and business groups first identified Black consumers as a distinct, lucrative consumer group.[11] In an effort to persuade American businesses to expand their sales beyond the White market, Claude Barnett of the Associated Negro Press sent out a series of letters informing advertisers that there was $1 billion, theirs for the taking, in the Black consumer market.[12] Barnett's letters offered tips on racially-targeted advertising best practices. These included appealing to Black racial pride, selling products in stores where Blacks could shop, and placing ads in Black media outlets.[13] Barnett also urged advertisers to feature Black models participating in activities that demonstrated their equality with Whites and their upward social mobility.[14]

White advertisers responded warily. They hesitated to act on Barnett's advice, despite the profits they stood to gain if his figure was correct. Many companies feared that advertising to Black consumers would earn their products the reputation of being Black goods, rendering them undesirable to White purchasers.[15] Many also doubted the accuracy of Barnett's numbers, believing that Black spending simply could not generate enough profit to justify the added expense of race-targeted marketing.[16] Others presumed that even if Black consumers could afford their products, they would not buy them in significant amounts.[17] Faced with the uncertainty of an entirely new market and plagued by racist attitudes toward Black consumers, most companies continued to put their faith in the trickle-down strategy or simply not to think about Black consumers at all.[18]

In 1932, Paul K. Edwards, a Fisk economics professor, published the article "The Negro Commodity Market" in the *Harvard Business School Bulletin* and the book *The Southern Urban Negro as a Consumer*.[19] Conscious of the potential pitfalls of a White man conducting research in the Black community, Edwards relied on his position at a historically Black college to earn the trust of his interviewees. He also employed a diverse group of field-workers to ensure the accuracy of his data. Even so, Edwards's social analysis of Black consumers traded in racist assumptions. He claimed that Blacks worked primarily in White homes instead of starting their own businesses due to their "constant awareness and fear of white disapproval of the assumption on their part of the role of entrepreneur and a lack of confidence in themselves."[20] This ahistorical and condescending view of Black labor ignored over a hundred years of constrained choices for Blacks, in employment and every other social sector.

Edwards's findings concluded with advice that echoed Claude Barnett's recommendations. Edwards noted that the inclusion of Black models in advertising, particularly when they appeared respectably dressed or alongside White models, appealed to Black consumers.[21] Racist portrayals of Blacks in advertising could drive Black consumers away.[22] Exhibit A was Aunt Jemima.[23] Quaker Oats has used this stereotypical and, in some circles, still iconic Mammy-shaped bottle and spokesperson to sell pancakes since 1889.[24] Black consumers rejected this degrading portrayal of Black women, preferring other products.[25]

Edwards noted with surprise his discovery that Black consumers care more about brand names and product quality than White consumers do.[26] He found that Black families purchased significant amounts of butter but showed little or no interest in butter substitutes, despite their lower price. Edwards also emphasized that personal appearance was very important to Black consumers.[27]

Around the same time that Edwards released the results of his studies, the National Negro Business League produced a report estimating Black spending power at $1.65 billion, a significant increase from Barnett's previous $1 billion figure.[28] A separate industry handbook sought to quell White manufacturers' fear that Black consumers would taint their products and drive away their White consumer base. It insisted that advertisers could target Blacks without Whites ever being the wiser.[29]

As time went on, Black consumers became harder to ignore. Black income rose 300 percent between 1940 and 1950.[30] American involvement in two world wars spurred national production, making additional jobs available to Black workers, particularly Black women, who stayed behind and filled vacant positions when both Black and White men left to fight.[31] Increasingly higher numbers of advertisers chased a cut of this emerging market.[32] By the end of the 1940s, companies selling soft drinks and food began active campaigns in Black media outlets. These outlets previously limited advertising almost exclusively to Black beauty products, cigarettes, and alcohol.[33]

An essay by David J. Sullivan in the March 1, 1943, issue of *Sales Management* helped new advertisers create successful campaigns targeted at Black consumers. The essay provided corporations with a set of rules to avoid offending potential Black customers.[34] Sullivan was the national expert on Black consumers before World War II. He opened the first Black-owned independent sales and marketing agency in the United States.[35] His essay "Don't Do This—If You Want to Sell Your Products to Negroes!" instructed:

> 1. Don't exaggerate Negro characters, with flat noses, thick lips, kinky hair, and owl eyes. They don't exist any more as a matter of fact. 2. Avoid Negro minstrels. Avoid even the use of white people with blackface and a kinky wig for hair to depict a Negro. We know, as well as you might, that they are phonies—minstrelsy is a dead issue. 3. Don't constantly name the Negro porter or waiter "George." He could be John, James, or Aloysius, for that matter. Nothing makes Negroes angrier than to be called "George." 4. Avoid incorrect English usage, grammar, and dialect. In other words, get away from "Yas suh, sho, dese, dem, dat, or dat 'ere, gwine, you all." (This last white Southerners use more often than Negroes.) Avoid also, "I'se, dis yere, wif," and others in similar vein. 5. Don't picture colored women as buxom, broad-faced, grinning mammies and

Aunt Jemimas. Negroes have no monopoly on size. Neither are they all laundresses, cooks, and domestic servants. By no means color them black. Use brown-skinned girls for illustrations; then you satisfy all. Don't refer to Negro women as "Negresses." 6. Don't overdo comedy situations, gag lines, or illustrations. Avoid, even by suggestion, "There's a nigger in the woodpile," or "coon," "shine," and "darky." 7. Don't illustrate an outdoor poster, car card, advertisement, or any other advertising piece showing a Negro eating watermelon, chasing chickens, or crap shooting. No race has a monopoly on these traits. 8. Don't picture the "Uncle Mose" type— the type whom Octavus Roy Cohen employs in his stories in Collier's and elsewhere. He is characterized by kinky hair and as a stooped, tall, lean and grayed sharecropper, always in rags. The U.S. Chamber of Commerce says, and facts prove, that Negroes spend more money for clothes per capita than do white people in New York City and other large cities. 9. Always avoid the word "Pickaninny," or lampooning illustrations of Negro children. They are as dear to their parents as are other children, irrespective of race. 10. Don't insult the clergy. The day of the itinerant Negro preacher has gone long since.[36]

Integration of Sullivan's advice into national advertising was slow. A study of magazines comparing advertisements from 1950 with ones from 1980 revealed that Whites appear predominantly in ways that they like to think of themselves but that Blacks appear as Whites like to think of them.[37] There were some notable exceptions. Pet Milk broke new ground when it created the radical "Happy Family" campaign targeting Black consumers.[38]

That campaign was the brainchild of Black ad executive W. Leonard Evans Jr.[39] In the 1940s, Evans coauthored a major study of Black consumer habits in New York; Washington, DC; and Philadelphia.[40] Based on the study's results, he created campaigns for clients that, in addition to Pet Milk, included Philip Morris cigarettes, Wrigley gum, and Armour meat products.[41] All of these products represent significant health risks for Black consumers, who suffer from food- and smoking-related illnesses and deaths at higher rates than White consumers do.[42]

The Pet Milk Happy Family ads appeared in Black publications, including the *Birmingham World*, the *Washington Afro-American*, and the *Los Angeles Sentinel*, between November 5, 1949, and March 29,

1958.[43] Carefully designed to appeal to Black consumers, the ads contained unique copy and did not simply replicate White ads using Black models. Instead, there were four general themes, each one tracking studies that revealed Black shoppers' preferences. The ads focused on upward mobility, homemaking as a career, fatherhood, and career success resulting from higher education and hard work.[44] The families featured in the ads owned homes where they cheerfully entertained friends and neighbors and cultivated blooming gardens.

Although likely not as prevalent as Pet Milk's campaign made it appear, home ownership for Blacks did increase after World War II. Changes to mortgage financing and the ability of some returning soldiers to take advantage of the GI Bill's mandate to create home loans for veterans brought the American dream within reach for some Black families.[45] An early Pet Milk ad showed Helen and John Norman and their twins, preparing for a move: "It's a big year for the Normans—in March [1950], they'll start their new house on Birmingham's Elsberry Drive."[46] The ad reported that John juggled three jobs—teacher, tax consultant, and typewriter salesperson—to make home ownership possible.

Despite the happy face that this ad put on the Normans' hard-won achievement, reality was not so gentle. Segregation cabined Black families into poor urban neighborhoods.[47] The GI Bill excluded all but a few Black veterans. White violence sought to discourage Blacks from moving into previously White neighborhoods.[48] These efforts included six bombings of homes in Birmingham, Alabama, the Normans' destination, in 1949, the year that Pet Milk ran the Happy Family ad showcasing the Normans' upward mobility.[49]

The Happy Family campaign misleadingly exaggerated Black women's domesticity in their own homes.[50] Portraying them on leisurely shopping trips with their children and merrily performing their household chores, these ads overlooked the reality that the homes in which most Black women cooked and cleaned were not their own. Neither were the children they spent their days caring for.[51] Employers underpaid Black women compared to White men and women, making it necessary for them to work harder to achieve the same income levels. Black women also faced the challenge of financial instability caused by the absence of Black wealth. Many White families amassed wealth through inheritance, home ownership, and other financial and social advantages denied to Black families.[52] The need for Black women to work outside the home made them perfect targets for formula advertising.

In a separate advertising campaign initially intended solely for White consumers, Pet Milk began adopting sets of triplets in 1934. The company provided the multiples' families with free formula in exchange for the use of their stories.[53] When the Fultz sisters were born in 1946, Evans Jr., mastermind of the Happy Family campaign, saw a unique opportunity to secure a contract with the country's first recorded set of identical quadruplets. Including the Fultz girls in Pet Milk's multiples campaign would expand the very limited set of products advertised to Blacks at the time.[54]

Formula was an ideal product to break this barrier. It signified elevated social and economic status, despite the reality that it was working mothers who needed formula the most. This gave formula marketers two significant entry points into the market of Black women. First, the false but persistent message about formula's high nutritional value relieved Black mothers of some of their guilt about leaving their infants to go to work.[55] Second, the trend of associating formula with wealth branded them as sophisticated consumers.[56] Pet Milk's timing was prescient. The post–World War II baby boom ushered in a large crop of new mothers as quarry for formula companies.[57]

In magazines, on television, in newspapers, and on the internet, the most common image of a Black woman breastfeeding is not a blissful, nurturing, middle-class Black version of the idealized White mother. Instead, it is a bare-breasted African woman, adorned in traditional dress and jewelry.[58] These types of depictions make breastfeeding by Black women appear to be a primitive practice, appropriate for an anthropological, dehumanizing gaze.[59] This "savage" woman stands in stark contrast to the beatific nursing White mother that a quick Google search for images of breastfeeding women will reveal.

Ironically, most nonstereotypical images of Black women breastfeeding appear in formula advertisements.[60] The formula companies use these positive portrayals to create a feeling of goodwill for their product, promising to deliver a bonding, nurturing relationship between Black mother and child without the hassle and unpredictability of actual breastfeeding.[61] Pet Milk's Fultz Quads campaign was the first to put this marketing strategy to the test. Carnation Milk sought to follow in Pet Milk's footsteps, but it was not nearly as successful.

The Tigner Quads

After losing its bid for the Fultz girls to Pet Milk, Carnation Milk jumped at the chance to adopt a new set of Black quadruplets for a marketing campaign. At 1:03 a.m. on Thursday, August 23, 1946, nearly three months after the Fultz sisters were born, thirty-one-year-old Lucille Tigner gave birth to four healthy babies over the course of eight minutes in the charity ward of Multnomah County Hospital in Portland, Oregon.[62] Although her doctors told her to expect them, she said she "thought they was just a-teasin' [her]."[63] Lucille's sister had also given birth to quadruplets, but they had all died in their first eight months.[64] Lucille and her sister are the only known case of two siblings giving birth to quadruplets.[65]

Each of Lucille's new babies was healthy and weighed around five pounds, even though they had arrived a month early.[66] They took after their mother, who was six feet tall and weighed 210 pounds. Lucille was "decidedly feminine," with "partially straightened hair" and a "soft Arkansas drawl."[67] Hospital attendants reported that the babies "were kicking up a staccato din in their incubators."[68] Lucille named them Joe, Jessie May, Josephine, and Jerry.[69]

Their father, L. D. Tigner, was thrilled but nervous about their arrival. "When the neighbors came over this morning and told me what had happened I jumped out of bed and started shakin' all over," L. D. told reporters.[70] He had moved to Portland during the shipyard boom several years earlier and worked as an electrician in the shipyards before they closed down.[71] After that, he worked as a cook on the Southern Pacific Railroad but lost his position in May, three months before the babies were born.[72]

The babies thrived, coming out of their incubators after only twenty-four hours.[73] Lucille succeeded in breastfeeding one-day-old Jessie May.[74] As the family posed for pictures, Lucille joked with reporters, telling them, "I used to think one was a lot of work. Now look what I've got!"[75] L. D. was optimistic about his ability to find a job soon, declaring, "Where there's a will there's a way."[76] White reporters at the *Oregonian*, who proudly reported on the Tigner quads for years to come, commented immediately on their race. An editorial about their birth said, "There they lie four little black pearls and if we had our way about it we should engage Paul Robeson to sing them a lullaby when they are a little older."[77]

As soon as the quads left their incubators, Carnation Milk sent an emissary from Milwaukee with an offer in hand for the Tigners.[78] Only four days later, attorney Neal R. Crounse petitioned probate judge Ashby C. Dickson to approve a contract between Carnation and the Tigners that would allow the company "to exploit the babies' pictures for advertising purposes."[79] The *Oregonian* declared that "fortune had suddenly smiled on the dusky quadruplets."[80] But part of Crounse's petition was a request to sign guardianship of the quadruplets over from their parents to Alton J. Bassett, a White attorney.[81] The judge agreed to this provision, explaining that "various firms, persons and corporations desire to enter into contracts relative to the sponsoring of said minors for advertising purposes . . . [so] it is necessary and expedient that a guardian be appointed."[82]

Crounse selected Bassett in part for his "knowledge of negro affairs and his interest in promoting better race relations."[83] The court charged Bassett with overseeing the agreement with Carnation, which promised to set up a $25,000 estate for the quadruplets' benefit.[84] The company would make an initial $4,000 cash payment to the Tigners and then provide $175 a month toward the quads' expenses, half of what Pet Milk paid out each month for the Fultz girls' upbringing.[85] Carnation would also give the Tigners a five-year supply of milk. In return, the quads would have to drink Carnation Milk exclusively and do occasional modeling for the corporation's ads. The contract limited Lucille and L. D.'s access to the money. They could use only 10 percent of the upfront cash payment for their own and their other children's needs.[86]

Suddenly, a variety of corporations wanted to jump on the bandwagon of advertising to Black consumers. The *Oregonian* reported that "countless firms, producing every kind of product from baby foods safety pins and diapers to household equipment have made flattering offers in exchange for endorsement of their wares."[87] It does not appear that any of these other bids ever came to fruition.

With the four babies still in the hospital, L. D. took a break from job searching to try to find a new place for the family to live. Their small one-bedroom apartment already housed the quadruplets' two older sisters, thirteen-year-old Manda Lee and eight-year-old Mary Lee, and their eighteen-month-old brother, Robert Lee.[88] Bassett optimistically opined, "When the time comes I doubt if [L. D.'ll] have any trouble going back to the railroad or working elsewhere if he wants to do so."[89] Lucille returned home, and the *Oregonian* photographed the babies in the hospital without her, observing that Josephine was "obviously . . . tossing a comment over her shoulder" and Joe did "not seem to be registering approval."[90] The paper's prognosis of the Tigners' situation was positive: "All they have to do is absorb milk, and keep well, and grow up and go to school and to college" to reap the rewards of their deal with Carnation Milk, their "fairy godmother."[91]

Under Bassett's guardianship, the babies got new names: August Joe, Beatrice Josephine, Carole Jessie, and Dee Jerry.[92] The newspapers approvingly christened them the ABCD, or Alphabet, babies.[93] Observing their developing personalities, *Oregonian* writer Polly Predmore said that Beatrice "manifested considerable feminine curiosity about life in general and visitors in particular. The other three just acted hungry."[94] Predmore reported that the doctors gave them one hundred to one chances of survival, which were good odds.[95] She wrote, "Quadruplets are a rarity in any shade . . . with about one chance in a million of survival for all. Among the 15,000,000 Negroes in this country, there is only one other set of living quadruplets."[96] She referred, of course, to the Fultz sisters, who were even rarer, being identical. Predmore also mused, "Perhaps fate dealt these four little aces to the world to act as tiny ambassadors of good will in a world all too prone to think in terms of color rather than human beings."[97]

By October, the babies had doubled their birth weights and outgrown their cribs.[98] Even though the all-charity Multnomah hospital was overcrowded and understaffed, its administration reassured Bassett and the Tigners that the infants could stay there until they had a home to go to.[99] On November 1, the court approved Bassett's proposed modification of the agreement with Carnation.[100] The new contract reduced by $85 the already meager $175 monthly payments for expenses in exchange for the advance of a lump sum to purchase a house.[101]

Like the Fultz's farm, paid for by Pet Milk, the house that Carnation bought for the Tigners had a nursery with a display window.[102] The

Sunday after the babies turned six months old, the "chocolate brown and big-eyed" Tigner quads went on display.[103] Curious onlookers paid twenty-five cents to see them during a two-and-a-half-hour period.[104] The admission price went into a fund for their welfare.[105]

After signing the deal with Carnation, Lucille no longer tried to breastfeed her babies. Instead, Miss Olive Oleson, of the Visiting Nurses Association, showed their new nurse, Pinky Lee Ross, "how to make formula and sterilize bottles and other modern tricks."[106] The growing quads drank twenty bottles of Carnation Milk a day.[107] When they turned one in August 1947, the *Oregonian* predicted that their days of celebrity and comfort had come to an end. Noting that the "healthy and bright-eyed" children would soon start to walk, Ann Sullivan reported that they would not be able to afford shoes when they did.[108] The salary of their full-time nurse, Betty Lou Gentry, was one hundred dollars a month, and their Carnation allowance was only ninety dollars.[109]

"The children get all their milk from the company and will as long as they need it. But milk and a nurse aren't all year-old babies need," Sullivan asserted.[110] They were still wearing the clothes they received as newborns. Sullivan also noted that "from now on they [would] only share the limelight about once a year, on their birthdays."[111] In her eyes, they were "has-beens."[112] But she thought that their siblings had it even worse. Their little brother "had been the cherished baby, but the little ones took precedent. . . . So in the winter time, Robert Lee plays in the basement. He has few toys."[113]

As with the Fultz sisters, celebrity was not enough to raise a Black family out of poverty. Even corporate sponsorship could not stave off the consequences of living in a racist society. On February 4, 1948, the *Oregonian* published a letter to the editor from the Tigners' White "grocery man," S. E. Campian, under the heading "Quads' Dad Needs Job."[114] The letter described his unsuccessful efforts to find work and the dwindling amount of groceries that L. D. could afford to buy for his seven children.[115] L. D. had placed 137th on the civil-service exam.[116] "I say Tig, what can you do? There are a lot of things I could do if they would let me, he says. I can wait on table do any kind of labor, drive truck or maybe—then he hesitates and goes on: They wouldn't let a negro do that. He pays taxes, eats, sleeps and just about everything that you or I do except have a chance to support his family."[117]

Campian's appeal to *Oregonian* readers to help find work for L. D. was similar to Elma Saylor's plea for toys for the Fultz sisters in the *Pittsburgh Courier*. Both dispelled the illusion that corporate sponsorship led to prosperity. The *Oregonian* ran a picture of L. D. holding a broom in front of the quads in their crib.[118] "Quads get milk and nurse services from milk company but household of ten makes grocery, fuel and clothes buying difficult without a steady income," the caption read. "Being a negro has made the hunting a little harder."[119] The *Oregonian* was a White newspaper serving a White city. Its efforts were not as successful as the *Courier*'s. L. D. remained unemployed, and his relationship with Lucille deteriorated.

On the Tigner quads' second birthday, on August 22, 1948, Dee was in the hospital recovering from a hernia operation.[120] The *Oregonian* announced that the other three would "attend a silver tea in their honor from 3 to 6 p.m. at the Blessed Martin day nursery. The public may view them there at that time."[121] That year, Lucille gave birth to twins. Two days short of the quads' third birthday, Lucille swore out a warrant for L. D.'s arrest for nonsupport of their children.[122] Bassett assured reporters that none of this would "affect the material welfare of the quads who have an income from a legacy established by Carnation Milk company."[123]

Bassett's confidence in their situation was misplaced. As the quads prepared to enter school at six years old, the *Oregonian* reported that nurse Betty Lou Gentry would "dress them in their finest—which is far below par."[124] Worried about how they would fare at school, Gentry shared that "they [hadn't] yet been near a school and [seemed] apprehensive about going—but go they must."[125] She said, "They are very shy and won't fight for anything. They haven't anyone their size in the neighborhood except two younger twins to play with."[126]

Even more disturbing, Gentry said, was that they lived "in a huge white house that needs paint and repairs and [would] start to school at a disadvantage. They need clothing, the special uniforms required at the Catholic school by October, shoes, underclothing, warm outer coats, hats, a more balanced diet, and many, many things including beds in which to sleep. The four now sleep in three cribs—one of the four originally purchased for them having completely worn out some time ago—and the remaining three are much too small, especially as two have to sleep together."[127]

Unlike the Fultz sisters, the Tigners did not receive enough money from their corporate sponsor to dress properly. Whereas the Fultz girls wore fancy matching dresses, the Tigners could not even afford underwear. Once the Tigner quads started school, Gentry, their nurse, planned to leave them to take care of her own family.[128] Lucille could not care for the four of them and her five other children. Bassett put out a plea for a foster family to take them in: "They will need a foster home when the nurse leaves where they can have individual love and attention, help with their tutoring, discipline and proper food. Today they are shy, backward and won't fight for their rights. They need clothing from inside out and will need much more as the future unfurls."[129]

The foster home never materialized. But like the Fultz sisters, the Tigner quads became separated from their family. They went to live in charitable institutions—the boys at St. Mary's Home for Boys in Beaverton and the girls at Christie School at Marylhurst College.[130] They reunited once a year for their birthday. When they turned eight, a couple from Milwaukee sponsored a beach party for them.[131] On that carefree occasion, they got to "eat[] birthday cakes and do[] the things other children do on their birthdays."[132] When they were nine, they went on a two-week camping trip run by a Catholic organization at Cougar Mountain.[133] By this time, the girls were taller than the boys. They aspired to be housewives when they grew up.[134] August wanted to be a boxer or a basketball player.[135] Dee had simpler ambitions: "I want to grow up and be a plain man."[136]

More trouble was in store for the Tigners. In 1956, Lucille turned herself in to the police after throwing boiling lye in her abusive partner's face in an act of self-defense.[137] The prosecutor charged her with aggravated assault and booked her into jail, setting bail at $1,500.[138] In 1957, L. D. was convicted of gambling.[139] On the quads' eighteenth birthday, in 1964, August was the only one who had graduated from high school.[140] He worked as a busboy at the Sheraton.[141] Dee, who was "much more sophisticated," worked at the Imperial Hotel.[142] Both boys lived with Lucille. Their sisters shared an apartment.[143] The Tigner boys accomplished what the Fultz sisters never could: a lasting reunion with their mother.

In return for its $25,000 investment in the Tigner quads, Carnation only ever ran one ad featuring them. It appeared in *Ebony* in 1949, with their four disembodied heads and a simple caption: "Famous Tigner

Quads Raised on Carnation Milk Born August 22, 1946 to Mr. and Mrs. L. D. Tigner of Portland, Oregon. Two boys and two girls, now 'going on three'—all doing fine."[144] The turmoil of the Tigner household likely made it impossible to orchestrate photo shoots and appearances.

The failure of this corporate adoption to pay off highlights the extraordinary nature of the Fultz sisters' experience with Pet Milk. Pet Milk needed complete control over the girls to make their campaign work. Without Fred Klenner's self-interested intervention, they could not have achieved it. They also needed to invest a significant amount of resources into their models. Nothing less could guarantee a successful marketing campaign targeted at Black women in the 1940s and 1950s.

Race-Targeted Formula Marketing from the 1950s to the Present

The Tigner quads ad in *Ebony* included a direct appeal to Black mothers. At the top of the page, under the caption, "She was a Carnation baby. . . . Now she's a Carnation mother," there are two pictures of Josephine Burch.[145] The first is an image of a baby in a bonnet in a stroller. The text below reads, "As a baby, little Josephine (now Mrs. Bernard Burch) was well fed with Carnation Milk, and today is one of the millions of grown-ups enjoying happier, healthier lives as a result of early Carnation feeding."[146] The second picture shows Josephine as an adult, looking straight into the camera, with a baby's head beside her shoulder. Underneath, it reads, "Mrs. Burch with her own 'Carnation baby' Cheryl Ann at four months. Josephine Burch is a Consulting Home Economist, expert in foods. She knows the high value of Carnation—for all milk purposes."[147] This attribution of expertise to Mrs. Burch was radical during a time when almost all formula advertisements, even those in Black magazines, featured White mothers.

Formula companies continued to advertise in *Jet*, *Essence*, and *Ebony* magazines. After the success of the Fultz Quads campaign, Pet Milk adopted triplets from Cincinnati, Ohio.[148] The *Ebony* ad claims that their mother, Ruth Cave, "who graduated from a school for beauty culture before her marriage, now has a full-time job with triplets, keeping house, cooking—but loves her job as a homemaker! She's one of the many young homemakers who have found how easy it is to serve better meals at lower cost with Pet Milk."[149] When the ad ran in 1952, it was very rare for a Black woman to stay at home with her children. But advertising ignored this reality. Pet Milk Happy Family ads in *Ebony* in 1952 and 1953 also featured Black housewives, as did a 1961 Carnation ad.[150]

A 1976 Enfamil ad in *Parents* magazine of a seated Black baby extols the benefits of formula over cow's milk.[151] It explains, "Cow's milk provides nutrient levels needed by calves. These levels are modified in Enfamil."[152] A 1984 Gerber ad in *Essence* portrays a Black mother holding a bottle to her baby's mouth and asks, "What's better than formula?"[153] A 1991 Gerber ad in *Ebony* depicts a Black woman lovingly breastfeeding her baby.[154] It insists, "We hope you breast-feed your baby. But if you ever need a formula, talk to your doctor about Gerber Baby Formula."[155] A similar 1993 Gerber ad with a light-skinned Black mother claims, "We know that your breast milk is best for your baby. That's why there simply is no better formula than Gerber for your baby's nutrition."[156]

In 1994, Mead Johnson began advertising toddler formulas in *Ebony*. These types of formula seek to take the place of solid foods and cow's milk in young children's diets. A 1995 Carnation ad for follow-up formula has three White babies and one light-skinned Black baby sitting in a row.[157]

Much of modern advertising now reaches parents through social media platforms such as Facebook and Twitter. A "Similac dad" Facebook ad from 2015 shows a Black dad holding a very light-skinned baby girl and encourages parents to "relax their own rules."[158] A 2017 Similac Facebook ad features a dark-skinned Black woman holding a light-skinned baby.[159] A 2018 Enfamil Facebook ad shows a little Black girl on her own wearing a button that says, "I'm an Enfamil baby."[160] The erasure of the parents from this ad and the implication in the others that the baby has one White parent diminish the roles of Black parents in their children's upbringing.

On television, formula ads usually feature families bonding. They claim that specific ingredients in their products promote healthy digestion, mental performance, and overall healthy development. Online, formula companies have their own websites and put banner ads with discount codes on third-party sites such as Amazon and Walmart. Similac spent $1 million on internet advertising in 2015.[161] The company's site features a StrongMoms Rewards Club offering "expert nutrition guidance" as well as discounts and free samples.[162] The site provides ideas and advice for three stages of parenting: pregnancy, new baby, and toddler. Its home page has a video of a Black mother giving birth to a White-looking baby. The Enfamil home page boasts that its products have "brain-building nutrition." It has an image of a Black woman in the section titled "For Mom."[163]

The most powerful formula marketing now takes place on social media. The centerpiece of a Similac campaign using the hashtag #EndMommyWars is a video, "Mother Hood," depicting a standoff between camps of parents, including breastfeeders versus formula feeders and cloth- versus disposable-diaper users.[164] One of the camps consists only of dads. As the different groups assemble on a playground, their criticisms of each other become stronger until they decide it is time to battle. One mother lets go of her stroller as she goes to join the rumble. It starts to roll down a hill. The "moms" forget their differences as they all rush to save the baby from impending doom. They succeed. A voiceover encourages them to stop judging each other and join the "sisterhood of motherhood." The video got more than twenty million views.

Formula corporations also get free advertising by encouraging mothers to make their own videos on social media platforms using the companies' hashtags. Moms receive rewards for this labor in the form of discounts. The World Health Organization's *International Code of Marketing of Breast-Milk Substitutes* prohibits this marketing strategy. Other exploitative marketing tactics employed by formula companies include positioning themselves as reliable sources of information for breastfeeding mothers, offering general health advice about infants, normalizing formula use by featuring "real" moms in their advertisements, engaging mothers through social media, and advertising "specialty" formulas.[165]

Formula marketing matters. Women exposed to formula advertisements during pregnancy or shortly after giving birth are less likely to breastfeed exclusively and more likely to use formula in a baby's first ten weeks.[166] Formula advertising inspires an expectation of breastfeeding failure. It misleadingly presents formula as a solution to normal infant behaviors, such as fussiness and spitting up.[167] It confuses consumers about whether formula is superior, inferior, or equivalent to breast milk, particularly in combination with the product's endorsement by health care practitioners and institutions.

Corporate messages that loving Black families use formula resound loudly in the absence of positive images of Black women breastfeeding in the media and popular culture. Many Black women cite the absence of positive role models, in their personal lives and in the surrounding culture, as a reason to choose formula feeding over breastfeeding. Even though formula advertising also targets White mothers, abundant images of breastfeeding White mothers exist to counter its messages and present a range of viable possibilities. In contrast, when Black infants and children are visible on television and in magazines, they often serve as commodities employed to increase corporate profits.

Pet Milk's Darling Quads

Although Pet Milk intended the Fultz Quads campaign to last only ten years, it ended up spanning the sisters' infancy, childhood, and adolescence.[168] To promote its product, the company featured the girls in traditional newspaper and magazine ads and booked them for celebrity appearances and musical performances. In many significant ways, Pet Milk treated the Fultz sisters differently from its other multiples. Through Fred Klenner, Susie Sharp, and Elma Saylor, the company sought to control every aspect of their lives.

Dr. Klenner's personal goals guided his interactions with the girls. In their first few years, he sought to protect them from any health hazards that would jeopardize their survival or his experiments. He insisted that Pet Milk's first photo shoots take place at the nursery he designed on the farm that the company had bought for them.[169] He positioned himself as their quasi-guardian, requiring Pet Milk to consult with him before booking their early appearances.

Beginning on October 17, 1949, when the girls were almost three and a half, Pet Milk ran a series of advertisements in popular Black magazines and newspapers that praised the girls' excellent health. These ads boasted that "since birth Pet Milk has been their only milk." The company took full credit for the girls' beauty and robustness, proclaiming, "Now half past three the Fultz quads are still thriving on the extraordinary milk."[170]

Because consumers used Pet Milk both as infant formula and as evaporated milk for drinking and baking, the girls' utility as models was at least twofold. As tiny infants, they miraculously survived on a diet of Pet Milk. Their ongoing health served as a testament to Pet Milk's healing powers. As little girls, they were lovely, boasting smiles and dimples that would make any product appealing. In this capacity, they promoted Pet Milk as a staple in their favorite desserts.[171] To reach as many mothers as possible, Pet Milk's campaign included, in addition to print ads, large posters displayed in grocery stores across the country. The company also published a calendar with different images of the girls to brighten each month.[172]

In 1950, when the girls were four, Pet Milk ads claimed that "good milk for this famous four is good milk for your baby!" The advertisement went into detail about the girls' dietary habits: "The little girls had their first feeding of Pet Milk when they were only 11 hours old—have been drinking Pet Milk ever since—are still drinking *only* Pet Milk."[173] In May 1951, just before their fifth birthday, the sisters participated in Virginia's fifth annual Peters Park music festival as the "Pet Milk Kids," receiving accolades for their musical talents.[174] Pet Milk reaped the rewards. In the four years after Pet Milk adopted the Fultz sisters, the company sold more of its product than it had in the previous sixty-one years.[175]

When the girls began their second year of elementary school in Milton, the *Pittsburgh Courier* called them "the most spectacular of the 90,000 Tar Heel children returning to school this month."[176] The newspaper claimed that "four more vivacious girls have probably never gone to school."[177] The principal of Caswell County Training School, Nathaniel Dillard, called them model students. In the same article, the *Courier* made a new plea for its readers to donate to the girls' education. In light of their persistent love and talent for music, the paper asked readers to give them the gift of a piano.

Despite the enthusiasm of Principal Dillard and the *Courier* reporter, Elma saw the young girls struggling, academically and socially.[178] Pet Milk expected them to be ready on command for photo shoots and appearances. The company's demands required a high level of maturity from the girls, but the sisters lacked the emotional stability that would have come from living with their parents and siblings. They could not afford private tutors who could have helped them make up the school lessons that they frequently missed. The $350 monthly allowance that Pet Milk gave the Saylors did not stretch to cover all their expenses, much less provide for any extras.[179] Elma took her salary out of that amount. The fashionable clothes and accessories that Pet Milk wanted the girls to wear were expensive. Often, there was nothing left over for nutritious food or other basics that would have helped them cope with their rigorous travel schedule. Despite their cheerful and comfortable appearance, the girls lived in perpetual poverty.[180]

To the outside observer, the sisters' lives seemed glamorous. Later, reflecting on their childhood, Catherine Fultz agreed with Elma that their schedule was too grueling. "I didn't feel like a celebrity because I was tired," Catherine lamented.[181] "We had to get up at 5 in the morning to take pictures and get dressed. They were always pulling us out of school, and we'd be gone for days or weeks at a time, traveling all over the country."[182] Still, the trips the girls dreaded the most were the ones they made every two weeks to Dr. Klenner's office. The doctor performed physicals on the girls, injected them with vitamin C, and replenished the supply of pills that he instructed Elma to give them daily.[183] Brief reunions with their mother during these visits helped to offset their unpleasantness, but the looming pain of imminent separation often overshadowed the joy of these visits.[184]

At age six, the girls visited the North Carolina legislature. They sang to House members, who made them honorary pagettes.[185] In 1953, when the girls turned seven, Pet Milk sponsored elaborate birthday festivities in Reidsville's community stadium. During the event, the company cordoned the girls off from the packed crowd and from their family members. After this humiliation, their sisters and brothers never attended another one of their birthday parties again.[186] The girls received their most useful gift that year from North Carolina Mutual insurance company.[187] After they danced and sang "Fairest Lord Jesus, Ruler of All Nations" for the company's staff, they each eagerly opened a department-store box, prettily wrapped in a bow, with a winter coat inside.[188]

That same year, Elma and Charles started charging money for the girls' performances. At their first paid show, the sisters began a tradition of wearing makeup. They performed in front of three hundred people at G. C. Hawley High School, a historic site for Black education in North Carolina.[189] At the beginning of the twentieth century, there were no free public schools for Black children in North Carolina beyond elementary school. The only option for Black parents wanting to continue their children's education was to pay room and board to Mary Potter High School, located in the city of Oxford, North Carolina.[190] Things began to look up in 1936, when Grover Cleveland Hawley became the principal at Creedmoor Colored School and established its high school department.[191] Hawley worked tirelessly to gather resources for the school. He raised enough funds from the Parent Teacher Association to buy a school bus and upgraded the school's facilities using lumber from the dismantled barracks at nearby Camp Butner, which housed prisoners of war during World War II.

Creedmoor High School's students were the children of tenant farmers, small-farm owners and entrepreneurs, and Camp Butner employees. When its first class graduated in 1939, the school board changed the school's name to G. C. Hawley High School. Several years later, in 1952, Hawley oversaw the opening of G. C. Hawley Middle School. Its students contributed to this opening by clearing the land for the building themselves, carrying saws, axes, hoes, and other equipment on the school bus to get the job done. Later, in the 1970s, a fire forced the merger of G. C. Hawley and the then predominantly White Creedmoor Elementary School. Their integration occurred overnight, without incident.

In 1954, the Fultz sisters performed ten song-and-dance numbers, in addition to a skit titled "Dolly Has the Flu," at G. C. Hawley High School.[192] The show marked the beginning of the Saylors' efforts to train the girls for careers as entertainers. Elma and Charles believed that the girls were unlikely to succeed academically. Even with social advantages, good jobs for Black women were scarce. Elma took their performance training very seriously, escorting them to music classes with the local teacher, Mrs. M. J. Harris, three times a week, and to tap and ballet class in Danville, Virginia, once a week.[193] Pet Milk also showed interest in developing the girls' creative talents, assets that would likely increase its sales. The company invested in a recording of the girls singing and dancing to test their cinematic appearance.[194]

Elma also enthusiastically encouraged the girls academically. She was proud to report that their grades had improved to As and Bs.[195] While Catherine and Ann enjoyed spelling, Alice and Louise liked to read and do art. Louise's real passion was performing. Even without a big audience, she loved to clown around for her sisters. All four girls delighted in the trips to the beauty parlor that preceded their performances, and the glamorous looks that they sported afterwards. Living their lives in the spotlight, they were already "acutely sensitive about their looks" at seven years old. Elma cultivated this preoccupation with their physical attributes and encouraged the girls to be "feminine to the core."[196]

On their eighth birthday, the sisters got a special surprise. One of their idols, actor Juanita Hall, flew to Greensboro to bring them gifts from Pet Milk.[197] Born in the small town of Keyport, New Jersey, Juanita attended her local public school and sang in her church choir. After these humble beginnings, she went on to attend the Julliard School in New York and embark on a successful singing career. Her first big performance was in *Show Boat* in 1928. After that, she sang in a number of Broadway shows between 1943 and 1947, including *The Pirate, Sing Out, Sweet Land, Saint Louis Woman, Deep Are the Roots,* and *Street Scene.* Broadway composer Richard Rodgers (famous for his partnership with Oscar Hammerstein) discovered her singing in a nightclub. In 1949, he gave her the role that catapulted her to fame, Bloody Mary in *South Pacific.*[198] The Fultz sisters, who dreamed of following a similar path, were absolutely thrilled to meet her.

In the summer of 1954, at age eight, the sisters traveled on an airplane for the first time. *Ebony* publisher John Harold Johnson flew them to Chicago to make an appearance in the Bud Billiken parade.[199] Bud Billiken was a fictional character who regularly appeared in the *Chicago Defender* newspaper. He lent his name to an annual parade celebrating African American life.[200] In a short article publicizing the 1954 parade, the *Chicago Tribune* described Billiken as "the legendary god of things as they ought to be and godfather of Chicago's Negro children."[201]

Johnson, who featured the girls on the cover of *Ebony* four times in their lives, wanted the young celebrities to march in the parade alongside other Black personalities.[202] The event's most famous participants included boxer Joe Louis, known as the Brown Bomber, and track-and-field star Jesse Owens. Owens set a record by winning four gold medals at the 1936 Olympics in Berlin.[203] His victories disappointed Adolf Hitler, who had hoped to establish Aryan superiority at the competition through German dominance over all its categories.

At nine years old, the girls were reluctant for the summer of 1955 to end, but the year ahead held exciting things in store. In March 1956, they were flower girls at the wedding of North Carolina's Herbert Hope and Kate Shirley Jeffries. *Ebony* and other news outlets documented this honor, elevating the happy couple to temporary celebrity status by association. Trying to make sense of the ritual, Alice asked why there was a ring. Louise complained to the officiating minister, "Reverend, did you have to tell him to kiss her?"[204] Another highlight of their year was riding in a parade float with celebrity dog Rin Tin Tin.[205]

At school, the girls played tricks on their teachers, playfully switching classes and identities. They were very affectionate with each other, constantly hugging and kissing.[206] They were also eager to establish their individual personalities. They often asked friends at school to switch clothes with them so they could stand apart from their sisters.[207] Contemporary Pet Milk ads proclaimed, "Our famous babies are big girls now!" and "Playing With A Foursome Is Four Times As Fun!"[208]

When the girls turned ten, Elma and Charles formally adopted them, ending any hopes the girls might have had of returning to their family and life on the farm. Charles, who suffered from diabetes, worked long hours to support them. Pet Milk continued to pay Elma's salary, and the girls still went to Dr. Klenner for regular checkups and vitamin C injections. Their lifestyle, which included jetting off to Miami to take part in the Orange Blossom parade that year, was completely alien to their fellow students.[209] At school, the sisters played mostly with each other. At home, they vied for the attention of their adoptive mother, who struggled to juggle the individual needs of four girls approaching adolescence.

In 1960, while in Chicago, the sisters met professional golfer and tennis player Althea Gibson. Gibson was the first person of color to win a Grand Slam title.[210] That same year, Pet Milk also introduced the girls to Floyd Patterson.[211] In 1956, at age twenty-one, Patterson became the youngest boxer ever to win the heavyweight champion title.[212] Later, he was the first to regain the title after losing it.[213] Catherine was afraid that Floyd would break her hand when he shook it.[214]

Although the contract with Pet Milk was set to end on the girls' fourteenth birthday, Elma convinced the company to extend it until they turned eighteen.[215] Elma was angry with Pet Milk for sharing so little of the profits it made from the girls with them.[216] Members of the press saw the arrangement differently. In the 1960s, Poppy Cannon White wrote a steady column, called "Poppy's Notes," for the New York–based *Amsterdam News*. The paper covered stories of interest to the African American community. Poppy was a White South African Jew. She was the widow of

Walter White, who headed the NAACP for over twenty years.[217] The couple married in India in 1949. It was Poppy's fourth marriage.[218] It lasted seven years, until Walter's death.[219] Poppy was a popular food writer most famous for her first book, *The Can Opener Cookbook*.[220] In 1975, her career ended abruptly when she either fell or jumped from the twenty-third floor of her New York apartment building.[221]

In one edition of "Poppy's Notes," the columnist asserted that Pet Milk took good care of the Fultz sisters. Of all the media coverage of the girls, this particular column seemed to bother Catherine the most when she reflected later in life on how the world had viewed them.[222] Poppy insisted that Pet Milk had treated the girls as more than just a public relations stunt. She claimed that the company made "a constant effort to protect the children against exploitation and the ravages of publicity" and "carefully considered" the girls' "individual interests and capabilities." She also referred to the girls as a "well advised investment" on Pet Milk's part.

In their teenage years, Pet Milk required the girls to appear frequently at social functions. In service to the company, they went to Pittsburgh to attend the National Medical Association convention with Louise Prothro, Pet Milk's home economist and field representative. They delighted the somewhat staid crowd at the conference by looking for opportunities to go out dancing.[223] They also made their first television appearance, on the *Roy Rogers Show*.[224] Pet Milk continued to throw birthday parties for them every year, complete with new dresses for the occasion, but the company failed to extend invitations to the Fultz family.[225]

The demands on the girls during these years were intense. Once they were in the middle of writing a history exam when Elma came to tell them that they had to leave immediately for a Pet Milk appearance.[226] To help them through these challenges, Louise Prothro spent more and more time with the girls, chaperoning their travels. She worked hard to raise their spirits, but they were often tired and lonely.[227] They stood apart from their classmates at school, and they never stopped missing Annie Mae.

In the summers, the sisters worked at the Skylight Café in Greensboro, the third-largest city in North Carolina.[228] Greensboro was thirty minutes away from Reidsville and over an hour from Milton. Skylight Café was a restaurant on East Market Street in the center of a thriving

Black business area.[229] Studded with barbershops and beauty salons, supper clubs, restaurants, a church, a movie theatre, a taxi stand, a dentist, a grocer, and a billiards hall, East Market was the focal point of Black life in Greensboro beginning in the 1950s.[230] The area thrived for almost two decades until 1968, when a redevelopment plan intentionally displaced all the Black businesses and drove away the Black community.

This transition mirrored many others across the country in cities where Whites resented Black prosperity. Zoning laws and development schemes took the place of arson and other forms of violence that had destroyed Black business centers in the past, but the result was the same. Economic segregation served White interests until Black enterprises became too successful. Racially targeted property laws often provided the means to shut down lucrative Black businesses. Their owners could not make enough money in the poor Black areas but could not afford rent or gain a foothold in the White ones. In the summer of 1961, before East Market Street fell prey to this pattern, the Fultz sisters found themselves in the center of all the excitement at the home of the Skylight Café's owners, Julius and Lucy Ann Thacker.[231]

That summer, the sisters waited tables, took piano lessons, and played music. Although Ann was the most outgoing sister, Alice was particularly good at earning tips because of her welcoming smile. Louise Prothro described her charm in a letter, saying, "Your humor darts out like unexpected lightning and your easy smile makes peace like a rainbow."[232] One day, during a lunch break at the café, Catherine turned her back on Alice for a minute. When she turned back around, she realized that Alice had eaten Catherine's sandwich as well as her own. This gave Catherine pause. Thinking about it, she realized that lately Alice had been gobbling up everything in sight. Catherine looked closely at Alice and asked her point-blank whether she was pregnant. Alice admitted that she was. Up to that moment, she had successfully hidden her condition, even though she was already quite far along.[233]

Alice's pregnancy came as a complete surprise to her sisters, considering how strict their foster parents were. Elma and Charles had a rule that the girls could not date until they turned eighteen. Whenever boys did come over to see them, Charles would sit in the kitchen with the door open. When he sensed that things were getting too quiet, he would yell, "Everything all right in there?"[234] The family's livelihood depended on the girls' carefully cultivated wholesome image. Alice's pregnancy threatened to destroy their reputations, and Pet Milk's too.

Elma could not let that happen. Alice had to leave before the press got wind of her condition. Acting quickly, Elma whisked Alice away to Chicago without her sisters for the remainder of her pregnancy and the birth.[235] There is no record of where and how Alice spent her time in the faraway city or of how Elma accounted to the press for her sudden disappearance. Catherine said that when Alice finally came back to Greensboro with her sweet, small boy, she was different. Before she left, she always had a clean-cut look, pretty but conservative. When she returned, Alice wore flashy red lipstick that matched her bright-red fingernails. Catherine felt compelled to ask her if she was still herself. Alice reassured her, "Yeah, it's me."[236]

Lucy Thacker had a bassinet ready for Alice's tiny, delicate-featured boy, and the girls took turns fawning over him. All their lives they were afraid of having multiples like Annie Mae. This fear made them cautious, perhaps overly so, when it came to boys. They were relieved that Alice had given birth to a single child, and all four sisters adored him. Although the baby was a good sleeper, the household painstakingly tiptoed around him when he napped.[237]

One day, shortly after Alice's return to their summer home, Elma and Lucy consulted in whispers in the kitchen. The girls did not think much of it until a couple from Winston-Salem, North Carolina, appeared at the Thackers' doorstep soon afterward. They did not stay long. As they headed to the door, they reached for Alice's baby boy, much to Alice's and her sisters' surprise.[238]

When Alice realized what was happening, she tried to grab the baby out of their arms, but she was not strong enough to stop them. The Thackers, who had orchestrated the adoption, let the couple leave with her baby, while Alice screamed and thrashed in agony. For the rest of the summer, Alice cried every night, her heart completely broken. Catherine felt her sister's pain and cried with her, berating herself for not thinking clearly in the moment.[239] If she had been smarter, she would have followed the couple to see where they took the baby, but the opportunity was lost forever. Alice never found out where her baby went, and she never had another child.

Despite her misery, Alice went back to school and continued to make public appearances for Pet Milk. But the things she used to love about her life, the glamorous clothes and exciting events, no longer made her happy. Alice would have struggled as a teenage mother but would have had no reason to give up her child if she had not needed to live up to Pet Milk's exacting demands. Her son's absence permanently altered her personality, making her bitter, stubborn, and outspoken. Even her appearance changed. Her face set into a regretful expression, and her mouth turned down.[240]

During the summer after their seventeenth birthday, the girls went to Livingstone College to study social graces.[241] Their training included making an entrance, standing on a receiving line, and taking their leave. Fred Klenner's sister-in-law, Judge Susie Sharp, continued to disburse their Pet Milk allowance of $350 a month.[242] Elma and Charles tried to get the company to pay for extra expenses but were not always successful. Once, Judge Sharp informed the Saylors that the company refused to accept a handwritten receipt from the girls' dentist for reimbursement.[243] Charles continued to sell insurance, and Elma worked as a substitute teacher throughout the girls' high school years to keep them in the debutante dresses that Pet Milk insisted they wear.[244]

As the girls approached the end of high school, their academic performance fell below the expectations of the prestigious colleges that had once vied for their future enrollment. With their grades, attending any college at all might not be possible. After they underwent testing at UNC–Chapel Hill for basic academic skills, a specialist recommended that the girls get remedial tutoring to get them on track to graduate from high school.[245]

Summer school was not an option for the celebrity sisters. In August, the National Association of Colored Women's Clubs sponsored a return trip to the White House for them. During their Rose Garden tour, President Kennedy suddenly appeared on the South Lawn for a ceremony involving trainees for a new defense communications system. Andrew T. Hatcher, assistant White House press secretary, introduced the Fultz sisters to the president, who did an exaggerated double take when he saw them. Photographers documented this fortuitous meeting, which rekindled the girls' iconic status in the Black community.[246]

The sisters also traveled to New York City, where Louise Prothro hosted them for a cocktail hour at the Overseas Press Club. At the event,

Louise praised Pet Milk's commitment to the girls "and their admirable way of guidance."[247] But this "guidance" and support would soon end. When the sisters graduated high school, they were on their own, released from their contract with Pet Milk. They struggled to establish themselves as adults. They had long lost the comfort of their family, and their academic standing was dismal at best. They had no money left from the years of monthly allowance Pet Milk had given them. Elma was no longer on Pet Milk's payroll.

Although the sisters had an extraordinary childhood and adolescence, the price of their fame was high. When it was all over, the girls felt the sting of separation from their family even more acutely. In their later years, they saw their exploitation by Pet Milk clearly. The company unapologetically used the Fultz sisters' bodies to sell its product. It thought nothing of sacrificing the girls' bond with their family at the altar of high profits. The devaluation of Black families and enduring stereotypes of Black mothers allowed the corporation to do this unchallenged.

Chapter 4

THE BAD BLACK MOTHER

From the moment they set foot in this country as slaves, Black
women have fallen outside the American ideal of motherhood.
—*Dorothy Roberts*, Killing the Black Body

To further their corporate and reputational interests, Pet Milk and Fred Klenner cavalierly arranged for the Fultz sisters' separation from their family. If they had any concerns about how this might affect the Fultzes, they gave no indication of it. Their perceptions of Black life and relationships likely relied on long-standing stereotypes. Tropes about Black men, women, and children provide cognitive shortcuts, allowing people to make quick judgments based on assumptions. Stereotypes eliminate the need to get to know people as individuals.

These stereotypes are dangerous. In 2018, security guard Jemel Robertson picked up an extra shift to help pay for his son's first Christmas.[1] When a man fired gunshots in Manny's Blue Room, the suburban Chicago bar that Jemel was guarding, Jemel pinned him to the ground before anyone got killed. When a White officer arrived at the scene and saw Jemel on top of the shooter, he immediately shot Jemel dead. The stereotype of Black men as criminals prevented the officer from pausing to assess the scene and recognizing Jemel for the hero that he was. Because of this stereotype, Cleveland police also killed Tamir Rice, a twelve-year-old boy playing with a toy gun in a park, within two seconds of laying eyes on him.[2]

Tropes about Black women and girls are equally harmful. Since slavery, they have dehumanized Black women, casting them as sexually accessible and as unfit mothers. The real-life consequences of these stereotypes

include Black women's over-incarceration and Black mothers disproportionately losing their children to the child-welfare system. The origins of
these stereotypes lie in three stock characters introduced during slavery.

Mammy

Mammy is a Black woman who takes exemplary care of White children.[3]
She was happy as a slave. Once freed, she continued to enjoy selflessly
serving White people.[4] She is buxom, dark skinned, and gently scold-
ing. She often wears a handkerchief over her head. She has deep religious
faith.[5] She is the strict domestic manager of White households—without her, everything would fall apart. Her children come second to the
White children she cares for.[6] Their needs are nonexistent or unimportant, as are her own. Void of desires, she is emotionally self-sufficient and
asexual.[7]

In *Mammy: A Century of Race, Gender, and Southern Memory*, Kimberly Wallace-Sanders describes the complexity of Mammy's dual maternal aspects: "Her devotion for the children she cares for is best illustrated
by her disregard for her own children."[8] Mammy's rejection of her children is not merely incidental to her love for the slave owner's children.
It is fundamental to it. One cannot exist without the other. It therefore
makes the most sense for Black women to rear White children. Wallace-
Sanders explains that "because of widespread theories of nineteenth-
century racial essentialism, African American women were thought to be
innately superior in their abilities as caretakers of white children."[9] Presumably, someone else, or nobody, would care for Black children.

Through popular folklore, "the mammy emerge[d] as a mother who
frequently displaces white mothers and has ambiguous relationships with
her own children."[10] This displacement often led White women to experience confusing and conflicting attitudes toward the enslaved women who
cared for their children. Jealousy, gratitude, and resentment complicated
this relationship. Emotions ran high, as interactions were often quite intimate, with many enslaved caregivers living in the slave owners' homes. In
this close and complex environment, White mothers often sought to establish their racial superiority.

In one modern version of this trope, Mammy has evolved into the
benevolent, all-knowing Aunt Jemima, purveyor of perfect pancakes to
White families.[11] In another, she is the much-desired Black nanny. This

figure is so endemic to the popular imagination that White onlookers often assume that Black women with light-skinned children are their nan-
nies, not their mothers. This perception may be more palatable to Whites
than the reality of a Black woman with a White male partner.[12]

During slavery and Reconstruction, the mythical Mammy did not
breastfeed her children, because she—and, by extension, all Black women—
lacked maternal instincts toward them. This lie obscured the reality that
slave owners and, later, demanding employers prohibited Black women
from nursing. This perception that Black mothers do not breastfeed persists into the present.

Jezebel

Jezebel is a Black woman with an insatiable sexual appetite.[13] She is young
and shapely. She is often light skinned with European features, denoting
her allure.[14] She recognizes her power over men and uses it to manipulate and deceive them into giving her attention and money. She reserves a
special lust for White men. She has no shame. Due to her voracious desire
for sex, it is impossible to rape or sexually abuse her.[15] She is a constantly
willing and available sexual partner, animal-like in her aggression.[16] Her
lasciviousness stands in stark contrast to the essential chastity and purity
of White women.

By portraying Black women as sexually insatiable, casting their bodies
as mere instruments of sexual desire, the Jezebel stereotype erased Black
women's humanity, including their maternal and spousal roles.[17] This
dehumanization made sexual assaults by slave owners and other White
men appear to be desired instead of a manifestation of White male exploitation and violence. Jezebel has evolved into the Video Vixen, always
half-naked and sexually available.[18] Black women who experience rape or
other forms of sexual assault and harassment still face indifference reinforced by this stereotype.[19] The modern Jezebel is the antithesis of a
nurturing nursing mother.

The Jezebel stereotype operates not only among White onlookers but
also sometimes as a "controlling image" internalized by Black women
and their communities.[20] Insidiously, it can make Black women more
self-conscious about breastfeeding in public. It can also lead the partners
and family members of Black mothers to admonish them for baring any
parts of their bodies outside the home.[21]

Similarly, the practice of compelling Black women to expose their bodies in public during slavery created an aversion to public nudity that persists today.[22] This history contributes to lower breastfeeding rates among Black women. If nursing mothers must restrict their breastfeeding to private spaces, they are unlikely to continue doing it very long, because infants require breast milk on demand to ensure adequate nutrition and milk supply.[23] The Jezebel myth sexualizes all forms of nudity, sublimating and erasing Black women's roles as mothers.

Sapphire

Sapphire is a sharp-tongued Black woman. She is loud, scathing, and quick to anger. Her obvious intelligence is intimidating, and she lords it over everyone. She dominates her household with an iron fist. Make the wrong move, and she will be quick to correct and punish you. In Regina Austin's words, she is "the stereotypical BLACK BITCH—tough, domineering, emasculating, strident, and shrill."[24] With her confidence and competency, Sapphire unnaturally usurps men's proper role in society as the authoritative breadwinners.[25] She is personally responsible for the disintegration of the Black family.[26]

Sapphire became popular as a character created for the *Amos 'n' Andy* show in the 1950s. This incarnation of the stereotype "is tart-tongued and emasculating, one hand on a hip and the other pointing and jabbing (or arms akimbo), violently and rhythmically rocking her head, mocking African American men for offenses ranging from being unemployed to sexually pursuing white women. She is a shrill nagger with irrational states of anger and indignation and is often mean-spirited and abusive."[27] During and after slavery, this trope justified the use of Black women as laborers instead of allowing them to care for their homes and children.[28] The modern version of this stereotype is the Angry Black Woman, who elicits no sympathy when she speaks up against injustice or simply raises her voice.[29] She exists in stark contrast to the calm, gentle, tender White woman.[30]

Sapphire also stands in opposition to Mammy.[31] Where Mammy subserviently aims to please, Sapphire is breaking balls. Sapphire is nobody's friend or caretaker. Instead, she is "devoid of maternal compassion and understanding."[32] Sapphire is not a nurturer and, therefore, not a breastfeeder. If a Black woman is domestic, she is Mammy. If she is sexual, she is Jezebel. If she is intellectual, she is Sapphire. In none of these polarized versions of Black womanhood is she a good mother.

Welfare Queen

The Welfare Queen is the quintessential modern version of the Bad Black Mother. She is a composite of Mammy, Jezebel, and Sapphire. Like Mammy, she is indifferent to her children's needs. But unlike Mammy, she is not soft or subservient. Instead, she is a "failed mammy," incapable of caring for children.[33] Like Jezebel, she uses her sexuality to get ahead in life, and like Sapphire, she is manipulative and harsh. Reminiscent of the Breeder stereotype in slavery that portrayed Black women as perpetual but indifferent mothers, this newer stereotype layers the dimension of criminality onto the old trope. The Welfare Queen's attitude and behavior inspire disgust in all decent onlookers.[34]

In short, the Welfare Queen is a morally and socially deviant single woman. She has children whom she fails to care for because the sole purpose of their existence is to make her eligible for government benefits.[35] She lives off her government checks without lifting a finger to help herself, society, or her offspring.[36] She has a heightened sense of entitlement and an irrepressible sexuality that makes her indifferent to the inevitable by-products of her wanton sexual activity.[37] Society has to pay the price for her behavior, because she cunningly evades doing so herself.

The *Chicago Tribune* introduced this term in the headline "'Welfare Queen' Jailed in Tucson" in an October 12, 1974, article about the arrest of Linda Taylor.[38] Taylor's husband, angry because she had taken his television set, tipped authorities off about her whereabouts. When apprehended in Arizona, Taylor was receiving welfare checks from Illinois. She had over fifty aliases, three cars, four buildings in South Side Chicago, and plane tickets to Hawai'i. Ronald Reagan made Taylor's story and the Welfare Queen myth famous when he used them on the campaign trail in 1976.[39]

The introduction of the Welfare Queen into the popular imagination engendered support for radical changes to social-benefit programs. When the federal welfare program began in 1935, the common image of a woman on welfare was that of a "Madonna-like" White mother who needed society's support to fulfill her important caretaking roles.[40] At first, Black women did not receive welfare. Because they had always worked, they appeared self-sufficient and undeserving of state assistance.[41] Even if the state had wanted to help Black families out of poverty at that time, the task was too overwhelming.

Later, when welfare benefits extended to unmarried darker-skinned women, social attitudes toward the program shifted. The initial goal of welfare was to raise children out of poverty. But as the color of program participants changed, so did attitudes toward it. Critics began to view welfare as a reward for some mothers' careless behavior instead of as a genuine attempt to help children.[42] A White woman who stayed home to care for her children was selfless, but a Black woman who stayed home with her kids was lazy. The concept of welfare lost its original association with the idea of women's, children's, and society's well-being.[43]

Other, more positive stereotypes of mothers simply exclude Black women altogether. The Soccer Mom is a middle-class White woman who spends all her time driving her kids around. She staunchly defends them, on and off the field.[44] The Soccer Mom's ferocity, although sometimes scary, pales in comparison to the wrath of the Angry Black Woman. The Tiger Mom similarly pushes her children to succeed in academics and extracurricular activities.[45] She is typically Chinese.[46] She is overly strict, demanding, and indifferent to her children's desires—for their own good. Although she is harsh to the point of being shrewish, her heart is in the right place.[47]

None of the stereotypes that apply to Black women allow for the possibility of good mothering. A Black mother is either lustful to the exclusion of all other concerns (Jezebel), cruelly sharp tongued (Sapphire), seeking only to please White people (Mammy), or duplicitous (Welfare Queen). There is no room for nuance or complexities. Cumulatively, these tropes become the Bad Black Mother, a ubiquitous character in news, politics, film, and the collective conscience. This figure guides law and policy and renders inequality socially acceptable, even correct.

Tracing the birth of the Bad Black Mother stereotype from slavery to its modern incarnations reveals how it affects Black women's breastfeeding rates. The case of Tabitha Walrond provides an illuminating example of how racial stereotypes, structural inequality, law, and breastfeeding collide in contemporary times. Tabitha faced criminal charges after losing her baby due to breastfeeding complications.[48] The exploitation of her tragedy by formula companies and the media echoed the experiences of the Fultz sisters fifty years earlier.

Bad Black Mothers in History

In 1786, the *Georgia Gazette* ran a story berating an enslaved woman named Hanna for running away with her five-year-old daughter while leaving behind "a child at her breast."[49] In reality, women in Hanna's community would care for and nurse her baby. Still, the White press saw no irony in condemning Hanna's behavior while approving of the frequent forced separation of Black mothers and children by slave owners.[50] Renowned civil rights scholar Dorothy Roberts identifies the *Gazette* article as the first depiction of the Bad Black Mother in America.

Whites commonly attributed the high rate of infant mortality among slave children to Black mothers' "carelessness and total inability to take care of themselves."[51] This could not have been further from the truth. Instead, infant mortality reflected poor nutrition, abuse, hard labor during pregnancy, and reduced opportunities to breastfeed. Ironically, lies about Black mothers' fatal incompetence did not prevent simultaneous development of the belief that they were perfectly suited to raising White children.

After emancipation, Black women continued to work primarily as domestic laborers. These jobs required long working hours, forcing Black children into others' care. After slavery became unlawful, Whites resisted giving up their positions of privilege over Blacks.[52] Physical and emotional abuse by White employers was common, reflecting the persistent devaluation of Black women's lives. At the turn of the twentieth century, White reformers blamed Black mothers for rampant social disorder. These accusers claimed that Black mothers' neglect of the care and education of their children created widespread social chaos.[53]

Blaming Black mothers for society's ills maintains the myth of White superiority. It also justifies disparate treatment across all aspects of society and reinforces racist stereotypes. It absolves the government from the responsibility to enact reforms.[54] Historically, identifying poor Black mothers as the source of social problems opened the door for New Deal policies that boosted poor Whites' social status while excluding Blacks. These innovative programs included the introduction in 1934 of home loans managed by the Federal Housing Administration and distributed unequally through the process of redlining Black neighborhoods[55] as well as the 1935 Social Security Act[56] and the 1944 GI Bill.[57]

Senator Daniel Patrick Moynihan strengthened the case against Black women in his 1965 report titled *The Negro Family: The Case for National Action*.[58] The report blamed Black mothers for poverty in the Black community.[59] Moynihan claimed that "the Negro community has been forced into a matriarchal structure which, because it is so out of line with the rest of the American society, seriously retards the progress of the group as a whole, and imposes a crushing burden on the Negro male and, in consequence, on a great many Negro women as well."[60] The report's stigmatization of Black families as inappropriately matriarchal relied on the Bad Black Mother myth.[61] It also laid the groundwork for supporters to embrace Reagan's Welfare Queen eleven years later.

Instead of seeing welfare as an appropriate government response to entrenched structural inequalities, people came to view it as a free handout for undeserving scammers. In 1984, political scientist Charles A. Murray bolstered this view in his influential and controversial book on American welfare policy, *Losing Ground*.[62] Murray posited that welfare encourages Black women to have more children, which harms rather than benefits them.[63] He asserted that abolishing welfare would help impoverished racial minorities get back on their feet. He believed this move would lead to enduring change instead of providing a Band-Aid solution.[64] In his view, welfare benefits allowed the government to usurp the roles of Black parents, ultimately damaging their families.[65] The myth of the Welfare Queen made this claim appear both palatable and reasonable.

Ten years later, Murray argued in *The Bell Curve* that the comparative social and economic status of different racial groups reflects not systemic racism but natural genetic variations in intellect and ability.[66] For Murray and his proponents, government intervention is wasteful and ineffective. Benefits are merely an unnecessary and unfortunate manifestation of White guilt.[67] Murray's philosophy, which denies the realities facing low-income communities of color, formed the basis of American welfare policy. It led to a reframing of family assistance as a windfall bestowed on the undeserving poor.[68]

The Welfare Queen myth also fueled mistaken belief in the false epidemic of crack mothers and crack babies. In the 1980s, a doctor at Northwestern University released a study of twenty-three babies whose mothers took cocaine while pregnant.[69] The study concluded that the cocaine had negative effects on the infants' development that would last throughout their lives. Media coverage of the report spread like wildfire, causing a moral panic.[70] Further research exposed that the study, whose sample size was too small to create reliable data, conflated the symptoms of premature birth with the effects of the mother's cocaine use. But the damage was already done.[71] Outrage about crack babies fed the War on Drugs. Black women faced prosecution for giving birth to crack-addicted babies.[72] Even Black babies did not escape the vitriol inspired by this lie. The media cast them as a burden on taxpayers and as living proof of their mothers' cruelty and indifference.[73] Although subsequent research definitively proved that they never existed, the myth of the crack baby persists.[74]

The false images of the Welfare Queen and the Crack Mother also linger, framing Black mothers as heartless, corrupt, and deviant. These myths justify disproportionate interventions into Black families by child services[75] and the over-criminalization of pregnant Black mothers.[76] They provide support for punitive welfare reform that requires new mothers to work outside the home, removing many Black mothers from their infants and disrupting breastfeeding.[77] They also guide the mistreatment of incarcerated Black women, who receive little respect for their motherhood.

Prisons often force women to give birth while shackled.[78] All but a handful of prisons separate babies born in prison from their mothers.[79] This practice denies mothers and infants, who end up with relatives or in foster care, the benefits of breastfeeding. It also echoes back to slavery practices. Women are the fastest-growing prison population. Since 1980, the number of women in prison has increased twice as fast as that of men.[80] In 2016, there were 1.2 million women in the criminal justice system.[81] Black women are disproportionately represented in this group. In 2015, although there were 52,700 White female prisoners compared to 21,700 Black female prisoners, Black women's imprisonment rates (103 per 100,000) were almost double the rates of Whites.[82]

Political scientist Shanto Iyengar tested the power of the Welfare Queen myth. He found that when viewers saw the image of a Black mother on welfare, they commonly attributed her need for benefits to her personal failings instead of to public policy or any other structural factor.[83] Other studies demonstrate that many Whites have no significant interactions with Blacks that would counter this false perception.[84] Racial segregation accounts for many Whites' inability to filter stereotypical images presented by popular culture, including news media, through their own lived experiences. It also prevents them from understanding these stereotypes as incorrect and harmful. Instead, many Whites buy into a narrative script that equates welfare and poverty with single Black motherhood.[85]

Repeated exposure to this script reinforces the views that receiving welfare is a reflection of weakness; the government should cut spending on welfare; and women should take on traditional gender roles that render them financially dependent on men.[86] As Dorothy Roberts explains, "Part of the reason that maternalist rhetoric can no longer justify public financial support for mothers is that the public views this support as benefiting primarily black mothers. Maternalist rhetoric has no appeal in the case of black welfare mothers because most white Americans see no value in supporting their domestic care-giving. Many workfare advocates fail to see the benefit in poor black mothers' care for their young children."[87]

In 2017, 32.5% of adult TANF (Temporary Assistance to Needy Families) recipients were White, and 30.2% were Black.[88] That same year, 27.5% of child TANF recipients were White, and 27.8% were Black.[89] In 2016, 43% of Medicaid recipients were White, and 18% were Black.[90] Although Whites are the primary beneficiaries of welfare, imposing the face of a Black woman on the image of a welfare recipient transforms public perception of the program.

Bad Black Mothers in the News

The Bad Black Mother myth leads to the criminalization of acts performed by Black women that White women can get away with.[91] This criminalization begins in pregnancy and continues throughout motherhood. In *Cheating Welfare*, Kaaryn Gustafson chronicles how Black women on welfare often face criminal fraud charges for working extra jobs to afford food for their families because their benefits are inadequate.[92] Similarly, despite parents across the country using the addresses of friends or relatives to get their children into better-resourced public schools, two Black mothers, Kelley Williams-Bolar in Ohio[93] and Tanya McDowell in Connecticut,[94] received felony convictions for doing so. Ordinarily, schools deal with this type of boundary hopping by transferring the student to their districted school and issuing a warning to parents.[95]

Alexis Hutchinson was a soldier and a single Black mother who chose not to deploy because she could not find appropriate care for her infant son.[96] As a result, Alexis lost custody of her son and faced charges and possible jail time. Shanesha Taylor was a homeless, single Black mother who left her two children in a car while she interviewed for a job with Farmers Insurance because her child care fell through. She faced charges of felony child abuse.[97] Deborah Harrell, a forty-six-year-old single Black mother from South Carolina, could not afford child care for her nine-year-old daughter on her McDonald's salary.[98] Deborah's daughter went with her to work and played quietly on the family laptop.[99] After thieves broke into their home and stole the computer, her daughter asked to play in a nearby park during her mother's shift.[100] Three days later, a woman discovered her alone in the park and called the police.[101] Officers arrested Deborah and placed her daughter in the custody of social services.

After getting off a city bus in Atlanta, single Black mother Raquel Nelson and her children, a two-year-old she held in her arms and her four-year-old son, A. J., waited in the median for cars to pass so they could cross safely. A. J. wriggled his hand out of Raquel's and ran straight into a car driven by a drunk driver.[102] The Atlanta prosecutor charged Raquel with reckless conduct, improperly crossing a roadway, and second-degree homicide by vehicle. An all-White jury, all but one of whom admitted that they had never ridden a city bus, convicted her of vehicular manslaughter.[103]

Even Black mothers of children that police officers killed have received blame for their children's deaths.[104] Michael Brown was the eighteen-year-old victim of a police shooting in Ferguson, Missouri, on August 9, 2014.[105] Some commentators claimed that the bad parenting of his mother, Lesley McSpadden, was the cause of his death.[106] After Cleveland police shot and killed twelve-year-old Tamir Rice on November 22, 2014,[107] his mother, Samaria Rice, faced accusations, including some from police officers, that her parenting led to his death.[108] When a police officer shot sleeping seven-year-old Aiyana Stanley-Jones in the head during a raid on the wrong home on May 16, 2010, he initially blamed his action on her grandmother, who reached out to protect her.[109] In the Detroit Police Department's first version of the incident, Joseph Weekly, the first officer on the scene, falsely "reported to his sergeant that 'A woman inside grabbed my gun' and 'It fired. The bullet hit a child.'"[110]

On May 29, 2016, Cincinnati Zoo employees shot a seventeen-year-old gorilla named Harambe to prevent him from hurting Michelle Gregg's three-year-old son, Isaiah, who had fallen into the primate exhibit.[111] After she publicly thanked the zoo for protecting Isaiah, an online petition, signed by half a million individuals, stated, "It is believed that the situation was caused by parental negligence and the zoo is not responsible for the child's injuries and possible trauma. We the undersigned want the parents to be held accountable for the lack of supervision and negligence that caused Harambe to lose his life. We the undersigned feel the child's safety is paramount in this situation. We believe that this negligence may be reflective of the child's home situation. We the undersigned actively encourage an investigation of the child's home environment in the interests of protecting the child and his siblings from further incidents of parental negligence that may result in serious bodily harm or even death."[112] Internet memes compared Michelle, who is Black, to a gorilla, and Harambe became a symbol prominent in racist memes.[113]

In contrast, there was overwhelming support for Matt and Melissa Graves, the White parents of a two-year-old eaten by an alligator at Disney World.[114] And Michelle Schwab, a White woman who accidentally dropped her two-year-old son into a cheetah cage at the Cleveland Zoo, did not face calls for intervention by child services.[115] Instead, when wealthy White parents allow their children increased independence, some child development experts label this behavior "free-range parenting." They frame this philosophy as a deliberate and positive parenting choice.[116] When Black parents loosen the leash on their children, they face condemnation and retribution.

Bad Black Mothers in Popular Culture

The Bad Black Mother myth goes beyond newspaper headlines and political speeches. She pervades the cinematic experience, in all of her incarnations. As Robin M. Boylorn explains,

> "Bad" black mamas are common tropes in films where black women are scapegoated . . . as the precursor for pathology in the black family. Black mothers are blamed or implicated though rarely praised or celebrated.

> Working mothers are chastised for not being stay-at-home mothers; welfare mothers are demonized for not working; single mothers are blamed for not being sufficient "father-figures"; married women are expected to want to be mothers; young mothers are vilified for unplanned babies; older mothers are harshly judged for waiting too long.[117]

Mammy was the first Black mother to grace the silver screen. The character of Mammy initially appeared in minstrel shows in the 1820s and then on-screen in 1914's *Coontown Suffragettes*.[118] Since then, Mammy has appeared in a long list of films by White directors. These films span a century and include *The Birth of a Nation* (1915), *Her Fairy Prince* (1915), *Heart and Soul* (1917), *Hallelujah* (1929), *Mammy* (1930), *Imitation of Life* (1934), *The Buccaneer* (1938), *Gone with the Wind* (1939), *Mammy* (1951), and *The Help* (2011). In 1940, Hattie McDaniel was the first Black actor to win an Oscar. She won Best Supporting Actress for her performance as Mammy in *Gone with the Wind*.[119] She needed special dispensation to be able to collect the award at the segregated Ambassador Hotel where the ceremony took place.[120]

Over fifty years later, Whoopi Goldberg followed in McDaniel's footsteps. Goldberg was the second Black woman to win the Best Supporting Actress award, for her performance as Oda Mae Brown in 1990's *Ghost*.[121] Goldberg's role fell in line with the stereotype of the "Magical Negro."[122] Magical Negros are saintly Black characters, alone in a predominantly White universe, whose sole purpose is to enrich the lives of the White characters around them.[123] White directors have also created roles for Black women that perpetuate the Jezebel, Sapphire, and Bad Black Mother myths. These include Pam Grier's eponymous role in *Foxy Brown* (1974); Adrien Lenox as Denise Oher, a real-life mother of eleven children, in *The Blind Side* (2009); and Halle Berry as Khalia in *Losing Isaiah* (1995) and Leticia in *Monster's Ball* (2001).

Berry won the Best Actress award for her portrayal of hypersexual Leticia in *Monster's Ball*.[124] Some critics launched personal attacks against her for accepting the role and engaging in an explicit sex scene with her co-star, Billy Bob Thornton.[125] Actor Angela Bassett fed into this criticism by stating publicly that she turned down the role because she refused to play a prostitute on film. Bassett added that she blamed Hollywood, not Berry, for the stereotyping.[126]

Decades of White cultural production entrenched stereotypes about Black women in popular culture. This legacy eventually led to the incorporation of these stereotypes into the work of Black cultural creators and into the tastes of Black cultural consumers. Today, some of the most controversial Bad Black Mothers exist in films created by Black filmmakers and directed at Black audiences. Tyler Perry's overwrought caricature of a Black mother, Madea, exemplifies this stereotype. The character appears in a dozen popular films, including *A Madea Family Funeral* (2019), *Madea on the Run* (2017), *Boo 2! A Madea Halloween* (2017), *Boo! A Madea Halloween* (2016), *Madea's Tough Love* (2015), *Madea's Neighbors from Hell* (2014), *A Madea Christmas* (2013), *Madea Gets a Job* (2013), *Madea's Witness Protection* (2012), *Madea's Big Happy Family* (2011), *Madea Goes to Jail* (2009), *Madea's Family Reunion* (2006), *Diary of a Mad Black Woman* (2005), and *Madea's Class Reunion* (2003). Martin Lawrence also created and portrayed a stereotypical matriarch, Big Momma, in three movies, *Big Momma's House* (2000), *Big Momma's House 2* (2006), and *Big Mommas: Like Father Like Son* (2011). Eddie Murphy played a similar character in *Norbit* (2007).

The popular Madea and Big Momma characters have inspired harsh criticism by cultural scholars for their degradation of women and their perpetuation of stereotypes about Black mothers. Several critiques center around the harmful effects on Black women's self-image and eating habits that these characters, who are both unrealistically large, could engender.[127] Madea, Big Momma, and a host of other Bad Black Mothers in film are direct descendants and modern incarnations of Mammy, Sapphire, and Jezebel: vicious, unaffectionate, and grotesquely sexual women. One writer deemed this hybrid of stereotypes Sapphmamibel.[128] This composite character seems not to have a nurturing bone in her body. She appears disinterested in and incapable of nurturing children through breastfeeding.

The Bad Black Mother also appears in serious films, played convincingly by skilled actors that include Loretta Devine as Marguerite Slocumb in *Kingdom Come* (2001), Tasha Smith as Jennifer in *Daddy's Little Girls* (2007), Taraji P. Henson as Yvette in *Baby Boy* (2001), and Kim Wayans as Audrey in *Pariah* (2011). One critique of the character Audrey in *Pariah* asserts that "such a representation supports E. Franklin Frazier and Senator Patrick Moynihan's infamous and specious characterizations of African American women as emasculating, causing fathers and husbands to desert their families as well as precipitating racial inequality."[129] Audrey is a modern Sapphire.

Perhaps the most extreme version of the contemporary Bad Black Mother in film is the character of Mary Jones, the mother of the protagonist in director Lee Daniels's *Precious: Based on the Novel "Push" by Sapphire* (2009). Actor and comedian Mo'Nique won the Best Supporting Actress award for playing Mary.[130] Critiques of the role as perpetuating harmful stereotypes about Black mothers abounded. Armond White, then chief film critic for the *New York Press* and chair of the New York Film Critics Circle, controversially attacked the film as "a sociological horror show" that was "full of brazenly racist clichés."[131]

White asserted that "[*Precious*'s] agreed-upon selection of the most pathetic racial images and social catastrophes helps to normalize the circumstances of poverty and abandon that will never change or be resolved."[132] He also decried the film's effect on White audiences:

Worse than *Precious* itself was the ordeal of watching it with an audience full of patronizing white folk at the New York Film Festival, then enduring its media hoodwink as a credible depiction of black American life. A scene such as the hippopotamus-like teenager climbing a K-2 incline of tenement stairs to present her newborn, incest-bred baby to her unhinged virago matriarch, might have been met with howls of skeptical laughter at Harlem's Magic Johnson theater. Black audiences would surely have seen the comedy in this ludicrous, overloaded situation, whereas too many white film habitués casually enjoy it for the sense of superiority—and relief—it allows them to feel.[133]

The character of Mary is a quintessential Welfare Mother who physically, sexually, and emotionally abuses her daughter. Her dialogue consists mainly of curses and invective.[134] Other critics describe her as "an unredeemed monster who brutalizes her daughter"[135] and "a callous and indifferent mother, consumed by afternoon television and psychologically dependent upon welfare."[136] Mary embodies all of the worst clichés about Black mothers. Not satisfied with collecting her own welfare checks, she takes her daughter's as well. She puts her own needs first, always. In her most horrifying revelation, Mary attempts to justify the fact that she allowed Precious's father to rape her by Mary's need to maintain his affection.

The terrible largeness of Mary's literal and figurative evil provides support for the myth that welfare is primarily for single Black mothers who cheat the government and are poor due to their own deep failings. This portrayal arises directly from the dog-whistle politics that Ronald Reagan relied on to spread the Welfare Queen myth.[137] Confronted with this repulsive portrayal of Black motherhood, the viewer cannot imagine a scenario in which Mary lovingly breastfeeds her ironically named daughter.[138]

Seven years after the Oscars honored Mo'Nique for her portrayal of Mary, Naomie Harris received an Oscar nomination for her work as Paula, the mother of protagonist Chiron in the 2016 Best Picture–winning and universally acclaimed[139] film *Moonlight*, created by Black auteur Barry Jenkins.[140] Paula is another single Black mother who selfishly puts herself before her child. In this case, she does so in the service of her crack addiction. Unlike Mary, Paula alternates between bestowing affection on her child and cruelly rejecting him, but this unpredictability is equally destructive. Both Jenkins and Harris consciously tried to avoid harmful stereotypes with the role. But despite their efforts, a single Black mother who neglects her son for crack addiction falls squarely into the realm of the Bad Black Mother, no matter how nuanced the portrayal.[141]

Harris initially turned down the role but changed her mind after discussing her fears with Jenkins. She describes their conversation:

> I said to Barry, "I have fears about taking on this role." He said to me, "I understand your fears, but the reality is I want to tell my story, and my story necessarily involves that of my mother." And I thought, "Here, for the first time, is someone who has a vested interest in ensuring that she doesn't become stereotyped, and that she is given her full humanity." And what I felt in doing it and reading it was that she has a complete arc. So I thought I could understand where she starts off in trying to be a good mother, trying to hold down a job, doing this on her own, the pressures of all of that, how she gets into crack addiction and how she ultimately comes out of it. I didn't think it was stereotypical.[142]

Nonetheless, the character of Paula reinforces the stereotypical assumption that Black mothers are incapable of nurturing their children.[143] Paula's failings are particularly glaring in comparison to the kindness of Teresa (played by Janelle Monáe), the girlfriend of Juan (Mahershala Ali)—the benevolent drug dealer who becomes a father figure to young Chiron (Alex R. Hibbert). The contrast in the ability to nurture between a biological Black mother and a Black mother figure without biological children underscores the disassociation of Black mothers from their children that has been a through line in common perceptions of Black motherhood since slavery.[144]

If the cultural landscape included a range of Black women in film, flawed mother Paula would fall in the middle, somewhere between Mary Jones and Katherine Johnson (played by Taraji P. Henson), the heroic mathematician of *Hidden Figures* (2017), or Sharon Rivers of Barry Jenkins's 2018 *If Beale Street Could Talk*. Regina King won the award for Best Supporting Actress for her portrayal of Sharon, a loving, accepting mother, willing to take any steps necessary to secure the happiness of her teenage daughter, Tish (Kiki Layne), soon to be a mother herself. Jenkins gives us a foil to Sharon in Mrs. Hunt (Aunjanue Ellis), the mother of Fonny (Stephan James), Tish's childhood friend turned lover. But in this female-centered film, even Mrs. Hunt's harsh disapproval of Tish and Fonny's expected child seems rooted in maternal concern. The three Black mothers in the film provide complexity, highlighting different aspects of Black motherhood. Sharon emerges as a rare figure in American cinema: a completely good Black mother.

In contrast, *Moonlight*'s Paula joins a long line of stereotypical Black women that the Oscars have celebrated and Whites have adored. They include Effie the entertainer (Jennifer Hudson in *Dreamgirls*, 2006), Patsey the slave (Lupita N'yongo in *12 Years a Slave*, 2013), and Minny the Maid (Octavia Spencer in *The Help*, 2011). *Moonlight*'s Oscar victory, although surprising and affirming in some ways, confirmed that White institutions consistently reward roles and films that fall within their comfort zone. *Moonlight* was excellent, but so were *Daughters of the Dust* (1991), *Selma* (2014), and *Tangerine* (2015). The Academy overlooked these complex and stunning films about three generations of Gullah women living on an isolated North Carolina island, a turning point in US civil rights history, and a Black, transgender sex worker.

The fictional Bad Black Mother has even bled into news media, making the stereotype appear real.[145] In 2009, the well-publicized child abuse inflicted by Black mother Antoinette Nicole Davis on her five-year-old daughter Shaniya echoed the brutality brought so convincingly to life on screen in the same year by Mo'Nique.[146] Officers charged Davis with child sex trafficking after they found Shaniya's body on a North Carolina road.[147] In response, political commentator Melissa Harris Perry observed,

> In a country with tens of thousands of missing and exploited children, it is not accidental that the abuse and murder of Shaniya Davis captured the American media cycle just as *Precious* opened. The sickening acts of Shaniya's mother become the story that underlines and makes tangible, believable, and credible the jaw-dropping horror of Mo'Nique's character.[148]

Perry's comments explain how fiction and reality can blur, allowing stereotypes to do the work of affirming political and social viewpoints. In this case, they supported social myths about Black women's criminality. In other cases, they shape perceptions of Black women's willingness and ability to nurture and breastfeed their children.

Generally, good Black mothers are simply absent from popular images of parenting. Denene Millner explains:

> Pick up any parenting journal of record; rarely will one see an image of a black mom tending to and loving on her children, much less participating in any kind of discussion on ordinary motherly concerns like teething or breast-feeding. Instead, chroniclers of modern family life tend to see little value in our voices and experiences outside of a racial context rooted in the effects of poverty or black-on-black crime on our kids or how we processed Trayvon Martin's death. Society, in turn, perpetuates the idea that we're all poor, strict disciplinarian, welfare-sapping single moms with no men to speak of and kids we barely love, who are destined for prison or early graves.[149]

One potential source of positive role models is celebrity mothers. In the age of *TMZ* and *Us Weekly*, these women undergo intense scrutiny of their parenting choices. White mothers have many celebrity role models validating their choice to breastfeed, including Angelina Jolie, Jennifer

Garner, Gwen Stefani, and Alyssa Milano, but there are few, if any, Black celebrity mothers that publicly advocate and practice breastfeeding.[150]

Thandie Newton of *Westworld* and Kandi Burruss of *Real Housewives of Atlanta* have posted breastfeeding selfies, and Serena Williams has engaged in online conversation about it.[151] Although celebrity news outlets reported that Beyoncé nursed her daughter Blue Ivy while eating on a New York restaurant's patio in 2012, there are no photographs to prove it.[152] Still, Beyoncé's highly public celebration of her pregnancy and motherhood may generate positive attitudes toward Black motherhood.[153]

Beyoncé announced her second pregnancy on February 1, 2017, with a beatific Instagram picture of herself against a backdrop of flower wreaths, dressed in lingerie, with a sheer veil over her head.[154] The pic's caption read, "We would like to share our love and happiness. We have been blessed two times over. We are incredibly grateful that our family will be growing by two, and we thank you for your well wishes, —The Carters"[155] The picture broke the record for most-liked Instagram post of all time. Experts set about analyzing it. Phillip Prodger, head of photographs at London's National Portrait Gallery, declared that "it's a wonderfully clever blend of references, showing Beyoncé as a Renaissance Madonna. . . . With its arched garland of roses, it calls to mind one of my favorite paintings, the famous 'Madonna in a Rose Garden' painted by Martin Schongauer in Colmar, Alsace, in 1473."[156]

On July 14, 2017, one month after giving birth to the twins, Beyoncé posted another stunning image on Instagram.[157] With it, she introduced Sir and Rumi Carter to the world and broke her own Instagram record.[158] The picture echoed the first one, with Beyoncé and the twins posed before a wreath of roses. She wore a flowing flowered dress and a long sheer veil. White Twitter users accused Beyoncé of using her children to maintain her brand.[159] They expressed outrage that she dared to compare herself to the Madonna. In contrast, White celebrity mothers, including Angelina Jolie and Katie Holmes, who celebrated their twins and babies on national magazine covers received overwhelmingly positive responses.[160] The backlash against Beyoncé's joyous images is evidence of the tenacity of the Bad Black Mother trope.[161]

Even presumably well-intentioned embraces of Beyoncé's vision of strong Black motherhood have fallen back on derisive tropes. At the 2017 Grammys, award-winning singers and self-professed fans of Beyoncé, Faith Hill and Adele expressed their desire for Beyoncé to be their "mommy."[162] They directed this evocation of slavery's Mammy myth at arguably the most influential Black woman in the United States at the music industry's largest event of the year. Their pleas reinforced the White vision of Black mothers' proper role as nurturers of White children instead of their own.[163]

Tabitha Walrond

Tabitha Walrond, a nineteen-year-old Black woman from the Bronx, consistently defied the stereotype of the Bad Black Mother during her pregnancy. Despite the heartbreak she experienced from her boyfriend Keenan Purcell's rejection when she told him she was pregnant, she resolved to keep their unborn child and raise him on her own. When Medicaid officers repeatedly turned her away because of a computer error, she never gave up. She survived a difficult birth and was determined to breastfeed her infant. Tabitha did everything right.

Tabitha gave birth to Tyler Isaac Walrond on June 27, 1997.[164] Four months before the birth, Tabitha, who received New York public assistance, had attempted to enroll Tyler in her health insurance plan (HIP). She ran up against a mountain of bureaucratic red tape and mistakes.[165] After several trips to three different offices in New York, Tabitha still could not get a Medicaid card for Tyler.[166] Tabitha's city caseworker informed her that she would have to wait until after Tyler's Social Security card and birth certificate arrived to get the card.[167]

Following her caesarian section, Tabitha developed a fever and blood clots that required medication, which prevented her from breastfeeding for ten days.[168] Four years earlier, at age fifteen, she had undergone breast reduction surgery.[169] During her extended post-birth hospital stay, Tabitha's doctors failed to inform her that these two factors put her at significant risk for problems with breastfeeding.

In the first few weeks of his life, Tyler steadily lost weight, but Tabitha did not realize it. It is normal for nursing mothers not to notice weight loss in their infants, even when it is significant, because they are together all the time.[170] Tabitha could not bring Tyler for a checkup because no doctor would see him without a Medicaid card.[171] Not suspecting that anything was wrong, Tabitha continued to breastfeed Tyler exclusively. On August 27, 1997, only eight weeks after his birth, Tyler became very ill. Tabitha rushed him to the hospital, but Tyler died from malnutrition in the taxi before they arrived.[172] Tabitha received Tyler's Medicaid cards and HIP membership several months later.[173]

Insufficient milk syndrome, or hypernatremia, may affect up to 5 percent of mothers like Tabitha in the United States each year, leading to dozens of infant deaths.[174] A tragedy similar to Tabitha's struck a mother in Ohio, when dehydration after exclusive breastfeeding led to her infant's leg amputation.[175] In Virginia, insufficient breast-milk supply caused another baby to suffer permanent brain damage.[176] In Colorado, Zion Cox, the son of a nurse and a minister, who were both White, died of malnutrition from low breast-milk supply.[177] In Zion's case, doctors saw him shortly after his birth but assured his mother, Ann, that everything was fine. Ten days later, a blood clot caused by dehydration cut off oxygen to his brain. Driven by the desire to create something meaningful from Zion's death, Ann went on to devote her life to providing medical care to impoverished rural communities.[178] A Denver newspaper lauded her efforts and portrayed her as a selfless woman seeking to honor her child's memory.[179] Similar incidents around the country involving White families prompted some states to change their laws regarding minimum hospital stays.[180]

Following Tyler's death, there was no outcry. There were no calls to reform the medical system to give low-income Black mothers and children adequate care so that what happened to Tabitha and Tyler would never happen again. No media outlet seized upon the story of a good mother who tried to provide her infant with the benefits of breastfeeding but fell victim to systemic racial disparities in medical treatment.[181] Tyler's death did not serve as a rallying point for increased resources for Black women who want to breastfeed. Instead, the New York prosecutor brought charges against Tabitha for second-degree manslaughter.[182]

Drawing on narratives from Tyler's paternal relatives, who described Tabitha as a "monster," the prosecutor theorized that Tabitha deliberately starved Tyler to death to get back at his father.[183] Keenan had left Tabitha for another woman after she informed him that she was pregnant and refused to get an abortion.[184] Later, in the waiting room for her six-month prenatal appointment, Keenan told Tabitha that his new girlfriend was pregnant.[185] Upset by the news, Tabitha asked the doctor at the beginning of her appointment if it was possible to get an abortion, but never mentioned it again. The prosecution argued that this single question to the doctor, along with the time she asked a friend about abortion when she first found out about the pregnancy, were evidence of her desire to kill Tyler.[186] During the trial, the prosecution and local media made no mention of the systemic obstacles that Tabitha encountered in her diligent attempts to obtain medical care for Tyler.

The Bronx district attorney sought to prove his theory by contrasting photos of Tyler from immediately after his birth with ones from after his autopsy. As reported by CNN,

> Bronx District Attorney Robert Johnson, in closing arguments Wednesday, showed jurors a photograph depicting a round-faced Tyler, taken just after birth, along with graphic autopsy photographs showing a gaunt and skeletal baby. "On June 27, 1997, God gave Tabitha Walrond a baby boy," Johnson said, as he showed the birth photo. "And in eight weeks," he continued, lifting up the autopsy photos, "this is what she did to him. . . . What god-awful sound does a crying baby make (when starving)?" Johnson asked the jurors. "Who heard it?" he went on. "The defendant." Johnson concluded by telling the jury to "do what he [Tyler] couldn't do. You speak for that little boy."[187]

Assistant District Attorney Robert Holdman also claimed that "the only thing that little boy knew in his short and helpless life was hunger and pain."[188] In May 1999, the jury convicted Tabitha of criminally negligent homicide.[189] In September 1999, the court sentenced her to five years of probation.[190]

The New York daily papers closely followed Tabitha's trial, featuring multiple headlines sensationalizing Tyler's death by "starvation."[191] They commented, "Deputy Chief Medical Examiner Yvonne Milewski . . . who has visited mass graves in Yugoslavia, was visibly shaken and her voice began to quiver when she looked at the pictures of Tyler."[192] In contrast, "Walrond, wearing a fleece sweater over a blue denim dress, remained calm yesterday even during the most critical testimony."[193]

Under the headline "Breast-Feeding Mom Recalls Watching Underfed Baby Die," the *New York Post* reported, "The prosecutor asked her how Tyler felt in her arms the week before his death. 'He felt like Tyler, he felt like my baby,' Walrond said. 'Did you feel his ribs?' Holdman pressed. 'When you changed his diaper did you move away the folds of skin around his butt? Did you feel his spine?'"[194] In "Jurors Shaken by Pix of Infant Who Starved," the *Post* said that Tyler's "leg was no bigger than a man's finger."[195] The article implied that Tabitha had ignored her mother-in-law Marcia Purcell's advice on clinics that would see him without a Medicaid card and lied about a doctor seeing him.[196] The prosecution and the media traded on the Bad Black Mother stereotype to cast Tabitha as deviant, ignorant, and cruel.

Newspapers also devoted significant space to the case of Black mother Tatiana Cheeks. Tatiana had an experience similar to Tabitha's, with a dramatically different result. Tatiana sought medical attention for her one-week-old daughter, Shannell Coppage, from a Brooklyn clinic. The clinic turned Tatiana away because she did not have either a Medicaid card or the twenty-five-dollar fee.[197] Five weeks later, in March 1998, Shannell died of malnutrition.[198] The Brooklyn district attorney charged Tatiana with criminally negligent homicide.[199] After prominent community members, including city councilperson Ronnie Eldridge, rallied around Tatiana, the prosecutor dropped the charges.[200]

Tatiana later brought a suit against the City of New York. In 2011, the jury awarded her two million dollars in damages.[201] Although Tatiana fared better than Tabitha in the justice system, the media's portrayals of both women's experiences served as warnings, particularly to Black women, that breastfeeding could be dangerous or even fatal. Much of the media coverage reinforced stereotypes of Black women on Medicaid—Welfare Mothers—as uncaring, lazy, ignorant, and selfish.

Assistant District Attorney Holdman claimed that Tabitha failed her son because of her emotional problems, which he claimed included narcissistic personality disorder.[202] He asserted that she lacked child care skills, reacted to her breakup with "extreme passive aggressiveness," and could not negotiate the Medicaid system.[203] Blaming Tabitha and "baby killer" Tatiana[204] for their infants' deaths made systemic support for breastfeeding Black women appear unnecessary. In this false narrative, Black women themselves, not institutional failings, make breastfeeding problematic.

The prosecution drew on the stereotype of Black mothers as cold and uncaring to bolster its portrayal of Tabitha as a cruel woman who savagely starved her child to exact revenge on her ex-boyfriend.[205] The manipulation of this racial trope in a court of law illustrates how deeply engrained it is and how de-mothering Black women can serve the needs of the legal, political, and social systems.[206] Tabitha's story reveals how systems fail Black women and then punish them for this failure.[207] It revives the myth, born in slavery, that Black mothers cannot and therefore should not nurture their own children. In some cases, such as Tabitha's, their breast milk is deadly. It follows logically that the government should not waste resources supporting breastfeeding Black mothers.

The exploitation of Black women by the formula industry, begun by Pet Milk's Fultz Quads campaign, continues today. Formula companies were eager to profit from Tabitha's loss. The Pharmaceutical Research and Manufacturers of America (PhRMA), an organization that includes the major infant-formula companies, partnered with CBS and Johns Hopkins School of Medicine to dramatize Tabitha's story on the then-popular medical drama *Chicago Hope*.[208] The show's producers decided to cast Tabitha's character as a middle-class White woman instead of as a low-income Black woman.[209] This choice served to divert attention from the structural issues that prevented Tabitha from accessing proper medical care. Instead, the episode emphasized the criminality and danger of breastfeeding.

Had Tabitha's character been Black, many viewers would have blamed her infant's death on the mother instead of on the hospital's insistence that she breastfeed. Usually, when a person belonging to a non-White racialized group commits a crime, society views the act as consistent with, or evidence of, bad traits that arise from the criminal's group membership. The person's actions confirm and perpetuate existing stereotypes, such as the Black male "Thug" or Muslim "Terrorist."[210] But when a White person commits a crime, reports attribute it to the individual's qualities (such as being a "lone wolf") or circumstances, not to the fact that they are White.[211]

In the *Chicago Hope* episode, titled "The Breast and the Brightest," a White mother and father rush their baby to the emergency room. The baby dies seconds after getting onto the table.[212] One of the show's regular characters, a White woman named Dr. Diane Grad, has just returned to work, leaving her infant at home with her husband. Grad is outraged by the emaciated appearance of the couple's baby. She declares loudly that the prosecutor should charge the mother with murder. Another doctor, a Black man named Dr. Keith Wilkes, instructs her to calm down and wait for the autopsy report to determine the cause of death. The report reveals that the baby died of cardiac arrest resulting from dehydration due to insufficient breast milk. The parents insist that the real cause of death was the hospital's baby-friendly contract. They claim that hospital policy discouraged them from formula feeding even when it was medically necessary. The couple sues the hospital for entering into the baby-friendly contract with them.

Meanwhile, Grad experiences the challenges of new motherhood acutely when she meets her Black neighbor, who is also a new mother. The neighbor has not yet returned to work and appears to be able to manage her home life successfully. Grad's baby then develops a fever, exacerbating the doctor's feelings of inadequacy. Grad rushes the baby to the emergency room, where a Black doctor, Dennis Hancock, reassures Grad that she is not a bad mother. Grad then apologizes to the mother of the infant who died for accusing her of murder. The mother is indifferent to Grad's words because she is consumed with guilt over her failure to keep her baby alive.

PhRMA publicly stated that it sponsored the episode in order to educate viewers about "the risks associated with breastfeeding."[213] The script successfully frames baby-friendly hospital policies as dangerous. In doing so, it casts a negative light on efforts to decrease the distribution of formula in hospitals. It portrays the White mother as innocent and appropriately distraught. Through a powerful medium that reaches millions of viewers, the episode reconfigures Tabitha's story to allow the demonization of Black mothers to remain in place while furthering the agenda of the formula corporations by discouraging government intervention to promote breastfeeding.

Ignoring the challenges that Tabitha Walrond and Tatiana Cheeks faced as low-income Black women trying to navigate the medical bureaucracy, the episode portrays baby-friendly hospitals and breastfeeding advocates as the bad guys. It also relies on the Magical Negro trope, embodied by the wise Black characters (the two Black doctors and the Black new mother) who guide the White woman (Dr. Grad) to a spiritual revelation.[214] Once the White woman achieves her epiphany, the audience can experience the Black characters' wisdom as truth. In this case, the "truth" revealed is that breastfeeding kills and formula saves babies' lives. In reality, medical research links formula feeding to thousands of deaths a year. Formula feeding also deprives countless more infants of the im-munological benefits of breastfeeding. If breastfeeding reached near uni-versal levels, it would prevent more than eight hundred thousand deaths a year worldwide.[215]

The real-life absence of legislation requiring hospitals to adopt baby-friendly practices reinforces the misleading message of "The Breast and the Brightest." The episode represented an innovative marketing strategy that evolved from the legacy of the Fultz Quads campaign. Now, formula companies reserve television for their traditional advertising and rely on social media for more creative messaging. From the 1940s to the present, the formula companies have not hesitated to manipulate racial realities for profit. But marketing and structural racism are not the only causes of low breastfeeding rates in the Black community. Laws and policies are also to blame.

Dr. Klenner and one-year-old Ann. "Quadruplets'
First Birthday," *Ebony*, May 1947, 14–18.

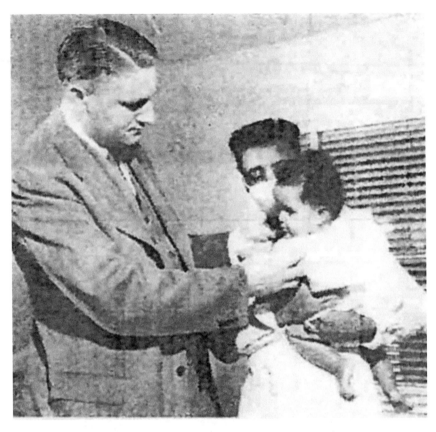

Dr. Klenner and nurse holding Ann. "Quads are
Growing Up," *Ebony*, November 1955, 25–28.

To readers of Ebony magazine, these pictures (this page and previous
page) of Dr. Fred Klenner holding baby Ann, who he named after
his wife, likely looked like racial progress. But a closer look at the
photographs reveals more. In the first photo, Dr. Klenner holds Ann
at arm's length. Above, a Black nurse holds the baby instead of Fred.
Dr. Klenner had no qualms about exploiting the girls, but it appears that
he was not comfortable touching them. His strictly segregated waiting
rooms were further evidence of this discomfort.

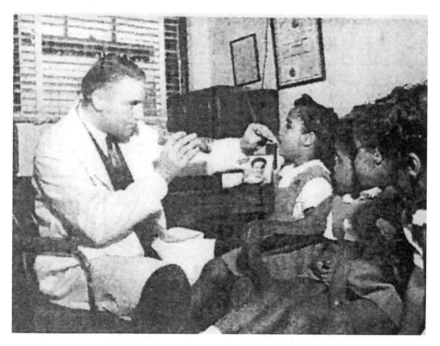

Checkup with Dr. Klenner. "Washington Birthday Party
for the Quads," *Ebony*, August 1950, 47–50, 52–55.

Ebony's publication of this photograph documenting Dr. Klenner's
care of the girls well past their infancy made a radical but misleading
statement. His very public special interest in the girls' health seemed to
foreshadow a new era. But, in fact, Klenner's care was a manifestation of
self-interest. By tying his fate to the sisters' celebrity status, he elevated
himself above his previous reputation as a 'quack.' His gain came at the
expense of the Fultz family.

"Oh, for the life of a quadruplet," seems to be mood of envious older Fultz children staring in window

Siblings and two of the quads. "Quadruplets'
First Birthday," *Ebony*, May 1947, 14–18.

Ebony's speculative caption captures the stark differences between the lives of the Fultz girls and their siblings, despite sharing a home and family. The image clearly demarcates the effects of White intervention into their lives. The new babies are literally on the inside while their siblings can only gaze in from outside. Soon, the young celebrities would lose touch with their brothers and sisters completely. Their siblings, in turn, would resent Pet Milk's influence over their family forever. Their older sister Doretha told Greensboro News and Record reporter Lorraine Ahearn that the girls "always thought they were better than us."

Pet Milk ad, "Four Little Babies." Pet Milk, "Four Little Babies Become Four Little Ladies," advertisement, *Pittsburgh Courier*, October 22, 1949, 5.

TOT QUARTET: The famed Fultz Quadruplets of Readsville, North Carolina, the world's only identical Negro Quads, who will be 4 years old on May 23rd, are shown in this latest photo in front of their farm home with their parents. Left to Right: Mary Alice, Mary Louise, Mary Catherine and Mary Anne. Their parents Pete and Annie Mae Fultz plan a huge birthday party with a cake. All the neighbors have been invited.

The girls at home with Annie Mae and Pete.
"Tot Quartet," *New York Age*, May 13, 1950, 14.

Pet Milk ad, "This Famous Four." Pet Milk, "Good Milk for This Famous Four," advertisement, *Pittsburgh Courier*, August 5, 1950, 5.

Family photo, ca. 1950 (L to R: Pete and Annie Mae, grandmother, siblings, and Fultz sisters with Elma above them). Charles L. Sanders, "The Fultz Quads: Grown-Up, Disappointed and Bitter," *Ebony*, November 1968, 212–20.

The intervention of Dr. Fred Klenner and his corporate partner, Pet Milk company, set the girls apart from their family and peers. This family photo showcases this separateness, with the four girls in matching stylish clothing watched over by the hired nurse who would eventually take the place of their mother, Annie Mae. The photograph seems to signal the inevitability of their ultimate severance from their family.

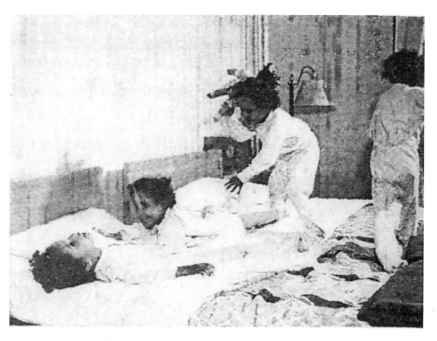

Quads playing in bed. "Washington Birthday Party for
the Quads," *Ebony*, August 1950, 47–50, 52–55.

These photographs (above and on the following page) of the sisters
playing and praying in a hotel room in Washington, DC would have
represented to Ebony readers the achievement of the American dream.
Far from their rural home and birth into a tenant farming family,
the girls appeared to be living a glamorous, enviable life. While the
photos portray the girls engaging in normal activities, the setting is
anything but.

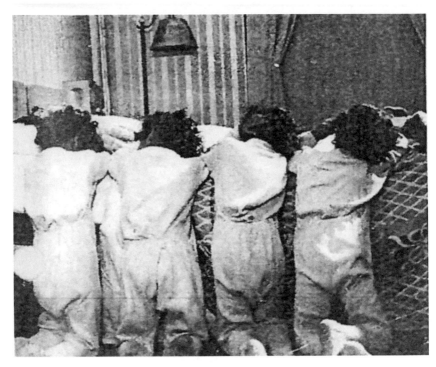

Quads praying at bedtime. "Washington Birthday Party
for the Quads," *Ebony*, August 1950, 47–50, 52–55.

President Truman meets the girls, ca. 1950. Charles L.
Sanders, "The Fultz Quads: Grown-Up, Disappointed
and Bitter," *Ebony*, November 1968, 212–20.

This iconic photograph of the girls with President Truman secured
their status as Black celebrities. Although Ebony could not convince any
White House official to pose with the young girls, a fortuitous run-in
with President Truman showed Ebony readers that America valued their
sweethearts.

Pet Milk ad, fifth birthday. Pet Milk, "The Fultz Quads Celebrate Fifth Birthday," advertisement, *Ohio State News*, May 26, 1951, 4-B.

The girls in tutus. "Famous Fultz Quads Are 8 Years
Old," *Washington Afro-American*, June 8, 1954, 5.
Courtesy of Afro American Newspapers.

President Kennedy meets the sisters, ca. 1962. Charles L.
Sanders, "The Fultz Quads: Grown-Up, Disappointed
and Bitter," *Ebony*, November 1968, 212–20.

Ebony's picture of the Fultz sisters, now young women, with President
Kennedy, reminded readers of their once treasured sweethearts. The
girls seem to know their audience, staring into the camera, paying little
attention to the president smiling at them. Although no longer Pet Milk
poster girls, the Fultz sisters retained their celebrity status in the Black
community. But their story was bittersweet, and predictable. Released by
their corporate godfather, they faded from the national spotlight. Their
once promising careers never materialized. After this last brush with
fame, they became part of the past, with little ever written about them
again.

Chapter 5

WHEN FORMULA RULES

The following warning appears on a can of CVS Health Advantage Infant Formula Milk-Based Powder with Iron:

> Important Notice: Breast milk is best for babies. Before using any infant formula, ask the advice of your health care professional. Powdered infant formulas are NOT sterile and should NOT be fed to premature infants or infants who might have immune problems unless directed and supervised by your baby's doctor.[1]

The label also asserts that "this milk-based infant formula features a unique blend of nutrients to support growth and development: prebiotics, which support the immune system; DHA & ARA which may support brain and eye development; and lutein."[2] The claims that formula creates immunities and promotes development seem to contradict the label's first statement: that breast milk is best for babies. The message is confusing at best. But what if the label simply said that breastfeeding was better for your baby?

The potential for warning labels on formula to make some mothers feel guilty has been an argument consistently put forth against requiring them. Proposed labels, endorsed by the World Health Assembly, state that breastfeeding is more beneficial to babies' health than formula feeding.[3] In the United Kingdom, formula products bear these types of warnings.[4] Many advocates believe that these labels do not go far enough.

Proponents lobby for large warnings placed prominently on the fronts of cans. They believe these types of labels are more likely to affect consumers in countries that import formula. Opponents object that these warnings will hurt some women's feelings.[5] Should that possibility take these warnings off the table? Or are corporate interests seeking to ensure an uninterrupted flow of profits by strategically insisting that it must?

The Fultz Quads campaign persuaded many Black mothers that formula was best for their babies. But marketing alone cannot explain the vast disparities in breastfeeding rates between Black and White mothers. A complex web of intersecting laws, policies, and practices obstruct the ability of Black women to initiate or sustain breastfeeding. Their collective effect is to leave many Black women with no real choice in the matter. The multifaceted aspect of the problem makes identifying and eliminating obstacles complicated. Social and emotional factors also contribute to the difficulty of devising viable solutions. This chapter explores the most significant contributors to low breastfeeding rates in Black communities.

The laws and policies examined here do not explicitly mention any racial group. They are facially neutral. Yet they have a disparate impact on individuals depending on their race, class, and other intersectional identities. The role of class in the laws and policies that push Black women toward formula use is much more obvious than the part that race plays. In many cases, receipt of government benefits, such as WIC or welfare, depends solely on socioeconomic status. It rarely, if ever, relies on race. In many cases, Black women suffer more from laws and policies that disadvantage poor women because of their overrepresentation in that group. But they are also uniquely situated, historically and presently, to use formula more because of their race.

Laws and policies related to breastfeeding fall roughly into two categories. The first encompasses affirmative practices that affect breastfeeding rates. The second consists of failures to act. The affirmative practices in the first category include the free distribution of formula through WIC and welfare-to-work reform. The second category covers the decision of the United States not to sign on to the World Health Organization's *International Code of Marketing of Breast-Milk Substitutes,* the lack of regulations requiring baby-friendly practices in hospitals, selective lactation support, and the rejection of warning labels for formula products, despite known harms. Between these two classifications lie workplace accommodations for pumping milk, parental leave policies, and laws protecting the right to breastfeed in public. These laws and policies signal a desire to protect and encourage breastfeeding, but their reach is limited, often by race and class.

WIC and Formula Distribution

The largest purchaser of formula in the United States is the federal government.[6] One of the most significant and controversial contributors to high formula use among poor women is the distribution of free formula through the USDA's Special Supplemental Nutrition Program for Women and Children (WIC).[7] The USDA buys formula that it then gives to WIC participants. WIC recipients are, by definition, low income.[8] They are also disproportionately women of color, particularly Black women.[9] The program does not distribute formula based on individual circumstances, such as difficulties with breastfeeding or work demands. Instead, formula is available to all participants for a period of six months.

Of the 7.7 million people that receive WIC,[10] approximately 58.7% are White, 20.3% are Black, 11.1% are Native American or Alaskan natives, and 4.1% are Asian or Pacific Islanders.[11] For the purpose of collecting WIC data, Latinx count as an ethnicity, not a race, and make up 41.6% of WIC participants.[12] All these categories are intrinsically misleading, because they are both overinclusive and underinclusive. Equating Native Hawaiians with Bangladeshis and Chinese under the umbrella term of Asian reveals nothing about the effects of free formula distribution on specific racial or national groups. Nonetheless, the data provides some sense of the racial disparities in program participation.

In the general US population, 76.6% of people identify as White, 13.4% as Black, 1.3% as Native American or Alaskan natives, and 5.8% as Asian or Pacific Islanders.[13] The percentage of the population that claims a Latinx identity is 18.1.[14] Comparing these numbers with the WIC participation statistics reveals that Black women and children are significantly overrepresented in the program, and White women and children are underrepresented. These disparities reflect social and economic inequalities.

More than half of the infants in the United States receive WIC.[15] The overrepresentation of Black women who receive free formula from WIC corresponds with and likely contributes to their higher use of formula.[16]

Across the board, WIC participants breastfeed at lower rates than other women do.[17] Only 14.5% of the mothers receiving WIC report breastfeeding exclusively up to six months, compared to 27.6% of non-WIC mothers, a number almost twice as high.[18] This gap more than doubles at one year, when roughly 10% of WIC participants breastfeed, compared to 38% of non-WIC participants.[19]

In addition to giving out free formula, WIC provides support for mothers who want to breastfeed. This support varies by state and regional offices. In some areas, WIC provides invaluable assistance for new mothers struggling with breastfeeding. But the challenges of breastfeeding can often appear insurmountable when formula is free and readily available. One Black mother in the program confided, "You want to know the truth? If WIC stopped giving formula, we would breastfeed."[20] Another Black mother asked her WIC worker for formula to give her infant during her intense weekend work schedule. Her worker responded, "Uh-uh. You either one or the other. . . . We gonna get you on Similac. Forget breastfeeding."[21]

When an infant is six months old, WIC stops distributing formula.[22] At that point, it is generally too late for mothers to switch to exclusive breastfeeding.[23] Once infants have gotten used to drinking from a bottle, which requires very little work on their part, it is difficult for them to switch to the more arduous task of breastfeeding. Also, most women will find it almost impossible to produce enough milk to satisfy their infants' hunger if they have not exclusively breastfed during the first six months. After formula has stepped in to respond to some or all of a baby's need, the mother's body will stop producing enough milk to meet that need. Through WIC, the formula companies create captive consumers. The large number of WIC participants who begin purchasing formula once the program cuts off their free supply makes it profitable for the formula companies to offer irresistible deals to the USDA.

Infant formula accounted for $927 million of WIC's $6.7 billion budget in 2010, or just over 12 percent.[24] The USDA gets most of the money it spends on WIC formula purchases back in the form of rebates. The Child Nutrition and WIC Reauthorization Act of 1989 regulates these rebates. Under the act, states must go through a competitive bidding process with formula manufacturers to award their WIC contracts.[25] The company that wins the contract becomes the exclusive brand for WIC in that state. This earns them prominence on drugstore shelves and a label associating them with the WIC program. These advantages serve as evidence of the government's endorsement of the brand to non-WIC participants. They are also a form of free advertising.

WIC distributes formula vouchers to eligible participants, who then give them to drugstore or supermarket cashiers when they check out.[26] After receiving the vouchers from the stores, the formula company sends the negotiated rebate to the state.[27] Rebates range from 85 to 98 percent of the purchase price.[28] The full amount of the rebate goes toward the state's WIC program. This funding dramatically expands the number of participants that the program can serve.[29] In 2016, $1.7 billion in rebates to states supported approximately 1.7 million participants monthly, representing about 22.5 percent of the program's caseload.[30] These rebates make the formula industry's support essential to the WIC program's bandwidth and success.

The formula companies do not give these rebates to the government out of altruism. They benefit immensely from this arrangement in several ways. First, formula has an extremely high profit margin, so the corporations do not stand to lose as much from the rebates as the 85 to 98 percent figures suggest.[31] Second, mothers can get formula from WIC for only six months. During that time, they develop a loyalty to the brand that WIC gives them. They then buy that brand once it is no longer free.[32] To hold on to these customers when pediatricians advise switching to milk or water at age one, the formula companies market toddler, or follow-up, products. Third, the companies partially compensate for the losses they incur from the rebates by raising retail prices. This price increase creates a cross-subsidy by non-WIC participants of WIC participants' formula use.[33] Families outside the program pay more so that those inside it can get their formula for free. Fourth, the boost in goodwill from WIC's endorsement increases overall sales, raising profit margins even higher.[34]

The relationship between WIC participation and increased formula use has put the program in the crosshairs of breastfeeding advocates, fueling a high-stakes public health controversy. Attaching WIC's name to formula brands can cause consumer confusion. This practice implies that the government recommends formula use, or at least views it as equivalent to breastfeeding. Providing formula free for the first six months of motherhood obscures its high cost. That cost can make breastfeeding more appealing to low-income parents.[35] It includes bottles and other paraphernalia in addition to the retail price of formula, which is approx imately twenty dollars per 12.5-ounce can.[36] A can will last anywhere from three to five days, depending on the baby's appetite.[37]

Realistically, breastfeeding is costly too. Feeding a baby on demand requires the mother and the baby to be close at all hours. This makes all but the most accommodating jobs difficult or impossible to maintain.[38] Maternity leave in the United States is scarce if nonexistent. It generally depends on state policies and corporate generosity. The alternative, expressing milk at work, also has associated costs, including breast pumps, bottles, and lost work time.[39] Taking time off from work to stay home with an infant often has career-long negative repercussions.[40] But breast-feeding results in significant savings on medical bills.[41] When supportive parental leave and accommodations are available, the negative effects of a temporary leave from work smooth out over time.[42]

Some breastfeeding advocates, while recognizing that WIC participation can make formula use more likely, still laud the program for its efforts to promote and support nursing. WIC's website asserts that the program "recognizes and promotes breastfeeding as the optimal source of nutrition for infants."[43] This declaration is more than lip service. In many states, WIC provides substantial lactation support through its Breastfeeding Support program.[44] This program provides new mothers with home and clinic visits by peer counselors and lactation consultants. WIC also provides breast pumps and other necessary supplies to mothers who need them.

The uncertainty regarding the extent to which other circumstances common among WIC participants, such as poverty, may contribute to disparities in breastfeeding rates also muddies the waters of this controversy.[45] It is clear that infants fed exclusively with formula miss out on significant health benefits.[46] It is also clear that the formula companies profit from WIC's support. Increased formula use, supported by either WIC or individual consumers, also benefits the USDA.

The USDA is an agency tasked with multiple and conflicting mandates. One of these is the distribution or disposal of surpluses generated from the Farm Bill's subsidies for agricultural commodities. The Farm Bill provides support for dairy, soy, and corn farmers, among others.[47] Subsidies protect these industries from the market forces of supply and demand.[48] Farmers of these commodities produce more than consumers want. It then falls on the USDA to get rid of what the farmers cannot sell. In 2018, this task became more difficult after China imposed retaliatory tariffs on US soybeans and corn.[49] Chinese tariffs on US corn imports went from 1 percent to 25 percent.[50] In 2017, the United States exported half of its soybeans to China.[51] After China raised the import tax on soybeans from 3 percent to 25 percent in 2018, Chinese purchases of US soybeans fell by 94 percent.[52] The burden on the USDA to make up for this decline is immense.

One way that the agency disposes of surpluses is by using its other programs to purchase products that contain subsidized commodities.[53] Infant formula consists mainly of corn (syrup) and either milk or soy. Using WIC to increase formula sales and thereby create a demand for three major commodity surpluses benefits the agency, if not its constituents.[54]

Do self-serving incentives for the USDA to promote formula at the expense of mothers' and infants' health suggest the need for a reevaluation of the policy of free, unmonitored formula distribution through WIC? Changing this practice would introduce a set of complicated questions. If poor mothers need or choose formula, shouldn't they be able to get it for free? How else will they feed their infants during the crucial six months when their babies cannot survive on water or food? If distribution were limited to cases of emergency or true need, who would decide which cases fit into those categories? Why should poor women have the important choice of how to feed their babies taken away from them when other women can make the same choice without governmental judgment or oversight?

If WIC did not distribute formula for free, some women might feel compelled to steal it. Many drugstores already keep formula products under lock and key, and penalties for formula theft are steeper than for other goods.[55] North Carolina passed a law in 2014 that made larceny of $100 worth of baby formula a Class H felony.[56] The state had previously reserved this category for thefts involving values of at least $1,000. The hyper-criminalization of formula theft often negatively affects women of color, contributing to the Bad Black Mother stereotype.[57] Some of the highly publicized cases of formula-theft rings have fueled support for increased surveillance of already marginalized populations, including low-income women of color.[58]

Another complicated aspect of the relationship between WIC and formula companies is the high level of influence it affords the industry over policy making. This sway is in addition to the corporations' already extensive lobbying efforts. In 2002, formula manufacturers began to offer some products with new additives designed to mimic the fatty acids in breast milk.[59] These additives made the formula products that contained them more expensive. To ensure continued sales at these higher prices, Congress introduced language that the industry requested into 2004's WIC reauthorization.

The new provision prohibited states from requiring manufacturers to include or omit specific ingredients in their WIC formula bids. Formula companies consequently submitted bids only for the more expensive versions of their product. This raised the price of the USDA's formula purchases by $91 million, more than one-tenth of the infant formula budget, without getting any more formula to participants.[60] It is unknown whether these additives provide any additional benefits. The Food and Drug Administration approved their safety but has never researched the companies' claims that the additives enhance brain development. More recently, the FDA has begun to question the truth of many of the claims made by formula companies.[61]

The partnership between the formula industry and the USDA undoubtedly helps some WIC participants. But its overall effects may be negative. It makes formula look like the better option for many consumers who have no reason to question the government's endorsement of the product. It positions formula as a staple food instead of as simply an option. It contributes to an official preference for formula use over costly reforms to government programs and services that could increase breastfeeding across race and class lines. And it appears to do more good for the USDA and its agriculture industry constituents than for the individuals that its mission mandates the agency to serve.

Welfare Reform

In 1996, a Republican-controlled Congress instituted significant reforms to the welfare system through the Personal Responsibility and Work Opportunity Reconciliation Act (PRWORA).[62] The PRWORA dismantled the Aid to Families with Dependent Children (AFDC) program and replaced it with Temporary Assistance to Needy Families (TANF).[63] Part of the putative motivation behind this change was the desire to create a path from welfare to work. The stated goals of TANF are to "(1) provide assistance to needy families so that children may be cared for in their own homes or in the homes of relatives; (2) end the dependence of needy parents on government benefits by promoting job preparation, work, and marriage; (3) prevent and reduce the incidence of out of wedlock pregnancies and establish annual numerical goals for preventing and reducing the incidence of these pregnancies; and (4) encourage the formation and maintenance of two parent families."[64]

Many aspects of these purported goals are problematic from a race and class perspective. Most glaringly, the emphasis on the importance of marriage and its relationship to prosperity and parenthood appears to express a preference for the traditional nuclear family. This type of "model" family exists primarily in the White and Asian middle classes.[65] The modern reality is that two-parent, married households are falling out of favor. In 2015, the Pew Research Center reported that less than half of the children in the United States live with two parents who are in their first marriage.[66]

Black women are significantly less likely than White women to marry. In the forty to forty-four age range, 10 percent of White women are unmarried, compared with 30 or 40 percent of Black women.[67] At all ages, Black women marry at the lowest rate.[68] One reason for this disparity is the mass incarceration of Black men. Being locked up makes men unavailable and less likely to earn a wage that can support a family upon release. Black women are less likely than other groups to marry outside their race.[69]

Interracial heterosexual marriages inevitably result in at least one partner losing or gaining social status. White men do not gain race or gender privilege from marrying Black women, so they often limit these relationships to sexual or casual ones. In 2017, 64 percent of all Black–White marriages involved Black men and White women.[70] These matches provide societal status benefits for both parties and continue to be much more common than the pairing of Black women with White men. White women gain some privilege associated with maleness from marrying Black men, who, in turn, benefit from their acquired affiliation with Whiteness.

Another, relatively recent, phenomenon documented in the Pew report is that women have become the primary breadwinners in many households.[71] There are racial disparities in single-parent households, with Black women being the most likely to head a single-parent household. TANF's focus on promoting marriage thus seems to condone middle-class White practices while condemning those of many Black families.

The first stated goal of TANF, to keep children cared for in their own homes, conflicts with the practical effect of the program—sending new mothers out of the home to work. The most significant difference between AFDC and TANF is that TANF gives states the ability to fashion their own work requirements and sanctions. This results in a wide range of policies that vary according to where recipients reside.[72] Under TANF, states can impose heavy conditions on welfare recipients, including work requirements and lifetime limits on receiving welfare.[73] States can also create exemptions to work requirements for mothers of young children, called the age-of-youngest-child exemption (AYCE).[74] Under AFDC, mothers received a thirty-six-month AYCE.

Beginning in 1996, the PRWORA allowed states to give no AYCE. Four states provide new mothers with no exemption.[75] Michigan requires women to report to work once their babies turn six weeks old.[76] Nineteen states have an AYCE of less than twelve months, and twenty-eight states allow twelve or more months.[77] Exemptions also vary according to how many children a woman has. They allow the most time at home for the first child and significantly less for each additional child, even though children's needs do not differ based on how many siblings they have. Education level can also affect benefits.[78] With Black women overrepresented in the program, these new requirements disproportionately affect their ability to stay home and breastfeed their infants during the first six months, as recommended.

After the welfare-to-work shift instigated by TANF, breastfeeding rates significantly decreased for women receiving benefits, particularly after their babies reached six months of age. At that point, the rates fell from their AFDC level by 22 percent.[79] Breastfeeding rates also fell by 9 percent overall at this time, possibly due to increased work demands or to a national shift, brought on by formula marketing, in attitudes toward nursing.[80] Costs associated with this decline included increased health care expenses and mothers' absenteeism from work.[81] Medicaid likely covered these higher health care costs, because most women on TANF live below the poverty line.[82] In 2003, researchers found TANF's effects to be worst in states that had work requirements of at least eighteen hours a week combined with regular enforcement of sanctions imposed on the families of women who did not meet these requirements.[83]

Examining the effects of these policies over a decade later, in 2016, analysts found that mothers with young infants forced out of the home to work experienced more symptoms of depression.[84] They were less likely to breastfeed or to read to their children.[85] The study found that despite these negative effects of maternal employment during the first year, work begun or engaged in during subsequent years had either neutral or positive effects on mothers and children.[86] These results support the practice in Canada and other countries of requiring employers to provide a full year of parental leave.[87]

TANF's stricter work requirements were a success, however, in terms of increasing maternal employment.[88] The number of single mothers working in the 1990s increased by 20 percent. [89] TANF accounted for 13 percent of this increase.[90] But these apparent economic benefits led to decreases in maternal and child welfare.[91]

Overall, it appears that TANF has not achieved its first two stated objectives, to have children cared for at home and to reduce dependence on government assistance. The costs of taking mothers out of the home earlier do not appear to justify the benefits. Many lawmakers, including President Trump, mistakenly believe that most women on welfare are Black.[92] This misperception likely explains their willingness to trade higher employment numbers for lower maternal and infant well-being.

Dehumanizing stereotypes about Black mothers have always accompanied laws and policies that disproportionately harm them. The Welfare Queen has come to represent all Black mothers. Since Reagan popularized this myth in 1976, Republicans and Democrats alike have relied on it to support welfare cuts.[93] Media, from newspaper articles to Google searches, add to the stereotype by illustrating stories about welfare and poverty almost exclusively with images of Black women.[94] This leads policy makers and the public mistakenly to equate welfare with Blackness.[95] This association, in turn, leads to increased support for welfare cuts.[96] When it comes to welfare reform, stereotypes drive policy more than statistics do.

WHO Ban on Formula Advertising

In 1981, one hundred and eighteen countries voted to adopt the World Health Organization's (WHO) new *International Code of Marketing of Breast-Milk Substitutes*.[97] Three countries abstained. The United States was the only country to oppose it.[98] This opposition went against the intention of the State Department. It was a direct response to heavy lobbying efforts by the formula industry.[99]

The WHO developed the Code in response to evidence of high infant mortality rates linked to formula feeding internationally and evidence that advertising increases formula feeding rates.[100] A parent's exposure to formula advertising or marketing during an infant's first two weeks of life, when breastfeeding can be most challenging, significantly increases decisions to stop breastfeeding.[101] Among women with uncertain feeding goals or breastfeeding goals of twelve weeks or less, exposure to formula promotion shortens exclusive and overall breastfeeding duration.[102]

The WHO Code prohibits direct or indirect contact between marketers and pregnant women or mothers of infants and young children.[103] It sets standards for pictures and information on formula labels, the distribution of information and educational materials about infant feeding, the provision of free samples and supplies, and interactions between companies and the health care system.[104] It bans the advertising and promotion of formula to the public, formula promotion by a health-care-system facility, donations or low-price sales of formula to health care institutions or organizations, and financial or material inducements to health care workers or their families to promote formula.[105]

Designed to guide government regulation of corporate advertising, the WHO Code did not even consider the possibility that governments might market formula products themselves. The US government appears to be the only one that actively associates itself with and promotes formula.[106] It does so by engaging in practices the WHO Code would likely not allow if it had considered them. These include disseminating materials to new mothers with infant formula logos and images in addition to distributing free formula through WIC and in state hospitals.[107]

US medical professionals sometimes receive perks from the formula companies for promoting and providing their products to clients. These perks, which include free meals, speaking and consulting fees, and stock options, are similar to the ones that the same companies give to doctors to prescribe their pharmaceutical drugs.[108] When it comes to breast-feeding support, doctors often do not dispense useful information or guidance because they do not receive adequate training on the subject in medical school. Family members can rarely fill this void. When mothers and grandmothers have not breastfed, as is often the case in Black families, they have no advice to offer. Advertising steps in to fill this gap. Corporate-sponsored messages offer authoritative and often misleading statements on what is best for babies and their mothers.[109]

In her book, *The Big Letdown*, Kimberly Seals Allers describes how formula companies plant seeds of insecurity in mothers through their advertising.[110] They then soothe the resulting feelings of inadequacy about milk supply through assurances that their products can make up for women's innate deficiencies.[111] After all, formula is measurable and consistent. It makes babies full. When they are full, they sleep longer and fuss less. Formula does not depend on a mother's presence or her perfection. In countless subtle ways, the formula companies create and then exploit women's fears that their bodies, in this and so many other regards, may not be good enough.

Formula marketing takes many forms. It is on YouTube, Hulu, Google, television, Spanish radio, and social media. It is in newspapers and magazines. Data-mining technology targets ovulating women with formula ads.[112] Websites run by formula companies offer free advice from medical experts to young mothers. Formula representatives "train" drugstore employees in the benefits of their products. Pediatricians' waiting rooms offer pamphlets created by formula companies, which stock these doctors' cupboards with free samples. Most hospitals have plenty of free formula but are short on lactation support.

A Carnation pamphlet from the 1950s made no bones about discouraging hesitant mothers from trying to breastfeed. It read, "You do not have to nurse your child. Scientific evidence today indicates that children who have never been nursed are just as healthy, sometimes more healthy, both physically and emotionally, as children who are nursed. If you are reluctant to nurse your child, if it makes you feel tense or uncomfortable, do not attempt it."[113] This message persists in every form of formula advertising employed today. But if the United States signed on to the WHO Code, parents could make their infant feeding decisions free of undue and well-financed corporate influence.

Baby-Friendly Hospitals

The formula industry's most successful marketing strategy is the distribution of free formula in hospitals.[114] This tactic creates brand loyalty and effectively wins over significant percentages of women who would otherwise breastfeed.[115] This corporate achievement would not be possible without the government's direct support, through formula distribution in its own institutions, and indirect support, by failing to enact regulations that would halt this practice in private hospitals.

Evidence that the free distribution of formula in hospitals contributes to lower breastfeeding rates led advocates to campaign for legislation prohibiting the practice.[116] Hospitals promote formula by giving away coupons and formula samples to new mothers during hospital stays and in discharge bags upon their departure.[117] Providing new mothers with free formula strongly influences their infant feeding decisions. Women who are recovering from birth rarely request information about breastfeeding beyond what their physicians provide.[118] They are exhausted and often in pain. Insurance policies that require women to leave the hospital within twenty-four hours of a vaginal birth and forty-eight hours of a caesarian section eliminate or reduce the time necessary to guide parents through initiating successful lactation.[119]

The international standards for baby-friendly certification require hospitals to (1) communicate a written breastfeeding policy routinely to all health care staff; (2) train all health care staff in the skills necessary to implement this policy; (3) inform all pregnant women of the benefits of breastfeeding; (4) help mothers initiate breastfeeding within one hour of birth; (5) show mothers how to breastfeed and how to maintain lactation, even if the hospital separates them from their infants; (6) give infants no food or drink other than breast milk unless medically indicated; (7) practice rooming in—allowing mothers and infants to stay together twenty-four hours a day; (8) encourage breastfeeding on demand; (9) give no pacifiers or artificial nipples to breastfeeding infants; and (10) foster the establishment of breastfeeding support groups and refer mothers to them upon discharge from the hospital or birth center.[120]

These practices save money. Conversion to baby-friendly practices does not result in any significant increase in hospital expenses.[121] The costs of treating the broad range of illnesses and conditions that result from lower breastfeeding rates, including increased infant mortality, are far higher.[122] Research indicates that if 90 percent of families breastfed exclusively for six months and continued nursing until an infant's first birthday, the United States would save $13 billion and avoid approximately 911 SIDS-related deaths each year.[123] Another estimate posits that baby-friendly hospitals save between $500 and $1,500 in medical treatment per infant.[124] Despite these impressive statistics, only four state legislatures have enacted baby-friendly requirements.[125]

Rhode Island hospitals ended the practice of handing out free formula in 2011, with Delaware following suit in 2015.[126] Massachusetts had to implement the ban twice.[127] The state's first ban, enacted in 2005, had a short life.[128] In early 2006, then-governor Mitt Romney reversed the Public Health Council's decision to institute the ban. Romney replaced three of the council members who objected to this reversal.[129] His spokesperson justified Romney's opposition to the ban as a preference for freedom of choice.[130] But this rationale became suspect a few days later, when Bristol-Myers Squibb, home to Mead Johnson, one of the three major formula manufacturers, announced plans to build a large pharmaceutical plant in the state.[131] The second ban went into effect in 2012. In Maryland, the Department of Health issued guidelines in 2015 directing maternity wards to ban the bags.[132] Although the guidelines were voluntary, all Maryland's hospitals complied.[133]

New York's ban on free formula in hospital discharge bags began as a citywide initiative. Under a program designed in 2012 by then-mayor Michael Bloomberg, 76 percent of New York City hospitals agreed to remove formula from new mothers' sight. They promised to deliver it to patients only upon request and accompanied by information about the significant advantages of breastfeeding.[134] The Latch On NYC program encouraged hospitals to make it hard for new moms to obtain formula goody bags.[135] To get these departure "gifts," mothers had to ask for them. The new mothers would then have to sit through a lecture from hospital staff discouraging formula feeding except when medically indicated.

This experimental measure inspired considerable backlash. Many argued that Bloomberg's tactics would make mothers feel guilty and, in the words of blogger Lenore Skenazy, "suck the choice out of parenting."[136] In 2017, New York State stepped in, amending its regulations to prohibit the giveaways in coordination with other provisions designed to support breastfeeding. The state's Department of Health explained that "despite the well documented health benefits to infants and mothers, the percentage of newborn infants exclusively breastfed in the first few days of life is only 44% in New York, well below the national target of 70%."[137]

FDA Warnings and Demands

The Food and Drug Administration's mission is to protect public health by ensuring the safety and efficacy of products that individuals consume.[138] Infant formula is a food product that marketers and pediatricians often treat as a drug. The formula industry is so powerful that government oversight of it has been minimal. Even so, when it comes to false claims, the FDA appears to have some limits to its endorsement of the product.

In 2014, the FDA issued a warning letter to Nestlé, advising that statements on the label of the company's Gerber Good Start Gentle Infant Formula violated the Food, Drug and Cosmetic Act because they were misleading and misbranded the product. Specifically, the label stated that the product reduced the risk of developing allergies. The FDA advised Nestlé that there was no credible scientific evidence to support this claim. The letter asked for a response from Nestlé detailing the steps it planned to take to correct these violations within fifteen days. Nestlé's reply settled the matter with the FDA,[139] but the company soon faced two lawsuits making similar claims.[140] Plaintiffs alleged that statements on Gerber Good Start formula calling it hypoallergenic were false and misleading.[141]

A 2016 report published in *Clinical Pediatrics* found that thirteen of twenty-two labels on formula products made unsubstantiated claims about treating colic and gastrointestinal symptoms.[142] The report noted increased sales of the products that made these assertions.[143] Most parents will try anything that promises to stop their babies from crying. Paying a few dollars more for formula, or trying it for the first time, are not exceptions. Other formula products boast of their ability to boost infants' immune system, digestive capacity, and brain development, without scientific evidence to substantiate these claims.[144]

In response to the report, the FDA created a draft proposal to put unique demands on the formula industry to meet certain scientific standards before claiming that a product can prevent or treat specific medical conditions.[145] In 2018, the Changing Markets Foundation published the results of its investigation into scientific claims on Nestlé's infant formula products.[146] It concluded that "Nestlé is not driven by nutritional science, but instead by a sharp and prioritized focus on profit and growth at the expense of infants and their parents."[147]

Marketing formula to parents by appealing to their frustrations and challenges is problematic for many reasons. Even if a product does induce or increase certain behavior, that result might not be in the baby's best interest. For example, some formula products appeal to parents' desire to have their infants sleep longer, giving the caregivers some much-needed rest.[148] But sleeping for longer periods of time is not necessarily ideal for babies' health and development. The medical consensus is that wakefulness is better for infant health and safety.

Another potential point of intervention for the FDA would be the placement of warning labels on formula that many other countries have adopted. In addition to requiring warnings, UK regulations prohibit images of infants or breastfeeding mothers on formula products, as per the WHO Code. They instruct companies to avoid consumer confusion by making clear distinctions between infant formula products and those designed for older children. But enforcement of these requirements is weak. And breastfeeding advocates view most of the warning labels currently in use as inadequate. They would prefer messages that cover one-third of the product label, as on cigarette packaging in the United States.

In 2005, Iowa senator Tom Harkin proposed a bill that would impose requirements on US formula packaging that are similar to those in the United Kingdom.[149] The proposed law would mandate warning labels on formula cans and advertisements stating that the Department of Health and Human Services finds that "breast-feeding is the ideal method of feeding and nurturing infants" or that "breast milk is more beneficial to infants than infant formula."[150] The bill died after the Senate read it twice and then referred it to the Finance Committee.[151] Formula companies have always resisted this type of labeling, even though it may have a very limited effect on consumer habits. Many families who use formula do so because of their life circumstances or personal preferences, not because they do not know about its harmful effects.

It is true that for women who lack true choice about formula feeding, warning labels might add insult to injury. But most mothers are strong enough to ignore these labels if they are not helpful or to dismiss any unwanted emotions that they might provoke. For others, labels might provide exactly the prompt they need to question the claims by formula companies that their product is equivalent or superior to breastfeeding. Even if the labels have little potential to affect most parents' choices, their prospective good outweighs any possible harm. The greatest obstacle to their implementation is not resistance from mothers but from the formula industry.

Workplace Accommodation

Iesha Gray was driving for the US Postal Service when she had her baby Daveah.[152] She felt lucky because nursing Daveah was easy from the beginning. But within a month after returning from her maternity leave, she had no more milk. On her first day back, her supervisors did not respond when Iesha asked where she could pump. They gave her a long route that day, making it impossible for her to stop. She recalled, "I didn't pump all day. That's just the most painful thing you can ever feel, having to walk around for eight hours a day with milk swollen."[153] The next day, they told her that she could pump in her truck. She said no because it was dirty with dust and mail. Next, they said she could come back to the station for unpaid pumping breaks. The day she tried it, she ended up being away from Daveah for eleven hours. Eventually, she had to quit her dream job to be able to nurse her child.

Iesha's story is not unusual. Mothers who work full-time breastfeed at lower rates than part-time or unemployed mothers.[154] Ideally, working mothers could nurse their babies several times a day at a nearby daycare or at a private space at work, assuming that someone could bring their infant to them. If that is not possible, the alternative is pumping milk at work to deliver to caregivers later. This keeps up the milk supply by imitating the baby's feeding schedule and ensures an adequate amount of milk to cover the mother's absence the following day.

Without sufficient accommodations for breastfeeding at work, including a private place to express milk, a refrigerator to store the milk, and reasonably lengthy and flexible breaks, working women simply cannot continue to provide their infants with an adequate supply of breast milk. Most breastfeeding accommodation laws do not require employers to provide all these things. Overwhelmingly, these laws fail to protect low-income women, who have less power to negotiate for policies that meet their needs in the workplace.

Because higher-income women initiate and continue breastfeeding at the highest rates and require less protection, amendments to the Fair Labor Standards Act (FLSA) in 2010 sought to increase breastfeeding rates for low-income women.[155] These amendments require an employer to provide "a reasonable break time for an employee to express breast milk for her nursing child for one year after the child's birth each time such employee has need to express the milk."[156] They also mandate "a place, other than a bathroom, that is shielded from view and free from intrusion from coworkers and the public, which may be used by an employee to express breast milk."[157] The law provides an exception for employers with fifty employees or fewer if the employer can prove that complying would impose an undue hardship on the business.[158]

The FLSA has several significant shortcomings. The amendments are unlikely to increase breastfeeding rates for low-income working women. The act does not require employers to provide storage for a breast pump, supplies, and expressed milk, which are all necessary to pump at work. It also fails to provide protection against discrimination. Two-thirds of cases alleging breastfeeding discrimination between 2008 and 2018 led to the employee losing her job.[159] This discrimination includes cases in which employers refused to give breaks to employees who were in pain and leaking milk; fired them for asking for a break; denied them privacy to pump; forced them to expose their breasts to their coworkers, to their clients, or in public; and made lewd comments about their bodies or mooed at them.

The FLSA also does not apply to exempt employees—workers who earn a salary instead of an hourly wage.[160] These positions are generally classified as administrative, professional, or executive and do not come with minimum wage, overtime, and other protections. In some instances, these are higher-level employees who can manage their own time. These women usually do not need the law's protection. But workers earning hourly wages often cannot afford to lose any paid time, and the FLSA does not require employers to compensate employees for time spent pumping.

The District of Columbia, Puerto Rico, and twenty-nine states have laws related to breastfeeding in the workplace.[161] The other twenty-one states must follow the requirements of the FLSA. The FLSA does not preempt the laws in the six states that offer greater protection than federal law provides. Indiana compels employers to provide refrigeration or other cold storage for expressed milk and to offer employees paid breast-feeding breaks.[162] Colorado requires employers to provide unpaid breaks to pump for up to two years after birth instead of the one year mandated by the FLSA.[163] Both Maine and Vermont require pumping breaks for nursing mothers for up to three years.[164] Oregon's statute provides for break time for up to eighteen months, applies to employers with twenty-five employees or more, and offers additional protections for school-board employees.[165] Oregon's law also has statutory civil penalties for employers who fail to comply.[166] Tennessee's statute applies to employers with one or more employees.[167] California requires employers to provide a special room for pumping that is not a bathroom.[168]

Three states incentivize protection for nursing mothers by creating the opportunity for employers to earn the label of mother or infant friendly.[169] To achieve this designation, an employer must allow for a flexible work schedule, provide a private location for pumping, guarantee access to a clean, safe water source and a sink, and offer a hygienic storage place for expressed milk. Puerto Rico provides tax incentives to businesses that give women time to nurse. In spite of these promising advances in workplace accommodation laws in some states, there is little protection for women who work several jobs or work for small businesses, as many Black women do.

Parental Leave

Even the most generous workplace accommodation laws cannot compensate for the difficulties inherent in the separation of nursing mothers and infants. Feeding on demand ensures a supply best tailored to a baby's needs, and nursing instead of bottle-feeding provides the mother with greater health and psychological benefits. Extended parental leave, flexible schedules, the ability to work at home, and quality, affordable child care located near work represent the ideal approaches to parental and infant welfare.

The United States is the only industrialized country without a federal law mandating some parental leave. Only four states, New York, New Jersey, California, and Rhode Island, give paid parental leave.[170] A 2018 study of California and New Jersey revealed that more mothers breast-

fed after these states passed their paid-leave laws.[171] But the primary beneficiaries of these laws were higher-income women. In some states, including Hawai'i, parents can use short-term disability to cover parental
leave. This is problematic, though, because it leaves employees short if
they need the disability leave in the future. In most cases, the availability,
amount, and details of parental leave are up to the employer.

Some large corporations have stepped in to address inadequate state
leave policies after recognizing that generous parental leave policies help
their employees and their bottom line. In 2018, Starbucks and Walmart
introduced paid parental leave for hourly employees, a benefit they previously extended only to salaried employees.[172] McDonald's, IBM, and
Walmart also increased their parental leave benefits.[173] Several companies
introduced or expanded leave for salaried and hourly working parents
who did not give birth to their infants. These moves respond to a consensus among Americans that paid leave is important to families and the
economy.[174] Without it, many hourly workers lose their jobs because they
must care for their newborns and cannot afford child care.[175] The majority of these workers are Black or Latinx women.[176]

Employees who receive paid parental leave are more likely to reenter
the workforce within a year[177] and less likely to need government benefits.[178] They breastfeed longer, contributing to better health outcomes for
mothers and babies.[179] When a partner who did not give birth takes leave,
the result is greater equity in the home and workplace.[180]

Breastfeeding in Public

Unless a woman can comfortably breastfeed in public, she will either
abandon nursing or never leave the house. Babies do not wait until their
mothers are in a secure, pleasant place to be hungry. The 1999 Right to
Breastfeed Act provides women the right to nurse on all federal property.[181] All fifty states, the District of Columbia, and the Virgin Islands
have laws that allow women to breastfeed in any public or private location.[182] Wyoming, South Dakota, and Michigan exempt breastfeeding
from public indecency laws.[183] Puerto Rico requires shopping malls, air-
ports, and government centers that serve the public to have accessible areas designated for breastfeeding.[184] It also has a breastfeeding awareness
month.[185] Georgia law declares that breastfeeding is "an important and
basic act of nurture which should be encouraged in the interests of mater-

nal and child health."[186] It allows a mother to "breastfeed her baby in any location where the mother and baby are otherwise authorized to be."[187] Sixteen states and Puerto Rico exempt breastfeeding mothers from jury duty or allow them to postpone jury service.[188]

Although these laws technically protect women's right to breastfeed, they may be doing very little if women cannot be comfortable nursing. Very few women want to breastfeed in public. They do it because they must. Black women are even less likely to feel comfortable nursing in public because of the long history of their exclusion from purportedly public spaces. They may also hesitate because of the way stereotypes have trained others to see them and have made them hyperaware of their own bodies. One woman explains:

> The Black woman is so voluptuous. We have the hips, we have the butt, you have the breasts, so society has made us so cognizant of our bodies and being of a sexual nature only. That is so prone, you see it in TV, commercials, videos, I mean, especially in our youth. That is all you see, and it's almost like a body, but I'm still a Black woman. And so to put [breastfeeding] out there, that does create a lot of discomfort just because of how society sees us.[189]

Vigilante efforts to stop women from the practice are also a powerful deterrent that undermines the objectives of public breastfeeding laws. One woman recounts:

> One time I was at Wal-Mart and I was with my son, and I had one of those newbie raps, so you really couldn't tell I was breastfeeding and I'm walking through Walmart . . . this White lady walked up to me like "are you breastfeeding at Walmart" and I'm like yes, I am. Do you have a problem with that, I don't even know you. She was like, "shouldn't you go in the bathroom or something."[190]

This type of harassment is common. For breastfeeding laws to be effective, changes in perspectives must accompany them. Public education and structural support are necessary to transform attitudes and architecture.

Harm to Black Women and Children

Black women experience unique forms of subordination and marginalization that make them more vulnerable to formula promotion and structural obstacles to breastfeeding. Intersectional identities exacerbate these harms. Low-income women, women with disabilities, LGBTQAI women, gender-nonconforming individuals, and many others who do not fit into traditional societal visions of mothers may confront heightened barriers to breastfeeding. But race is a special factor. The disparities in breastfeeding between Black and Latinx mothers at all socioeconomic levels make this clear. Their divergent histories, related to immigration and strong ties to other countries on the one hand and the legacy of slavery on the other, transcend economic similarities and lead to different practices and health outcomes.

Black women confront systemic obstacles to breastfeeding while simultaneously facing discrimination in almost every other aspect of life, including housing, employment, education, and the criminal-justice system. Historical oppression has led to a ten-to-one wealth gap between Whites and Blacks.[191] Other factors contributing to Black poverty and overrepresentation in benefit programs include unequal pay for equal work, fewer job opportunities, mass incarceration, and employment discrimination. These injustices lead to reduced political power to challenge them.

Child Protective Services (CPS) surveys and targets Black women and more frequently removes their children from the home.[192] Black children are represented in foster care almost twice (1.8) as much as the general population.[193] When CPS removes a child from its mother, breastfeeding is not possible. High incarceration rates in the Black community also impede breastfeeding. Incarcerated women face many challenges to breastfeeding.[194] Even when their infants are with them, the possibility of remaining together for an extended period is uncertain. Inside, they have lost the presence and support of their families and communities. Black women with incarcerated partners must go to work to support their children. Black women are the least likely of any social group to have a stable partner in the home to help with child care and financial support.[195] In 2012, 67 percent of Black households were single parent.[196] This compares to 53 percent of Native American, 42 percent of Latinx, 25 percent of White, and 17 percent of Asian/Pacific Islander households.[197]

Single parents often work at jobs that breastfeeding accommodation laws do not cover. Supervisors in low-income sectors, such as fast food or retail, usually view their employees as fungible. These workers cannot risk losing their jobs by making demands, however reasonable, even when the law requires employers to provide accommodations. Black women, particularly single mothers, disproportionately hold low-income positions and work for multiple employers and small companies. In 2011, 38.1 percent of Black women held low-wage jobs, defined as paying poverty-level wages or less.[198] In the same year, only 23.4 percent of White workers held similar low-wage jobs.[199]

Another consequence that many Black women suffer from working at a low-wage job is the lack of a comprehensive health insurance policy that allows for an extended hospital stay after birth. This postnatal period, when a baby tries to latch on for the first time, is crucial for receiving lactation support. Hospitals in Black neighborhoods generally engage in fewer practices that promote breastfeeding than hospitals in White neighborhoods do.[200] The greatest disparities are in early initiation of breastfeeding, limited use of formula supplements, and rooming-in policies.[201]

After they leave the hospital, many Black women find themselves isolated. Many new Black mothers live in "first food" deserts—urban areas that lack support for breastfeeding in the form of weekly support groups, breastfeeding cafés, strong La Leche chapters, board-certified lactation consultants, and other community-support mechanisms.[202] Many cities with large Black populations, including New Orleans, Louisiana; Birmingham, Alabama; and Jackson, Mississippi are "first food" deserts. These cities also lack child care facilities properly trained in handling human milk. Their public health clinics frequently refer breastfeeding women who need support back to hospitals, which rarely, if ever, provide outpatient lactation services.

Physicians and nurses often make a cultural assumption that Black women simply will not want to try nursing, because their breastfeeding rates are so low. This attitude creates a self-fulfilling prophesy and a cycle of worse care and lower expectations. Doctors also are generally less attentive to Black women due to engrained and usually unconscious perceptions that their needs are trivial or fabricated.[203] This racist treatment has serious consequences. Black mothers die during childbirth at three or four times the rate of White women.[204] This is true across class and education levels. Even tennis star Serena Williams had a brush with death after giving birth to her daughter when doctors ignored her history of pulmonary embolisms.[205] She survived because she pushed back against their authority. Not every woman feels comfortable doing that, however, even in a life or death situation.

Free formula distribution by hospitals disproportionately lowers breast-feeding rates for mothers of color, first-time mothers, ill mothers, and mothers with less-than-average education levels.[206] Once a new mother arrives home, free formula samples arrive in her mailbox.[207] In some cases, she starts receiving formula from WIC immediately. If she needs to breast-feed outside the home while fulfilling life and family responsibilities, she may encounter aggressive opposition exacerbated by racism.

Black women often face pressure from their partners and mothers not to breastfeed.[208] In their study of low-income Black women in Baltimore, Maryland, researchers Margaret E. Bentley, Deborah L. Dee, and Joan L. Jensen found that the opinions of fathers and grandmothers strongly influence breastfeeding rates.[209] The views of fathers had a greater impact on women's decision to breastfeed than those of any other family member.[210] Fathers whose own mothers had breastfed often favored nursing, but others discouraged it due to feelings of ownership of their partners' breasts or fear of their partners exposing their breasts in public.[211] One father told his partner, "I think that breastfeeding out in [ ] public will cause you to get raped or something."[212]

Some advocates have spearheaded projects that made significant strides toward normalizing Black women breastfeeding in public and ensuring that it is safe. In Atlanta, Sojourner Marable Grimmett led a long-term and ultimately successful campaign to build a breastfeeding space in Atlanta's Hartsfield-Jackson airport.[213] Asking "Would you eat in the bathroom?" under a series of humorous and poignant photographs, the initiative led to the installation of four lactation pods in the busiest airport in the United States.[214] Atlanta is one of the country's most Black-populated cities.

The disproportionate impact of all these laws, policies, and practices on Black communities points to the need for systemic structural reform. The attribution of disparities in breastfeeding rates to cultural or social factors fails to recognize the significant impact of each of the factors described here and their collective effect. Which laws and policies could eliminate breastfeeding disparities, improve the health of Black women and children, and avoid the type of corporate and personal exploitation that the Fultz sisters endured? How might constitutional principles contribute to meaningful change? What can we learn from the laws and practices of other countries? Can the formal and informal markets for breast milk improve health outcomes until significant reform takes place? Without a strong social movement, can any of these solutions really work?

Chapter 6

LEGALIZING BREAST MILK

Breastfeeding is the most elemental form of parental care. It is
a communion between mother and child that, like marriage, is
"intimate to the degree of being sacred." Nourishment is necessary
to maintain the child's life, and the parent may choose to believe
that breastfeeding will enhance the child's psychological as
well as physical health. In light of the spectrum of interests that
the Supreme Court has held specially protected we conclude
that the Constitution protects from excessive state interference
a woman's decision respecting breastfeeding her child.
—Dike v. School Board, *Fifth Circuit (1997)*

When Pet Milk adopted the Fultz sisters in 1946, there were no protections in place for breastfeeding mothers. Law and policy have evolved since then, thanks mostly to public health advocates. But there is still a long way to go.

Constitutional Protection of Breastfeeding

The United States Constitution should include a positive right to health or healthy food.[1] If it did, it would follow in the footsteps of nations that have created legally enforceable rights to basic needs, such as food, water, and shelter, for their citizens.[2] The United States is unlikely to do this, though, because of its commitment to capitalism. Still, it may be that the Constitution as written provides some protection against racial disparities in breastfeeding.

Due Process

The Fourteenth Amendment provides that no state shall "deprive any person of life, liberty, or property, without due process of law."[3] This dictate also applies to the federal government through similar language in the Fifth Amendment.[4] The Fifth Amendment Due Process Clause protects some intimate acts and decisions—including contraception, marriage, abortion, and parents' right to control their children's upbringing—as fundamental, individual privacy rights. In 1997, in *Dike v. School Board*, the United States Court of Appeals for the Fifth Circuit held breastfeeding to be a constitutional right protected by Fifth Amendment Substantive Due Process.[5]

If the Supreme Court considered this issue and agreed with the Fifth Circuit that breastfeeding is a fundamental right similar to marriage or contraception, courts would have to subject any laws, policies, or government practices that restrict breastfeeding to strict scrutiny, the highest level of review.[6] Strict scrutiny requires the government's action to be necessary to achieve a compelling interest. "Necessary" means that there is no alternative that would be less restrictive of the right—here, to breastfeed. Most laws fail to meet this demanding standard.

But the Supreme Court has been reluctant to extend the list of fundamental rights arising under Fifth Amendment Substantive Due Process. This stems in part from the fact that these rights do not appear in the text of the Constitution.[7] The Court has also narrowed some of the privacy rights over time. Although laws restricting abortion rights initially received strict scrutiny under *Roe v. Wade*,[8] the law now protects a woman's right to an abortion only to the extent that the state does not place an "undue burden" on her ability to have one.[9] The lower courts do not agree on what exactly constitutes an undue burden. But if the Supreme Court adopted this standard for breastfeeding rights, courts would invalidate any laws or state practices that put a substantial obstacle in the way of women's ability to breastfeed.[10]

Abortion and breastfeeding rights have the common goals of preserving women's control over their bodies and allowing parents to make decisions about their children free from government interference. These shared objectives suggest that using the same standard for both makes sense. But it may be ill-advised to tie these rights together because abortion rights are highly contested, constantly under attack, and evocative of deeply religious objections.[11] In comparison, breastfeeding is relatively uncontroversial. A better strategy might be to compare breastfeeding rights to contraceptive rights. Contraception also concerns parenting and bodily integrity but is not as contentious as abortion.[12] A national poll found that 96 percent of people surveyed supported access to birth control and 77 percent did not see birth control as a controversial issue.[13] There are some religious objections to contraception but none to breastfeeding.

Even if Fifth Amendment Due Process rights have the potential to protect women generally from laws and practices that discourage breastfeeding, they do not contemplate the problem of racial disparities in breastfeeding. The Thirteenth and Fourteenth Amendments, created to eliminate the vestiges of slavery and ensure racial equality, are more likely candidates to reduce these disparities. But even these amendments will be difficult to deploy under a conservative Court.

Equal Protection

The Equal Protection Clause promises that no state shall "deny to any person within its jurisdiction the equal protection of the laws."[14] Under the Supreme Court's most recent interpretations of the Fourteenth Amendment, the Equal Protection Clause almost never provides protection for individuals from racial discrimination that results from facially neutral laws, policies, or practices.[15] Instead, a challenger must prove that a discriminatory purpose motivated the action.[16] It is very unlikely that a plaintiff would find evidence that an intent to prevent Black women from breastfeeding motivates food or welfare policies. At best, it might be possible to show that legislators and policy makers are aware of this effect but indifferent to it. Even that, however, is not enough to find an Equal Protection violation.

To get a court to review their challenge under strict scrutiny, plaintiffs could try to demonstrate that no other explanation for the law or policy aside from racial discrimination is possible.[17] Over a hundred years ago, the Supreme Court held that the city of San Francisco's denial of a permit to run a laundry in a wooden building to all Chinese laundry owners and only one White laundry owner was racially discriminatory. Chinese people owned 89 percent of the laundries in San Francisco. The Court held that discrimination was the only plausible explanation for this lopsided enforcement of an ordinance allowing only brick or stone laundries to operate without a permit.[18]

In 1960, the Court similarly found that redrawing a square electoral district into a twenty-eight-sided shape that excluded over four hundred

Blacks and no Whites had a racially discriminatory purpose.[19] There was no other possible reason for this bizarre reconfiguring of electoral zones. But these two cases were outliers.

If plaintiffs could not prove intent to discriminate against Black breast-feeding mothers, the challenged law or policy would receive rational review, the lowest standard. Rational review requires the law or policy to have a rational relationship to a legitimate government purpose.[20] The purpose does not need to be the true purpose.[21] If the government does not offer one, the court can make one up. Virtually every law passes muster under this standard.

The intersectional nature of the injury of low breastfeeding rates among Black women might make it possible to challenge some laws and practices as sex discrimination instead of or in addition to race discrimination.[22] Discrimination on the basis of sex receives intermediate review.[23] This is a lower standard than strict scrutiny, requiring the government to prove that the challenged act is substantially related to an important purpose. But plaintiffs claiming sex discrimination must still show that the government acted because of, not merely in spite of, the discriminatory effect of its action.[24] This requirement would likely doom any challenge on these grounds.

It is possible that a future Supreme Court, one that is more committed to racial justice, will expand Fourteenth Amendment protection by allowing plaintiffs to prove discriminatory treatment through the use of statistics that demonstrate a discriminatory impact.[25] This approach would encompass discriminatory behavior that stems not necessarily directly from racial malice but from inequalities entrenched in our legal system, institutions, and assumptions since the beginning of slavery.[26]

Allowing proof of discrimination through disparate impact would be helpful because even when it is possible to trace discrimination to individuals' behavior, sometimes people act on implicit or unconscious bias instead of an intentional desire to harm.[27] Proving discrimination by effect instead of intent would allow the Court to invalidate laws and policies that arise from structural and institutionalized racism in addition to unconscious racism. The law already allows for this type of proof in other cases, most notably in those involving housing and employment discrimination. It would make sense to extend proof of discrimination through disparate impact to the health discrimination context, where it will always be difficult to discern and prove malicious intent.

The Thirteenth Amendment

The Thirteenth Amendment guarantees that "neither slavery nor involuntary servitude, except as a punishment for crime whereof the party shall have been duly convicted, shall exist within the United States, or any place subject to their jurisdiction."[28] It applies more broadly than the Fourteenth Amendment because it is not limited to redressing state action.[29] Unlike the Fourteenth Amendment, it reaches private conduct. It also does not require a plaintiff to prove discriminatory or any other kind of intent. In theory, Thirteenth Amendment protection extends beyond pure slavery[30] to include "badges and incidents of slavery" in addition to "vestiges" and "relics" of slavery.[31] Low breastfeeding rates in the Black community trace directly back to practices established during slavery and thus represent an enduring vestige of that institution.[32]

Courts and scholars treat the Thirteenth Amendment very differently, relying on different sections of the amendment for their arguments to narrow or expand its coverage. Based on the text of section 1 quoted above, the Court has condemned and prohibited many modern incarnations of slavery or involuntary servitude.[33] But it has been reluctant to extend the amendment's application to cases that do not directly involve forced labor.

Section 2 presents another obstacle to an expansive interpretation of the amendment. Section 2 advises that "Congress shall have power to enforce this article by appropriate legislation."[34] The Court's desire to adhere to this text has largely doomed Thirteenth Amendment challenges that do not involve congressional legislation.[35] Legal scholars, however, envision broad application of the amendment to issues ranging from hate speech[36] to payday lending.[37] Their arguments rely heavily on constitutional principles as opposed to precedent.

Temporary Assistance for Needy Families

Even though there is no real comparison between the brutality of slavery and contemporary labor conditions, modern interpretations of the Thirteenth Amendment could lead to the elimination of TANF's welfare work requirements as forced labor or involuntary servitude. Under

TANF, many states provide no or minimal exemptions to work requirements for new mothers. TANF also increased sanctions for failing to fulfill work requirements and encouraged states to enforce these sanctions more often.

TANF dictates that states must reduce or terminate assistance to recipients who do not complete their job requirements.[38] There is a narrow exception for single parents who cannot find adequate child care.[39] Despite TANF's strong language, case workers exercise discretion in granting exceptions and waivers. They help favored recipients interpret complicated rules and do not enforce requirements equally. States disproportionately sanction Black families.[40] Black women are far more likely than Latinx or White women to have their cases closed for violating a work requirement.[41] In New Jersey, Black recipients have a 16 percent chance of receiving full sanctions, compared with 10 percent of White recipients.[42]

These sanctions can be unnecessarily punitive and unjust, often targeting families with lower educational levels who never received instructions on how to comply with the program's requirements.[43] The effects of the sanctions are unreasonably harsh. One-third of mothers cut off from the program through sanctions report having inadequate food, housing, and medical care as a result.[44]

Increased sanctions significantly reduce the number of families who participate in TANF, despite their eligibility.[45] The drastic consequences of not receiving or losing these benefits fall on some of the most vulnerable members of society, since all TANF participants live below the poverty line.[46] Approximately one-third are Black and one-quarter are Latinx.[47] Black participants often receive less assistance than White ones do. Almost twice as many Blacks (53 percent) as Whites (29 percent) live in a state with TANF benefits at or below 20 percent of the poverty line.[48] Further, 48 percent of Blacks, compared with 30 percent of Whites, live in states with benefits that cover less than one-third of the housing costs for a two-bedroom apartment.[49]

Single mothers make up 90 percent of all parents in the program.[50] Medical and family emergencies often prevent participants from fulfilling their work requirements. Despite recipients' lack of resources to mitigate the loss of benefits through sanctions, such as wealthy family members, forty-five states terminate benefits as a sanction for failing to meet work requirements.[51]

TANF forces a disproportionate number of new Black mothers to work, requiring them to leave their infants at home. This separation renders breastfeeding extremely difficult if not impossible.[52] The inability to breastfeed during the first six months of life, the minimum amount of time recommended by the American Academy of Pediatrics and the World Health Organization, deprives Black infants and their mothers of significant health benefits. This deprivation, accomplished by compelling mothers to perform a specific type of labor that is outside instead of inside the home, echoes the practice of removing mothers from their infants during slavery. These forced separations determined that enslaved infants would not receive the nourishment of their mothers' breast milk, leading to detrimental and sometimes fatal results.

Dietary Control Is a Vestige of Slavery

Interpreting the Thirteenth Amendment for the first time in the *Slaughter-house Cases*, the Supreme Court held in 1872 that it applied solely to the literal enslavement of African Americans.[53] Eleven years later, in the 1883 *Civil Rights Cases*, the Court extended the amendment's reach: "The [Thirteenth] amendment is not a mere prohibition of State laws establishing or upholding slavery, but an absolute declaration that slavery or involuntary servitude shall not exist in any part of the United States."[54]

The issue in the *Civil Rights Cases* was whether Congress had the constitutional authority to enact the 1875 Civil Rights Act guaranteeing equal access to hotels, inns, theaters, amusement parks, and public transportation. Denying Congress's authority to make and enforce this promise under the Thirteenth Amendment, the Court labeled the integration of private facilities a social right as opposed to a civil one.[55] It then interpreted "incidents" of slavery to refer only to legal, not social, impediments to equality.[56] The integration of privately owned businesses therefore fell outside the Court's definition of badges or incidents of slavery. The term *badges* initially referred only to physical markers, such as skin color.[57] The Court held that the sections of the Civil Rights Act prohibiting discrimination also could not stand under the Fourteenth Amendment. The amendment's guarantee of Equal Protection applies only to government action, not to businesses or individuals.

Despite this disappointing holding, some language in the decision opened the door to a more expansive interpretation of the Thirteenth

Amendment. Justice Bradley's majority opinion states that "it is assumed, that the power vested in Congress to enforce the article by appropriate legislation, clothes Congress with power to pass all laws necessary and proper for abolishing all badges and incidents of slavery in the United States."[58] Since he wrote these powerful words, the definition of badges and incidents of slavery has been fodder for debate.

The Court did not shed any further light on how to define this phrase until its 1968 decision in *Jones v. Alfred H. Mayer Company*, confronting an apartment owner's refusal to sell property to an interracial couple.[59] Acknowledging the role that segregation played in slavery and subsequent attempts to reinstate it, the Court identified racial housing segregation as an incident of slavery.[60] It held that Congress could prohibit private housing discrimination through the Civil Rights Act under the authority of the Thirteenth Amendment's section 2 because residential segregation is a relic of slavery.[61] Although this holding seemed to foretell future use of the Thirteenth Amendment to invalidate different forms of racial discrimination, *Jones* became an exception, not a rule.

The Supreme Court declined to extend similar protection to Black swimmers in *Palmer v. Thompson* in 1971.[62] Instead of integrating its pools after Jim Crow segregation became illegal, the city of Jackson, Mississippi, shut them down.[63] The city's White population swam at private pools instead, while most Black residents lost the opportunity to swim at all.[64] As a result of these measures taken by Jackson and other cities, 70 percent of Blacks in the United States today cannot swim.[65] The segregation of Blacks and Whites in public spaces such as swimming pools heralds back to the social norms of slavery in the same way that the housing segregation struck down in *Jones* did. The Court's refusal to extend *Jones* beyond housing discrimination does not bode well for other challenges, including ones grounded in health discrimination.

Interfering with a mother's relationship to her children, including her choice of what to feed them, is an incident of slavery similar to housing discrimination. In an 1846 Alabama case, *Lee v. Mathews*,[66] the court included slave-owners' property interest in enslaved mothers' children as one of the incidents of slavery.[67] In 1856, George Stroud published *Sketch of the Laws Relating to Slavery*, surveying laws governing slave owning in twelve states.[68] The second chapter, titled "Of the Incidents of Slavery—

the Relation of Master and Slave," describes laws pertaining to owners' control over slaves' food.[69] This control represented an important
method of dominating the lives of slaves and suppressing their freedom.
Control over food includes infants' first food, which slaves and slave owners alike believed should be breast milk.[70]

During the debates leading up to the Thirteenth Amendment's rati-
fication in 1865, Iowa senator James Harlan referred to some of the incidents of slavery that the amendment would enable Congress and the
Court to dismantle.[71] That the amendment would abolish slavery itself
was already settled and not a subject of the debates.[72] Harlan's list included slave owners' prohibition of the "parental relation."[73] Similarly, in
debates about the 1866 Civil Rights Act, Representative Russell Thayer
described the amendment as intended to guarantee natural rights.[74]
These natural rights would encompass the ability to parent, including
providing children with food and safeguarding their health.[75]

At that time, when there were no viable alternatives to mother's
milk,[76] depriving a mother of the right to breastfeed her child had dire
consequences. Formula did not exist.[77] Water does not contain nutrients
essential to survival. Milk was unpasteurized, and contaminated milk led
to millions of infant deaths.[78] The inability of some enslaved mothers to
breastfeed their children contributed to the low survival rates of Black infants compared with White ones.[79] That disparity remains constant today. Even now, infant mortality rates are 2.2 times higher for Blacks than
for Whites,[80] and breastfeeding rates are dramatically lower.[81]

Laws and policies that contribute to higher rates of deaths and diseases in the Black population represent incidents of slavery, because they
have evolved from the laws and practices that maintained slavery. People
who accept these disparities without questioning them often do so because they are accustomed to the racial inequality established in and perpetuated since slavery. When inequalities arise from race-neutral, institutionalized laws and policies, they often appear natural. Many people
attribute them to the personal failings of Blacks instead of to deeply entrenched structural deficiencies.

When Congress can reduce or eliminate racial health disparities, it
should. Congress enacted the PRWORA and is free to amend it. Legislators should also restore the previous broad exceptions to work require-

ments for new mothers. But because of the formula industry's influence over government, Congress probably will not. The courts will have to step in to protect Black mothers by invalidating these parts of the law.

Forced Labor

The Court has never questioned the Thirteenth Amendment's ability to prohibit forced labor that closely resembles slavery. But scholars and activists have pushed the Court for a more liberal interpretation of "compulsory" or "involuntary" servitude.[82] In 1883, the same year as the *Civil Rights Cases*, the Court struck down the 1871 Force Act in *United States v. Harris*.[83] Designed to keep the Ku Klux Klan in check, the Force Act criminalized conspiracy to deprive a person of equal protection.[84] Prosecutors charged a Tennessee county sheriff, R. G. Harris, under the act after he led an armed lynch mob into the state jail. The mob captured four Black prisoners, killing one of them despite the deputy sheriff's attempts to intervene.[85] Harris won his case on appeal when the Court held that the Thirteenth Amendment did not authorize the Force Act. It held the amendment inapplicable because the law did not implicate either slavery or involuntary servitude, even though the mob's violence clearly continued a tradition of racist violence begun in slavery.[86] The Court also held that the Fourteenth Amendment failed to provide a basis for the act because the law regulated the acts of individuals, not the state.[87]

In 1896, in *Plessy v. Ferguson*, the Court upheld the racial segregation of railroad cars based on its professed belief that the accommodations the rail company provided to both races were "separate but equal."[88] Because they were substantially equivalent, the segregated cars satisfied the Fourteenth Amendment's guarantee of equal protection.[89] Considering whether it had the authority to order integration of the railway cars under the Thirteenth Amendment, the Court rejected the idea, confining the meaning of slavery to "a state of bondage; the ownership of mankind as chattel, or at least the control of the labor and services of one man for the benefit of another."[90] In the 1906 case *Hodges v. United States*, the Court again declined to expand the meaning of the Thirteenth Amendment to include situations that did not involve "the entire subjection of one person to the will of another."[91]

In 1944, the Court provided insight into how it might respond to a Thirteenth Amendment challenge against TANF work requirements and sanctions in *Pollock v. Williams*.[92] The decision reinforced the Court's commitment to eradicate all forms of forced labor. The case dealt with a Florida law that made it a crime of fraud to accept advance payment for labor and then not perform the labor.[93] This type of law was popular in the South, where employers looked for ways to force farm laborers to work under even the most horrific conditions.[94] Blacks made up the majority of these farm workers, because laws following Reconstruction excluded them from most other jobs. These laws primarily restricted Black men to agricultural labor and Black women to domestic labor.[95] Under the Florida law, failure to pay back an advance without fulfilling a contract was proof of intent to defraud. Because of the fraud element, the failure to pay came with penalties much harsher than an ordinary default would entail.[96]

Brevard County sheriff H. T. Williams took Emanuel Pollock, a Black laborer, into custody for sixty days for failing to give five dollars back to his employer, J. V. O'Albora, after he quit his job. Pollock did not have the money to pay O'Albora back. The sheriff set Pollock's release bond at five hundred dollars (the equivalent of $7,200 in 2019).[97] The steep price of his release ran afoul of the 1867 Peonage Abolition Act.[98] The Supreme Court struck down the Florida fraud law and upheld Congress's authority to enact the Anti-Peonage law under the Thirteenth Amendment.

The Court justified this holding by stating that the amendment's goal is "not only to end slavery, but to maintain a system of completely free and voluntary labor throughout the United States."[99] The Court went on to explain that "Congress has put it beyond debate that no indebtedness warrants a suspension of the right to be free from compulsory service. This congressional policy means that no state can make the quitting of work any component of a crime or make criminal sanctions available for holding unwilling persons to labor."[100]

This language speaks directly to the issue of TANF sanctions imposed on mothers who refuse to stop caring for their infants in order to perform state-ordered labor outside the home. Infant care is an important, if undervalued, form of labor. Although this labor is uncompensated when performed by the child's mother, it is not free. If the mother does not do it, she must pay someone else to do it for her. In rare cases, a family member may be available to do this work, but that person's time also has value. Compelling a mother to perform one type of labor over another is an unconstitutional restraint on freedom. TANF allows the government, through work requirements, to remove the choice of labor from mothers and impose its own.

Under *Pollock v. Williams*, sanctions for failing to perform forced labor are unconstitutional penalties. Withholding benefits from families who need and qualify for them can lead to extreme consequences.[101] These include homelessness, inadequate nutrition, and medical crises.[102] This degree of punishment amounts to criminalization of the failure to comply with forced labor conditions. The burden of this criminalization falls disproportionately on Black women.[103]

The 1988 case *United States v. Kozminski*[104] provides another window into how the Court might approach TANF's work requirements and sanctions.[105] The case analyzed two statutes enacted by Congress under the Thirteenth Amendment that criminalized involuntary servitude.[106] It involved two intellectually disabled men, Louis Moltinaris and Robert Fulmer, who worked against their will on a dairy farm in Michigan owned by Ike Kozminski, his wife, Margarethe, and their son John.[107] Fulmer and Moltinaris labored every day for seventeen hours, at first for fifteen dollars a week and then for free.[108]

Margarethe found Robert Fulmer on the road near a farm where he was working. She picked him up, left a note at the farm simply stating that he was gone, and then took him to her own farm. Ike found Louis Moltinaris on the street in Ann Arbor. Moltinaris was homeless after a state mental institution had discharged him. The Kozminskis housed the two men together in isolated, squalid conditions. They subjected them to physical and verbal abuse, including threats of institutionalization. After a bull gored one man and the other lost his thumb, the Kozminskis denied them medical treatment.[109] When their relatives came asking after them, the Kozminskis told them that the men had no desire to see them. They also ripped the workers' phone out of the wall after they tried to make a call.[110] The Kozminskis kept the men docile by failing to provide them with adequate nutrition.[111] Fulmer and Moltinaris, who had the intellectual capabilities of an eight- and ten-year-old, tried to leave the farm several times, but the Kozminskis always brought them back.[112] Eventually, a herdsperson working on the farm contacted county officials about the situation. The officials rescued Fulmer and Moltinaris, moving them to an adult foster-care home.[113]

The central issue in the case was the definition of involuntary servitude for Thirteenth Amendment purposes. Reviewing previous holdings, the majority concluded that "in every case in which this Court has found a condition of involuntary servitude, the victim had no available choice but to work or be subject to legal sanction."[114] In other words, "our precedents clearly define a Thirteenth Amendment prohibition of involuntary servitude enforced by the use or threatened use of physical or legal coercion."[115] The Court elaborated on this definition, asserting that "'involuntary servitude' necessarily means a condition of servitude in which the victim is forced to work for the defendant . . . by the use or threat of coercion through law or the legal process."[116] Further, "the vulnerabilities of the victim are relevant in determining whether the physical or legal coercion or threats thereof could plausibly have compelled the victim to serve."[117]

Under this definition, TANF's system of work requirements and sanctions is a form of legal coercion.[118] Welfare recipients do not have a true choice of how to care for their infants. They must either leave them at home or relinquish their ability to support them. The *Kozminski* concurrence explains that "in some minimalist sense the laborer always has a choice no matter what the threat: the laborer can choose to work, or take a beating; work, or go to jail. We can all agree that these choices are so illegitimate that any decision to work is 'involuntary.'"[119]

Similarly, new mothers on welfare cannot realistically choose to forfeit state financial support. If they do, they will likely lose their ability to shelter, feed, and clothe their children. The state wields TANF's combined work requirements and sanctions as a tool of coercion, imposing or threatening to impose extreme deprivation on participating mothers who decide to care for their infants instead of working at state-mandated jobs.

Unconstitutional Conditions
In the United States, social assistance is not automatic. The government sometimes chooses to confer this benefit and can just as easily remove it. In most cases, there are no restrictions on the government's ability to tie conditions to receipt of benefits. But there are times when the govern-

ment cannot impose a condition because doing so would deprive an individual of a constitutional right. This is true even if the government could choose to withhold the benefit entirely.[120]

The Supreme Court has found unconstitutional conditions in only a handful of cases. It ruled that the state could not deny a woman unemployment benefits for deciding not to work on her Sabbath (a First Amendment free exercise of religion right).[121] It held that World War II veterans could not lose a property-tax exemption because they failed to take a loyalty oath (a First Amendment free speech right).[122] It also found that a state's one-year residential requirement for welfare benefits violated applicants' Privileges and Immunities right to travel.[123]

Tying new mothers' receipt of TANF benefits to their work outside the home violates their Due Process right to control their children's upbringing. The Court first established this right in *Pierce v. Society of Sisters*[124] and affirmed it in *Meyer v. Nebraska*.[125] The ability to choose how to feed a child is central to parenting. As the Fifth Circuit recognized, the choice to breastfeed goes beyond nutrition. It represents a fundamental decision about the bodies of both the mother and the child. Under the unconstitutional conditions doctrine, states should not be able to compel mothers to surrender their right to make this decision.

TANF's work requirements and sanctions impose an unconstitutional condition on the receipt of welfare. They are both a form of forced labor that violates the Thirteenth Amendment and an unconstitutional exercise of dietary control over infants' food. A successful challenge to TANF could open the door to greater constitutional protection against other laws and policies that similarly prevent Black mothers from breastfeeding. At the very least, the Due Process and Equal Protection Clauses and the Thirteenth Amendment provide grounding constitutional principles for challenges to government acts that perpetuate racial disparities in breastfeeding rates.

International Breastfeeding Laws

International practices and laws provide models for and cautions about how to approach the problems of racial disparities in breastfeeding rates and of low breastfeeding rates generally. Cross-nursing, which has fallen out of favor in the United States, is far more common and socially acceptable in other parts of the world. In some Islamic countries, children who share the same cross-nurse become "milk kin."[126] This term not only marks a unique, enduring bond but also draws a strict kinship boundary, making marriage between them impossible.[127] Similarly, in Morocco, "milk children" form a recognized relationship with their "milk mothers" that elevates friendships and business relationships in addition to creating incest boundaries.[128] In some parts of Ivory Coast, cross-nursing is an essential element of the practice of communal child-rearing.[129]

Some countries seeking to achieve high breastfeeding rates use oppressive methods to do so. In 2014, the United Arab Emirates' Federal National Council passed the Child Rights Law requiring mothers to breastfeed their babies for two full years.[130] In the event that a mother cannot nurse for medical reasons, the council provides the family with a wet nurse. The law gives fathers the right to sue their wives for failing to comply with this provision.

Out of the Blues, a Dubai-based group that supports women who experience postnatal illness and depression, organized against the severity of the Child Rights Law.[131] It called for the government to focus on supporting new mothers with comprehensive workplace accommodation laws and other measures instead of punishing women who face insurmountable obstacles to successful nursing.[132] Sheikha Bodour bint Sultan bin Muhammad Al Qasimi, a businesswoman and philanthropist, created the Sharjah Baby-Friendly Campaign in response to these objections.[133] The campaign arranged for the training of 95 percent of the Emirates' maternity- and baby-care professionals in lactation support.[134] Although this training represents a positive step toward providing assistance for breastfeeding mothers, it does not directly respond to the pressing issues raised by Out of the Blues.

In Indonesia, breastfeeding is a serious public health issue due to the scarcity of clean drinking water.[135] In an attempt to lower the country's infant mortality rates, the Indonesian legislature sought to eliminate the practice of feeding infants formula mixed with unclean water. To accomplish this, it enacted a law imposing penalties of one year of incarceration and $11,000 in fines on any person, including an employer or relative, who creates an obstacle to a mother breastfeeding during the first six months of a baby's life.[136] The law also bans formula advertising directed at mothers of babies younger than one year old.[137]

A high court in India sought to enact a similar law. It asked the government to declare breastfeeding a fundamental right and make it mandatory for the first six months.[138] The court's thirty-six-page order making the request opines that "delivery gives birth not only to a child, but also a mother."[139] It declares that "there is no substitute for mother's milk in the world and even the so-called 'divine nectar' could not be equal to mother's milk."[140] Forcing mothers to breastfeed for the first six months is highly problematic because it deprives them of the choice of how to parent and what to do with their bodies. The report also contains less-restrictive suggestions, including increasing maternity leave and providing maternity insurance and daycare centers to government employees.

The harshness of the UAE, Indonesian, and proposed Indian laws render them unlikely and complicated models for United States legislators to follow. But there are more moderate international approaches that target different aspects of the problem, from marketing to workplace accommodations to protection for public breastfeeding. In a radical approach to the problem of low breastfeeding rates, Venezuelan legislators contemplated banning formula bottles altogether.[141] This prohibition would harm infants who require bottle-feeding. It did not pass.

Laws prohibiting discrimination against mothers who nurse in public appear to be the most popular form of protection for breastfeeding internationally. In Australia, the 1984 Sex Discrimination Act prohibits businesses and other establishments from excluding breastfeeding mothers.[142] Scotland's 2005 Breastfeeding Act provides similar protection, imposing substantial fines for obstructing a woman nursing a child up to two years of age in a public place.[143] In Great Britain, the 2010 Equality Act forbids businesses from discriminating against breastfeeding women and holds companies accountable for customers' discrimination as well.[144]

Sao Paulo, Brazil, was the first city in the world to impose fines on public institutions and private corporations that forbid women from breastfeeding or otherwise discriminate against nursing mothers.[145] Sao Paulo legislators enacted the law after a guard at the city's Museum of Image and Sound told Brazilian model Priscila Navarro Bueno to stop nursing her child during an exhibition. Navarro Bueno publicly denounced the guard's action, describing it as a puritanical expression of conflicting and insulting attitudes toward female nudity. She asserted, "During Carnival women can show their breasts, but it is not permitted to do so to give milk to your child. It is absurd that women have to breastfeed in a hidden room."[146] Other outraged mothers took up Navarro Bueno's cause, leading protests around the city. Sao Paulo legislators succumbed to this pressure. The law also responded to Brazilian research revealing that breastfed babies had higher IQs, received more education, and landed better-paying jobs than their formula-fed counterparts did.[147]

Brazilian law prohibits all formula advertising and promotion.[148] Pakistani law similarly focuses on marketing, requiring labels on formula similar to those proposed by Iowa Senator Tom Harkin, warning, "Mother's milk is best for your baby and helps in preventing diarrhea and other illnesses."[149] Pakistani law also prohibits health workers from encouraging mothers with infants under one year of age to use packaged milk.[150] Legislators in Sweden concerned about formula advertising considered banning pictures of babies from formula ads but ultimately did not pass the law.[151]

Other countries' laws focus on ensuring that working mothers have adequate breaks and environments to express and store milk. The Philippines' 2009 Expanded Breastfeeding Promotion Act requires employers to give nursing mothers a place to pump and forty minutes within the work day in which to do so.[152] In Argentina, working mothers are entitled to two thirty-minute breastfeeding breaks a day until their child turns one.[153] Extensions beyond that time are possible with a physician's recommendation.[154] The Netherlands provides even greater protection for working mothers, requiring a nursing room for up to nine months after birth and one-quarter of paid work time off for breastfeeding.

In Norway, an impressive 99 percent of new mothers breastfeed, with 70 percent still breastfeeding exclusively at three months.[155] Norwegian law makes this possible by offering mothers the choice of receiving thirty-six months off from work at full pay or forty-six months off at 80 percent of their salary.[156] Public breastfeeding is both common and welcome.[157] Norwegian law also prohibits formula advertising, and images of baby bottles at showers or similar occasions are rare.[158]

Activist Elisabet Helsing is largely responsible for Norway's unprecedented breastfeeding rates. Her efforts transformed an infant feeding culture that originally resembled the one in the United States, where the formula industry persuaded women that its product was a symbol of wealth and modernity.[159] In the 1970s, Helsing wrote a book modeled on a La Leche publication that detailed the benefits of breastfeeding. She sought to distribute it widely to mothers.[160] Coincidentally, the minister of health at the time, Gro Harlem Brundtland, had recently returned from Harvard, where she was researching the decline in US breastfeeding rates. She approved the pamphlet and later became Norway's prime minister.[161] Although Helsing began her movement as a grassroots campaign, her lobbying efforts ultimately led to the introduction of baby-friendly hospitals and revolutionary legislation that provides support for all new mothers.[162]

Greek law similarly supports new mothers by offering them several options to reduce their time away from their infants. They can choose to work one hour less each day with no salary reduction for thirty months after the end of their maternity leave, work two fewer hours a day with no salary reduction for the first year after their maternity leave ends and one hour less a day for six months after that, or extend their maternity leave by three and a half months.[163] Breastfeeding mothers in Greece can also lawfully refuse to work at night until their children reach the age of one, or they can choose to receive leave with full pay.[164]

On the other end of the spectrum, breastfeeding in China is a particularly complicated and controversial issue. In 2014, 30 percent of rural and less than 16 percent of urban Chinese mothers breastfed exclusively for the first six months, prompting an inquiry by lawmakers into the feasibility of a formula marketing ban.[165] Cultural practices remain a significant barrier to increasing breastfeeding rates. The tradition of *zuo yuezi* provides new mothers with a month-long resting period. During that time, caregivers feed babies formula to spare the mother the exertion of nursing.[166] The legacy of an ancient tradition that forbids women from exposing any body parts to strangers also has a lingering effect on the acceptance of public breastfeeding.

Half of Chinese women have Caesarian births.[167] Afterward, they do not breastfeed or quickly abandon efforts to do so because their milk is not immediately available. Internal migration from agricultural to manufacturing regions is a common occurrence due to the lack of employment opportunities in rural areas. Moving requires women to leave their babies in the care of grandparents, who necessarily rely on formula feeding. In rural and urban environments, Chinese mothers lack sufficient leave, public facilities for nursing, and other necessary support for breastfeeding.[168]

China's formula industry garnered international attention in 2008, when tainted formula led to the deaths of six infants and made over three hundred thousand others ill.[169] Chinese parents scrambled to purchase foreign-made formula in response but did not increase breastfeeding.[170] The Chinese formula industry has faced charges of price-fixing and attempting to circumvent regulations prohibiting the free distribution of formula in hospitals and other health care settings. This ban on marketing through distribution does not preclude regular advertising and marketing techniques.[171]

Attitudes toward breastfeeding in China came to a head in November 2015 when an individual named Hanjia Xiaoguaixue posted a picture on Weibo (Chinese Twitter) of a woman named Yang breastfeeding her three-month-old daughter on a crowded Beijing subway train.[172] Under the picture, he wrote, "You're on the capital's subway, not a bus in your village. Do you really think this behavior is appropriate?"[173] After Beijing Tale, a popular community-service organization, reposted the picture and warned women against exposing their "sexual organs," the post went viral, inciting heated debate on both sides.[174]

Although likely the most well-publicized incident of its kind, it was not an isolated one. News media have reported other instances of Chinese women receiving criticism for breastfeeding in public, including one mother whose father reprehended her and another who a fellow female passenger scolded on a bus.[175] Responding to this harassment, Chinese breastfeeding advocates point to the dearth of public facilities for breastfeeding in China's parks,[176] shopping centers, and bus and rail stations.[177] Because the cost of Chinese real estate makes building designated spaces for breastfeeding unattractive to developers, laws requiring them are essential to their creation.[178]

There is little evidence that other countries face the dramatic racial disparities in breastfeeding rates that exist in the United States.[179] Norway, the country with the highest breastfeeding rates, has a relatively racially homogeneous population. It also has a social democratic government. Its economic policies seek to benefit all citizens. These differences suggest that it would not be simple to implement its policies in the United States. Still, it would be worth trying. Canada, which is racially and culturally diverse, provides new parents with thirty-five weeks of standard leave and sixty-one weeks of extended leave.[180] Like Norway, it has a social democratic government that seeks to support families. In Canada,

Black women practice exclusive breastfeeding at higher rates than White women do.[181]

Extended parental leave policies, affordable child care facilities located close to workplaces, and a formula marketing ban would go a long way toward transforming infant feeding practices in the United States.

Community- and Market-Based Solutions

When a mother cannot or does not want to breastfeed, an alternative source of breast milk, as opposed to formula, will help guard against infant mortality and provide other important health benefits to the child.[182] This breast milk might be available through the now less common but traditional practices of wet nursing or cross-nursing or through the more recent innovations of milk banks and private milk exchanges. Wet nursing and cross-nursing have certain advantages over bottle-feeding donated or purchased milk. Although the United States has banned BPA (bisphenol A) from baby bottles, there is evidence that plastic bottles continue to contain harmful chemicals.[183] Bottle-feeding can also delay jaw and dental development in some babies. Caregivers who encourage babies to finish a bottle may be overfeeding and disrupting their natural eating habits. And from an environmental perspective, bottle-feeding creates more waste than breastfeeding.

Some domestic caregivers serve as wet nurses, usually for additional wages.[184] Despite the benefits of wet nursing and some calls for its widespread revival,[185] the practice continues to involve complex race and class dynamics. Most domestic workers are women of color employed by White families. Many of these workers experience exploitation and abuse, with little recourse. Cross-nursing presents a potentially less problematic solution because it relies on an existing, equal relationship between the mother and the cross-nurse. But the practice is essentially taboo in the United States.

A scene in the 2009 film *Away We Go* illustrates this point. Maya Rudolph plays a pregnant woman who embarks on a journey with her husband to find an ideal parenting style. The couple is shocked and appalled when their friend, played by Maggie Gyllenhaal, casually offers her breast to a friend's hungry child.[186] A later scene reinforces the lack of boundaries that this act purportedly represents, when Gyllenhaal confesses that she and her husband have sex in the bed that they share with their children. Cross-nursing fares no better in real life, judging from the intense debate surrounding Salma Hayek's spontaneous decision to breastfeed a hungry infant she encountered during a humanitarian mission to Sierra Leone in 2009.[187] In 2003, Oklahoma charged attorney Shannon Denney with the misdemeanor of outraging public decency for stopping a newborn in her daughter's daycare center from crying by breastfeeding her.[188]

Both wet nursing and cross-nursing come with some risks. It is possible to transmit diseases such as tuberculosis, HIV, herpes, viral infections, and syphilis through breast milk. Also, a mother who cross-nurses may have a smaller supply for her own child, leading to nutritional deficiencies or the need to introduce a substitute. And because the composition of breast milk alters as babies grow, a cross-nurse's milk may not be ideal to feed to another woman's child. Differences in the physical act of breastfeeding relating to the rate that milk comes down and other mechanics can lead to confusion or frustration for the cross-nursing baby.[189]

Another viable alternative to formula feeding is to bottle-feed using another woman's breast milk obtained from either a milk bank or a private milk exchange. A range of services provide breast milk, from nonprofit milk banks to for-profit centers to informal or more formal medically supervised milk-sharing networks. Some women object to paying milk banks for breast milk because the economic exchange represents the commercialization of a process that should be natural. In this sense, milk banks are an extension of the medicalization of motherhood. But the procedures necessary to ensure that donated milk is safe are expensive. Emotionally, the opportunity to share and donate milk can create community and provide solace to mothers whose children cannot ingest their milk.

Informal milk sharing was a somewhat limited endeavor until the introduction of Facebook facilitated opportunities for networking and exchange.[190] Eats on Feets pioneered this movement and subsequently grew to fifty chapters across the world. Other groups, including Human Milk 4 Human Babies and MilkShare, also provide this service. Like wet nursing and cross-nursing, milk sharing carries the risk of transmitting disease. But milk-sharing advocates argue that formula similarly increases the likelihood that a baby will experience health issues.[191] And caregivers can take precautions, including inquiring about any medication taken by the milk donor and heat treating the milk before feedings, to guard against potential infections and other harms.

Unregulated, informal milk-sharing networks can reduce the supply of regulated, formal milk banks, as many women who donate their breast milk prefer to operate less formally. Milk banks offer the advantage of adhering to national standards that reduce the risks associated with unofficial exchanges, but not all women can afford this advantage. Equity of access and donor exploitation make milk banks problematic. In 2006, the first for-profit milk bank, Prolacta Bioscience, opened in California. Prolacta offers specialized services, producing "unique breastmilk derived fortification products to add to maternal or donor milk to increase the protein, calcium and other nutrient composition." [192] In 2013, Prolacta sold its fortifier for between $125 and $312 a bottle.[193] The value and expense of these products contribute to the problem of inequitable access. Prolacta and other private services have also come under fire for the low rates they pay donors, especially considering the high prices they charge. This exploitation has both race and class elements.

A feature in *Ebony's* September 1949 edition describes the role that Black women played as early milk donors. Describing milk banks as "a proxy version of the old-fashioned wet-nursing practice," the article reports that seventeen cities set up milk banks in response to "medical insistence that there is no proper substitute for mother's milk."[194] The article states that "in many of the milk banks, [Black] women are the biggest contributors. In Chicago last year more than half of the 212 donors were colored women."[195]

Controversy over the exploitation of Black milk donors came to a head in Detroit in 2015 after Medolac Laboratories and its partner, Mothers Milk Cooperative (MMC), targeted new Black mothers in Detroit to be "paid" milk donors.[196] Medolac justified its recruitment efforts on the bases that they would help solve the problem of low breastfeeding rates in the Black community, encourage "healthy behaviors," and provide the financial means to extend maternity leaves.[197] All of these rationales were suspect.

Selling breast milk to Medolac for one dollar an ounce would not generate enough revenue to cover a full-time salary.[198] And the idea that

Black women would refrain from drug use to keep their milk "clean" to sell but not to feed to their infants invokes the Welfare Queen and Crack Mother stereotypes.[199] Giving milk away instead of nursing would more likely shorten, not extend, breastfeeding because of the need to divide the supply between the baby and the milk for sale. Activists resisted MMC's campaign because it tried to force economically vulnerable women to choose between nurturing their infants and monetizing their milk to make ends meet.[200] It also continued the long tradition of commodifying Black women's breast milk and exploiting their reproductive labor. This resistance successfully shut down the program.[201]

Best Practices

The complex nature of racial disparities in breastfeeding requires a multipronged attack. Advocates should confront this problem through litigation based on constitutional arguments that seek to expand existing protections through broad interpretations of the Fifth, Thirteenth, and Fourteenth Amendments. They should also campaign for legislators to create generous leave policies through the Family and Medical Leave Act and comparable state statutes. They should lobby for free and accessible universal daycare and for the protection of breastfeeding at work and in public. They should champion the abolition of formula marketing to new mothers. And they should spearhead a social movement that will push for radical reform in social structures and a reimagination of gender roles and work-life balance.

Had different laws, policies, and social attitudes toward breastfeeding been in place when Annie Mae gave birth to her quadruplets, their story might have been different. Annie Mae might have received breast milk for her girls from community members or milk banks, making their reliance on formula avoidable. If the law had prohibited formula companies from using infants in their campaigns, Pet Milk could not have adopted the Fultz sisters. Fred Klenner would have quickly lost his influence over the girls' lives and health, and he would not have performed his vitamin C experiments on them. They would have stayed with their parents and siblings. They might have lived long, healthy lives. Instead, the lasting effects of the Pet Milk contract shaped their adult lives in unexpected and troubling ways.

Chapter 7

THE FULTZ QUADS AFTER PET MILK

In April 1964, *Ebony* magazine ran a glamorous photo spread document-ing the appearance of eighteen-year-old Catherine, Alice, Ann, and Lou-ise at the Zeta Phi Beta cotillion, a debutante ball and fund-raiser run by Black sorority Alpha Alpha Zeta, the sorority's chapter in Salisbury, North Carolina.[1] *Ebony* reported:

> For 57 of North Carolina's prettiest girls, it seemed that six giddy weeks of coming-out parties, dress-buying sprees and poise practice would end in the worst of disasters. Here it was that one glorious night in a girl's life—the grand Debutante Ball—and it looked as if no one would be there. Snow and ice had choked highways for miles around Salisbury's gaily-decorated National Guard Armory, and parents of some of the girls who lived 20 to 200 miles away had put a foot down: No driving tonight! Most likely stay-at-homes were the famous Fultz quadruplets who lived in Reidsville, 70 miles to the north. Their guardians, Mr. and Mrs. Charles A. Saylor, had looked out at the weather and announced that, debut or no debut, the trip to Salisbury was off. But whimpering, sad-eyed girls can change the most made-up of minds. Though hours late, the Quads and a dozen other girls finally skidded into Salisbury—just in time to get in on the tail-end of a terrific time![2]

For all the sisters knew, the Zeta Cotillion could be their last society ap-pearance sponsored by Pet Milk.[3]

The Saylors had already persuaded the company to give the girls $5,000 to get through their last year of high school.[4] Because of Pet Milk's relentless interruptions to their schedules, the sisters were graduating a year behind their classmates. The constant upheaval and the girls' low grades had dimmed their once-bright academic prospects. After purchasing their white lace and tulle dresses for the cotillion, the sisters had only $11.97 left for the rest of the year, and they had to split that amount four ways.[5] The Saylors hoped that Pet Milk would agree to one more year of support for the girls, who were still working hard to promote its brand.

H. E. O. Heinemann, Pet Milk's vice president and research chemist, knew full well that the company was done with the girls. Dreading the Saylors' reaction to this bad news, he wrote to Susie Sharp, Dr. Klenner's sister-in-law, for help. Sharp was the girls' former trustee and now a North Carolina supreme court justice. Heinemann told Sharp that he planned to deliver the disappointing news in person and asked her not to let them know ahead of time what he was going to say. He expressed his frustration with the family, saying, "Sooner or later, these people must realize that there is no golden future around the corner, that these are just four nice little girls, who must seek a way of livelihood in a normal, wholesome fashion."[6]

The offers of admission that the state's best Black colleges had given them during their childhood evaporated with the girls' subpar academic standing. Elma thought that they might follow in her footsteps to become nurses, but Susie Sharp dismissed the idea. Writing to their attorney after consulting Dr. Klenner's wife, Ann, Susie suggested that the girls might instead take on less demanding roles as nurses' aides or hospital-ward assistants. Ann proposed that the girls train to become beauticians. Sharp explained that "it is her information that Negro beauty parlors do a lucrative business."[7] Sharp further implored the Saylors not to tarnish Pet Milk's reputation by association, purportedly because "the colored people have been very proud of these children and the publicity which they have received."[8] She warned against creating the impression of another "foreign aid fiasco" if the Fultz sisters' futures reflected badly on Pet Milk's investment.[9]

Nervous about confronting the Saylors alone, Heinemann asked Louise Prothro, their corporate godmother and beloved chaperone, to accompany him. Prothro was a pioneer, one of the first two Black women to hold a national post with a major US company.[10] Prothro's educational credentials were impressive. Born in Macon, Georgia, on February 10, 1920, she earned a home economics degree at Massachusetts' Framingham State Teachers College and a master's degree in food and nutrition from Columbia University Teachers College.[11] She went on to teach home economics at Florida A&M University and to serve as a dietician at the Massachusetts State Reformatory for Women.[12] Prothro made history when Pet Milk appointed her its home economist and field representative in the early 1950s. In these capacities, Prothro represented Pet Milk at marketing conferences, contributed recipes to African American newspapers, and became the chaperone and confidante of Pet Milk's darling Fultz Quads.[13]

When Heinemann commandeered Prothro to join him for the dreaded confrontation with the Saylors, her journey to the South involved many more dangers than his. Prothro drove from Raleigh to Yanceyville alone with the help of *The Negro Travelers' Green Book*, a travel guide to hotels, gas stations, and restaurants that would serve Black patrons.[14] Yanceyville was not a place where Blacks could feel at ease. The town was infamous for a 1951 rape trial of a Black man that attracted onlookers all the way from Canada.

Matt "Mack" Ingram's truck broke down near Yanceyville in 1950. Ingram's stalled truck was about fifty feet away from Willa Jean Boswell, a seventeen-year-old White girl. Boswell objected to the way Ingram looked at her. Following Boswell's accusation, Ingram sat trial for "rape by leer," or assault with intent to commit rape.[15] After Caswell County dropped the initial charge, a jury convicted him of assault on a female. On appeal, a hung jury sent the case back down, and the county court tried and convicted Ingram again. This time, the North Carolina appellate court reversed the conviction. Acknowledging that Ingram "may have looked with lustful eyes," the court held that in the absence of any overt act, it could not convict him "solely for what may have been on his mind. Human law does not reach that far."[16]

Prothro joined Heinemann in Yanceyville without incident. Together they delivered the bad news and the parting gift of a memory book filled with pictures documenting the sisters' years as Pet Milk's poster girls.[17] The company's refusal to extend the contract left the family at loose ends. "I didn't know what was happening," Catherine said. "Everything stopped all of a sudden, and it was hard to adjust. This was what we'd known all our lives, and I felt like we'd been used big-time by the Pet Milk company and the Klenners."[18] Still, all was not lost. Prothro pulled strings to get the sisters into Bethune-Cookman, a historically Black college in Daytona Beach, Florida. Bethune was a nine-and-a-half-hour drive from their house in Milton, North Carolina.[19]

The sisters studied music at Bethune, hoping to expand and refine their talents to achieve their lifelong goal of becoming full-time, professional performers. But the independent college lifestyle did not suit the girls. Despite the efforts of Bethune officials and the Saylors, they simply did not take college seriously. At their guardians' urging, Bethune set up a special academic program just for them. Still, they almost never showed up for classes. They fared no better socially. One college representative blamed their inability to adapt on their unique relationship. The representative theorized that "all the emotional problems that multiple-birth people usually have made it impossible for them to adjust to college life."[20] After trying to support them for two years, the college ultimately asked them to leave.[21]

The sisters were uncertain of what to do next. They stayed in the South for a month before returning to Milton in defeat. Disappointed by this turn of events but hoping for a new start, the Saylors decided to move to Peekskill, in upstate New York, where Elma's sister and brother-in-law lived. Just fifty-seven miles from New York City, Peekskill would allow the girls to pursue their dream of breaking into show business. This ambition persuaded them to trade in the wood-and-brick house that Pet Milk had bought them in Milton more than a decade earlier for a public-housing apartment in Peekskill. After sending their furniture ahead, the sisters and their guardians drove north in two cars in December 1967.[22]

The Barclay Plaza housing project where they put down roots was their first experience with integrated living. The girls and their guardians kept to themselves. They did not even know the names of the mother and son in the apartment next to them.[23] After visiting the sisters for an *Ebony* feature, titled "The Fultz Quads: Grown-Up, Disappointed and Bitter," journalist Charles L. Sanders observed that "only occasionally does a white mother run out and snatch her kid from among the black children playing in the old-fashioned gazebo that's built on the project lawn."[24]

Their four-room apartment was very cramped. The four sisters, who were then twenty-one, shared the master bedroom, while Elma and Charles made do with the small one. The rest of the place consisted of a kitchen and a living room with a dining nook facing a fake brick wall.[25] Charles worked in a dime-store credit department to make the $170 monthly rent.[26]

As young women, the sisters had an appealing style, known at the time as "tuff." They wore white makeup to lighten their skin, sported fashionable clothes, and had arched eyebrows reminiscent of the 1920s.[27] They called each other Addish (Alice), Weezie (Louise), and Cat (Catherine). Only Ann went by her given name.[28] In Peekskill, they joined St. Peter's Episcopal, an integrated church, where Reverend Anthony P. Treasure invited them to sing in the church choir.[29] They still dreamed of being full-time entertainers, but in the meantime, they worked in a factory that made men's raincoats.[30]

Factory work was difficult and painstaking. Their jobs included making buttonholes using a stylus and crayon, pressing on a steam hot-header, and sewing with power machines.[31] During one shift, boxes fell on Catherine while she was working the presser, and the boxes forced both her hands under the machine. Even in her late fifties, the pain from that injury continued to haunt her.[32]

When the sisters had time off from the factory during the holidays, they worked in the toy section of the department store near the housing project. They also modeled for Virginia Slims cigarettes and for makeup advertisements. They liked modeling but could not earn enough from those gigs to give up their factory jobs.[33] They also studied fencing at the Ophelia DeVore School of Charm in New York. At night and on the weekends, they practiced their act. Each sister could play several instruments and sing. Collectively, they played the piano, organ, violin, viola, cello, guitar, and drums.[34]

The sisters performed as The Quads in nightclubs in New Jersey and the New York suburbs, still hoping to break into the Manhattan scene.[35] Wearing miniskirts and boots, they sang seamless melodies, sounding like "the Andrews sisters with the soul of The Supremes."[36] They worked hard but found it impossible to get ahead. When they learned that their father Pete Fultz was in danger of losing the family farm, they used up their savings to pay off the taxes on it.[37]

At first, the sisters spent their time in Peekskill, as they always had, mostly with each other. The only vice they had time to indulge in was smoking. They told the *Ebony* reporter that Peekskill boys were too wild for their tastes.[38] Yet only two years into the move, Ann, Louise, and Catherine married.[39]

Forever haunted by losing her son, Alice stayed single for the rest of her life.[40] While the other three continued to look identical, Alice's individuality became increasingly pronounced. She spoke her mind freely and was the first sister to forge a separate identity.[41] She cared less about her appearance than her sisters did, refusing their admonitions to pluck her eyebrows or wear wigs. Her rejection of feminine norms also extended to her behavior.

Although her sisters' marriages did not last, they laid the foundation for significant life changes. The factory jobs evolved into positions in nursing homes and then as nursing assistants. Eventually, the sisters stopped performing. Ann was the first to divorce her abusive husband.[42] When they were thirty-one, Catherine became the second sister to separate from her husband. Afterward, she had a daughter, Tasha, with a man who left them for his other family. Elma encouraged Catherine to put Tasha up for adoption, but after Catherine refused, Elma and Charles raised Tasha.[43] Louise divorced her first husband but was happy with her second one and her son, Wesley.

After her divorce, Ann moved away from New York and settled in South Carolina. There she hired a local attorney to investigate the contract with Pet Milk, hoping to get compensation for the corporation's exploitation of her and her sisters. Susie Sharp, then chief justice of the North Carolina Supreme Court, responded curtly to requests for information from Ann's lawyers.[44] Sharp flatly stated that she had not had any dealings with Pet Milk for more than twenty years. She also expressed her belief that the company not only had fulfilled but had exceeded its obligations to the Fultz sisters.[45] Fred Klenner passed away on May 20, 1984. He died one year before his son Fritz and his niece-in-law, little Susie Sharp, killed nine members of their family, including themselves, over a custody battle for Susie's sons.[46]

Elma Saylor died on April 10, 1989, at age sixty-eight. Her husband, Charles, died the following year, on December 22, 1990, at age seventy-one. Annie Mae died at age eighty, five months after Elma, on September 9, 1989, when the sisters were forty-three. Annie Mae's burial led to the girls' reunion in North Carolina. Being together again made them want to move closer to each other,[47] so Louise settled in nearby Greensboro, while Catherine and Alice decided to make Reidsville their home. There were few familiar faces left. Susie Sharp had retired and withdrawn from public life. Finally admitting to one another that they would never return to live on the family farm, the sisters decided to sell it. They got $60,000 for the house and land.[48]

Back in Reidsville, Alice hoped that she might finally learn what had happened to her son. With her parents and guardians gone, she set out to find her uncle, Bill Troxler.[49] When she did, it was too late. Bill was near the end of his life, and he would never communicate again. He died without Alice ever learning whether he knew the identity of the couple who had adopted her son.[50] Once he was gone, there was no one left to ask.

The sisters celebrated their forty-fourth birthday at the Reidsville Garden Center. The festive occasion attracted many locals. The sisters were still celebrities in their hometown, and its residents welcomed them with open arms.[51] But their joy was short-lived. At age forty-five, all four sisters were diagnosed with breast cancer.[52] Louise died only a few months after she learned of her illness. Her son, Wesley, was just four years old. Ann lived with the disease for five years, dying at fifty. Alice succumbed to her cancer at fifty-five.[53] Catherine survived without her sisters for seventeen more years, dying at age seventy-two.

Alice smoked until the day she died. She spent her last days in Annie Penn Memorial Hospital, the site of the sisters' birth.[54] There were still two pictures of the four identical baby girls on the hospital walls.[55] Right up to the end, Alice begged Catherine to find her son. "Her eyes went to the door every time it opened, hoping he would walk in the room," Catherine recalled.[56] After Alice slipped away, one of the funeral cars that had transported the girls back home from the hospital fifty-five years earlier took Alice's body to her grave.[57]

Life was hard for Catherine without her sisters, although spending time with her two grandchildren made her happy. At first, she survived in Reidsville on her friends' generosity. After she got a job as a cook in the daycare of Shining Light Holiness Church, she could afford a small garden apartment.[58] As the church cook, she made twenty-two breakfasts, snacks, and lunches five days a week.[59] She credited Annie Mae with her talent for cooking. She lived modestly, with only a few possessions, including two white plastic chairs, her will, a survey map of the farm, and a photo album filled with pictures from the sisters' childhood.[60]

Catherine never forgave Pet Milk for the way it treated her family. "They got over on us like a big, fat rat," she said.[61] She also blamed Dr. Klenner's daily vitamin treatments for their cancer.[62] Four quadruplets suffering from breast cancer is a rare occurrence. Although it is unlikely that genetics alone accounts for this anomaly, there is no way to know if vitamin D or Pet Milk or both or something else entirely contributed to this phenomenon.

Catherine's daughter, Tasha, is bitter that Pet Milk stole the childhood of her mother and aunts. Catherine's anger toward the company created an enduring challenge in their relationship. "Put it this way," Tasha observed, "I get along with her as long as we're not together."[63] Ann's daughter Linda had similar regrets about the lives of her mother and aunts. She lamented that "for all that was said, none of my four aunts ended up having much. Not even a place to stay."[64] But Doretha, the girls' older sister, saw things differently. She said, "They always thought they were better than us."[65]

The Fultz sisters' love of music and one another in the face of their loneliness and exploitation provides a model of resistance and strength. In their first few minutes of life, they showed the world that they were survivors. Their tiny bodies withstood Dr. Klenner's vitamin C shots, and they grew strong despite a diet dominated by Pet Milk's sugary concoction. The joy that they found in singing, dancing, and playing instruments lasted from their early childhood into their adult life. It sustained them through their separation from their family, their alienation from their schoolmates, and their unrealized dreams.

America unequivocally adored the Fultz girls. In 1946, when they were born, the country was on the verge of integration. The Pet Milk poster girls represented the beginning of a new era of White acceptance of Blacks as consumers, Blacks as models, and Blacks as equals. The landmark case *Brown v. Board of Education* that mandated integrated public schools came down nine days before their eighth birthday.[66] When they were eighteen, the Civil Rights Act of 1964 extended *Brown* to make all forms of segregation illegal. Three years later, the sisters moved from a historically Black college to an integrated housing project. The Fultz sisters grew up in and symbolized a more open America, even as racism shaped their lives.

Although most of the people who played a role in this story have died, the Fultz sisters' children keep their story alive and continue the quest for justice that Ann began when she first contacted a lawyer. The family also has a presence on Facebook, where they share family pictures, past and present. The page explains that "even though in their past so many people use[d] them to gain their success they just totally forgot about them after they started getting sick."[67] The Fultz sisters left a lasting legacy of love and laughter in the hearts they captured with their performances, photographs, and joy. Their triumphs and pain serve as reminders to resist stereotypes, challenge inequalities, and fight for legal and policy reforms that reflect and uplift the value of Black women's and children's lives.

Conclusion

"FIRST FOOD" FREEDOM

From a feminist perspective, encouraging women to breastfeed can be a form of oppression. Telling women what is best for them can be patriarchal and condescending. Under current employment and social conditions, nursing generally keeps women out of the workforce, hidden in the home, and tied to an infant's erratic feeding schedule. Maternity leave, even if temporary, paves the way for men to get and keep the best jobs, allowing them to earn the most money and wield the most power.

For many women, work and breastfeeding are fundamentally incompatible. As one woman explains, "If I had an option I wouldn't be working at all. But that isn't even an option right now. Maybe if I go back to work for six months and I can keep it up that long, possibly by then I can afford not to work."[1] But the reality is that most people could not save enough in six months to afford to take time off. Even in high-wage jobs, women who work and parent face unacceptable trade-offs. Society degrades, devalues, or ignores work that takes place in the home or involves the care of others.

Obstacles to "having it all" hit women of color hardest. They often earn less pay, work multiple jobs and longer hours, live in segregated communities, go to schools with fewer resources, and suffer from over-surveillance and criminalization. These pervasive racial inequities can lead to serious health disparities. Outrageously high maternal and infant deaths in the Black community are just one example of how health, racism, and sexism interact.[2]

Promoting breastfeeding for Black women is an act designed to further racial justice. The goal of this advocacy is to create true choice for every parent. This includes making formula or breast milk available to and affordable for parents who want or need it. Structural support for all options will raise up the health of Black women, children, and communities. This goal is directly in line with critical race feminist principles. Good health is the foundation for all social and civic participation and for the quality of life that everyone should enjoy.

To be effective, advocates of breastfeeding in the Black community should not direct their efforts toward changing the beliefs and behaviors of individuals. Instead, societal structures must change. We must work to dismantle the institutionalized, systemic obstacles—erected by law, policy, and corporate greed—to breastfeeding in Black communities. The role of education is to expose and challenge the lingering stereotypes that falsely make these barriers look like personal choices or failings.

Looking Ahead

To reverse the low breastfeeding rates in Black communities, a vast number of reforms are necessary. These changes must occur simultaneously in the law, the workplace, the medical profession, and the media. A social movement that explains and drives these advances is essential to their success.

Physicians and nurses working in hospitals located in Black neighborhoods should implement baby-friendly practices, including rooming infants and mothers together. They should offer lactation guidance and support around the clock, with formula available only on request or in the event of medical necessity. Pediatricians should provide lactation support before formula, and they should remove all forms of formula advertising and marketing from their offices. Their walls should display pictures of women of all races breastfeeding. Health and Human Services should fund and staff clinics to support new parents in Black neighborhoods, eliminating all "first food" swamps and deserts.

Workplace accommodation laws should apply to every employer, regardless of size, and cover both full- and part-time employees. These laws should require employers to accommodate pumping with privacy, sufficient paid break time, and access to proper refrigeration. There should be affordable daycare centers in every neighborhood that nursing employees can go to throughout the day without penalty or pay reduction. The Family and Medical Leave Act should mandate paid parental leave up to one year with a guaranteed position upon a mother's return. It should provide similar leave for co-parents. New mothers should receive welfare benefits free of conditions that require them to leave their home to work. WIC's expenditures on breastfeeding support should be equivalent to its formula purchases.

City, state, and federal laws, in addition to the Fifth Amendment, should protect mothers who need or wish to breastfeed in public. There should be comfortable places to nurse in all public accommodations. The United States should sign on to the WHO Code and prohibit all types of formula marketing to pregnant women and new mothers. The American Academy of Pediatrics should operate independently of the formula industry. Government campaigns that promote breastfeeding should feature images of women and infants of color.

Legacy and Laws

In 1946, Fred Klenner forever altered the lives of the four sisters who unexpectedly came under his charge. He also helped usher in over a half century of misleading, racially-targeted marketing. The contract with Pet Milk severed the Fultz sisters' relationship with their mother, echoing the legacy of separation of enslaved mothers and children. This exile of the girls from their family occurred in the service of the formula industry and its quest to exploit the social and economic vulnerabilities of Black women. The story of the Fultz sisters serves as inspiration for legal and social reform. Justice, morality, and constitutional principles require steps toward the reforms outlined in the preceding section to afford Black women the opportunity to nurse their children at will and to eliminate the disparities in breastfeeding rates that have persisted since slavery.

Although law and policy reforms can lead to incremental positive change, they seem unlikely in the present political climate. An administration less driven by capitalist concerns might establish a clearer division between industry and government, which could lead to regulation that distances formula companies from new mothers. It could also reduce or eliminate the agricultural subsidies that compel the USDA to support formula as a secondary market for milk and soy.

Ending the partnership between government and the formula industry would require limiting or eliminating industry lobbying and campaign contributions to prevent capture of government policy. But ties between the administration and corporations are on the rise, and Supreme Court cases signal a trend in the opposite direction. *Citizens United v. Federal Election Commission*[3] allows corporations to contribute to political campaigns. *Burwell v. Hobby Lobby*[4] held that a corporation could have a religion for purposes of the First Amendment. As wealth inequality in the United States increases, it becomes even less plausible that lower-income individuals will be able to leverage the political power necessary to spearhead legal and policy changes.

Beyond law and policy, dramatic changes in social and cultural beliefs are necessary. Centuries of racial stereotyping of Black women as bad mothers require extensive counterprogramming. Twenty-first-century popular culture has begun to provide us with some excellent Black mothers. Many fans revere pop queen Beyoncé as much for her fabulous motherhood as for her musical talent. Tracee Ellis Ross gives a nuanced and humorous portrayal of a Black mother on the critically acclaimed and beloved television show *Black-ish*. Bow (short for Rainbow) is a hardworking anesthetist and a present and caring, if sometimes realistically selfish, mother. The character of Bow is a direct descendant of Phylicia Rashad's Clair Huxtable, attorney and loving mother of five on the 1980s *Cosby Show*.

A 2017 episode of *Black-ish*, called "Mother Nature," opens with a clearly frustrated Bow walking into a room wearing her electric breast pump.[5] The episode explores Bow's battle with postpartum depression. Tension with her mother-in-law, Ruby, comes to a head when Bow discovers that Ruby fed her baby a bottle of formula instead of Bow's pumped breast milk. Bow's commitment to breastfeeding is unusual for a Black mother on television. It may even be revolutionary.

In 2018, the Gap posted an ad on social media featuring a Black woman breastfeeding her toddler.[6] The image was simple yet radical. The company received accolades from thousands of viewers thrilled by the ad's beauty and realism. The picture was not even part of the scheduled photo shoot.[7] Gap model Adaora Akubilo, who has natural hair, took advantage of a break to nurse her son. The photographer happened to notice them and grabbed his camera to capture the moment. The rest is history. The overwhelmingly enthusiastic response to the ad demonstrates a collective hunger for these types of positive images.

Across the United States, there are many activists and professors working to ensure that Black mothers have viable choices in infant feeding. Dr. Angela M. Johnson, Dr. Ifeyinwa Asiodu, and Dr. Chelsea McKinney, among others, have produced pioneering scholarship in this area.[8] Kimberly Seals Allers, Kiddada Green, and Anayah Sangodele-Ayoka run an annual Black Breastfeeding Week. Dalvery Blackwell and Angelia Wilks-Tate founded the African American Breastfeeding Network. Afrykayn Moon spearheads Breastfeeding Mothers Unite. Danielle Atkinson created Michigan's Mothering Justice. Anayah Sangodele-Ayoka is a nurse-midwife and innovative culture worker at momsrising.org. Reaching Our Sisters Everywhere (ROSE) and Black Mothers' Breastfeeding Association are organizations run by Black women dedicated to promoting and supporting Black breastfeeding.

To combat the dearth of positive images and the manipulative messaging of the formula companies, a group of Black mothers led by Nicole Sandiford created a blog and Facebook page, Black Women Do Breastfeed. The page's mission is "making the community of Black women breastfeeding more visible."[9] The site supplies information about lactation groups for families of color, serves as a forum for questions, and provides a platform for breastfeeding Black women to share their pictures, stories, benchmarks, and accomplishments.

A Birmingham, Alabama, group called Chocolate Milk Mommies works to remove the stigma from nursing Black women. Group member Rauslyn Adams explains the need for the organization's advocacy: "It is taboo within the African American home to breastfeed your child, let alone to do it past the age of 1. Breastfeeding has been seen by some African American women as reverting to 'slavery days.'"[10] To counter these negative associations, group members posed as goddesses nursing their children in a photo shoot celebrating Black Breastfeeding Week in 2017.[11] Their beautiful photograph signaled to breastfeeding Black mothers that they are not alone. They matter. This message must resound throughout the country. We cannot allow the history of the Fultz sisters and Tabitha Walrond to repeat. It is time to tell a new story about Black motherhood.

ACKNOWLEDGMENTS

This book would not exist without Osagie Obasogie. I am deeply thankful to Osagie for introducing me to my fabulous editor, Michelle Lipinski, for all the other ways he has supported my work and this project, and for his friendship.

I am also so grateful to:

Angela Harris, for giving me my first opportunity to write about food oppression—in an architecture class—and for being an unfailing mentor and friend since then. For all the drafts she has read and insights she has shared. For opening her home to me. For her cornbread and chocolate pie.

Robin Lenhardt, who decided that I needed a mentor and that it would be her. For all the support, advice, letters, encouragement, and inspiration. For the phone calls.

Angela Onwuachi-Willig, for the opportunities and conversations. For the card games, breakfasts, lunches, and dinners across the country and the world.

Mario Barnes, for opening so many doors. For his leadership, kindness, brilliance, and generosity. For always having time for a drink.

Ian Haney Lopez, for making me want to be a law professor. For pushing me to excellence. For putting my kids on their first surfboard. For his wonderful family.

Devon Carbado, for his support, empathy, and friendship.

Chuck Lawrence, for always having an open door and an inspiring idea.

Kaaryn Gustafson and Tonya Brito, for their support, friendship, and brilliant work.

Kimani Paul-Emile, for her crucial support of this project and her friendship.

Camille Gear Rich, for her wonderful insights and tremendous support.

Wendy Greene, for her thoughtful book recommendations.

Dorothy Roberts, Ange Marie Hancock, Kimberly Seals Allers, and Khiara Bridges, for their pioneering work.

Bennett Capers, Lisa Ikemoto, Jessica Clarke, Maya Manian, and Joy Milligan, for their time and invaluable comments.

Nicole Gonzalez van Cleve, for her help, advice, strength, humor, and phone calls.

Priscilla Ocen, for the adventures, celebrations, commiseration, and community. For her groundbreaking work.

Addie Rolnick, for the check-ins, nights out, last-minute questions, draft reads, and solidarity.

Bertrall Ross and Russell Robinson, for friendship and inspiration.

Glen Duncan, for showing me how to be a good person and an even better writer. For not letting me forget who I am. For all the Bloody Marys and billiards.

Lauren Kaminsky, for turning a Stanford workshop into a lifelong friendship.

Khara Jabola-Carolus, for being a kick-ass feminist, activist, leader, mother, and friend.

Molly Van Houweling, for giving me a home away from home in Berkeley.

BJ, Jodi, and Cammie, for the 'ōlelo, laughs, and food.

Kinohi Gomes, for helping Hawai'i feel like home.

Dean Rowan and Ellen Gilmore at Berkeley and Diane Burkhardt at Denver, exceptional librarians who made significant and thoughtful contributions to this book.

Mykie Ozoa, Rochelle Sagawa, Fern Grether, Sarah Williams, Jasmine Dave, and Tatiana Robinson, my talented, dedicated, and fierce research assistants.

Jasmine Gonzales Rose, for being with me on every step of this journey. For providing encouragement, comments, love, and chocolate.

Joe, for covering for me.

Alia and Serafino, for sharing their light, love, laughter, and wisdom with me every day.

NOTES

Introduction

1. "Quadruplet Girls Born to N.C. Negro Couple," *Asheville Citizen-Times*, May 24, 1946, 11.

2. "Quadruplets Born to Mute at Reidsville," *Daily Times-News* (Burlington, NC), May 23, 1946, 14.

3. "Quads Born to Negro," *Waco News-Tribune*, May 24, 1946, 11; and Melba Newsome, "I Think It Was the Shots," *O, The Oprah Magazine*, April 1, 2005, 232.

4. Lorraine Ahearn, "Four Sisters, One Love," *News & Record* (Greensboro, NC), August 8, 2002, http://www.greensboro.com/four-sisters-one-love/article _cdccc43c-bd23-5e85-931f-2ad69c4a1f40.html; and Jerry Bledsoe, *Bitter Blood* (New York, E. P. Dutton, 1988), 184–85.

5. "Fultz Quads 'More Amazing' than Dionne Quintuplets," *Pittsburgh Courier*, August 3, 1946, 22.

6. Lorraine Ahearn, "And Then There Was One," *News & Record* (Greensboro, NC), August 3, 2002, http://www.greensboro.com/and-then-there-was -one-they-were-four-of-the/article_7d5869a7-3b2b-5b7d-b5d0-044464d8aba3 .html.

7. Kimberley Mangun and Lisa M. Parcell, "The Pet Milk Company 'Happy Family' Advertising Campaign," *Journalism History* 40, no. 2 (Summer 2014): 71.

8. Chinwe, "The Fultz Sisters: The Fascinating and Tragic Story of America's First Identical Black Quadruplets," *Black Girl Long Hair* (blog), September 18, 2015, https://bglh-marketplace.com/2015/09/the-fultz-sisters-the-fas cinating-and-tragic-story-of-americas-first-identical-black-quadruplets/comment -page-3/.

9. Raymond A. Bauer and Scott M. Cunningham, "The Negro Market," *Journal of Advertising Research* 10, no. 2 (April 1970): 9–11.

10. Kimberly Seals Allers, *The Big Letdown: How Medicine, Big Business, and Feminism Undermine Breastfeeding* (New York: St. Martin's Press, 2017), 14–16.

11. Katherine M. Jones et al., "Racial and Ethnic Disparities in Breastfeeding," *Breastfeeding Medicine* 10, no. 4 (2015): 189–90, https://doi.org/10.1089 /bfm.2014.0152; and *Breastfeeding among Mothers 15–44 Years of Age, by Year of Baby's Birth and Selected Characteristics of Mother: United States, Average Annual 1986–1988 through 2002–2004* (Centers for Disease Control and Prevention, 2010), https://www.cdc.gov/nchs/data/hus/2010/014.pdf.

12. Nina Bernstein, "Placing the Blame in an Infant's Death; Mother Faces Trial after Baby Dies from Lack of Breast Milk," *New York Times*, March 15, 1999, B1.

13. Allan Whyte, "Young Mother Convicted of Criminally Negligent Homicide in Her Baby's Death: New York Authorities Victimize the Victim," *World Socialist Web Site*, May 22, 1999, www.wsws.org/en/articles/1999/05/walr -m22.html.

14. "Report on Baby's Death Prompts Delay in Trial," *New York Times*, March 18, 1999, B8.

15. Karen Houppert, "Nursed to Death," *Salon*, May 21, 1999, www.salon .com/1999/05/21/nursing/; and "Jury Convicts Mother in Starved Baby Trial," CNN, May 19, 1999, http://www.cnn.com/US/9905/19/breastfeeding .trial.02/.

16. Andrew Jacobs, "Opposition to Breast-Feeding Resolution by U.S. Stuns World Health Officials," *New York Times*, July 8, 2018, https://www.nytimes .com/2018/07/08/health/world-health-breastfeeding-ecuador-trump.html.

17. *Vital Signs: African American Health* (Centers for Disease Control and Prevention, May 2017), https://www.cdc.gov/vitalsigns/pdf/2017-05-vitalsigns .pdf; and "Overweight and Obesity among African American Youths," *Ebony*, May 2014, http://www.ebony.com/wp-content/uploads/2017/03/LHC_Afri can_American_Factsheet_FINAL.pdf.

18. Jones et al., "Racial and Ethnic Disparities," 189–90; and Alan S. Ryan and Wenjun Zhou, "Lower Breastfeeding Rates Persist among the Special Supplemental Nutrition Program for Women, Infants, and Children Participants, 1978–2003," *Pediatrics* 117, no. 4 (April 2006): 1140–43, https://doi .org/10.1542/peds.2005-1555.

19. Ruth Marcus, "Lobbying Fight over Infant Formula Highlights Budget Gridlock," *Washington Post*, July 14, 2010, http://www.washingtonpost.com /wp-dyn/content/article/2010/07/13/AR2010071304634.html.

20. George Kent, "The High Price of Infant Formula in the United States," *AgroFOOD Industry Hi-Tech* 17, no. 5 (September/October 2006): 1.

21. George Kent, "WIC's Promotion of Infant Formula in the United

States," *International Breastfeeding Journal* 1, no. 1 (April 2006): 8–9, https://doi.org/10.1186/1746-4358-1-8; and Ryan and Zhou, "Lower Breastfeeding Rates Persist," 1140–43.

22. Kent, "WIC's Promotion," 8.

23. Steven Carlson, Robert Greenstein, and Zoë Neuberger, *WIC's Competitive Bidding Process for Infant Formula Is Highly Cost-Effective* (Center on Budget & Policy Priorities, February 17, 2017), https://www.cbpp.org/research/food-assistance/wics-competitive-bidding-process-for-infant-formula-is-highly-cost; and Kent, "High Price," 1.

24. Sylvia Onusic, "The Scandal of Infant Formula," *Wise Traditions in Food, Farming and the Healing Arts*, Weston A. Price Foundation (December 9, 2015), https://www.westonaprice.org/health-topics/childrens-health/the-scandal-of-infant-formula/.

25. Michael Pollan, "You Are What You Grow," *New York Times Magazine*, April 22, 2007, http://michaelpollan.com/articles-archive/you-are-what-you-grow/.

26. Andrea Freeman, "The Unbearable Whiteness of Milk: Food Oppression and the USDA," *UC Irvine Law Review* 3, no. 4 (December 2013): 1252.

27. Andrea Freeman, "Unconstitutional Food Inequality," *Harvard Civil Rights-Civil Liberties Law Review* 55 (2019).

28. Katherine Unger Davis, "Racial Disparities in Childhood Obesity: Causes, Consequences, and Solutions," *University of Pennsylvania Journal of Law and Social Change* 14, no. 2 (Fall 2011): 321.

29. James M. Rippe and Theodore J. Angelopoulos, "Relationship between Added Sugars Consumption and Chronic Disease Risk Factors: Current Understanding," *Nutrients* 8, no. 11 (November 2016): 697, https://doi.org/10.3390/nu8110697; I. A. Macdonald, "A Review of Recent Evidence Relating to Sugars, Insulin Resistance and Diabetes," *European Journal of Nutrition* 55, no. 2 (November 2016): 17–23, https://doi.org/10.1007/s00394-016-1340-8; and "The Sweet Danger of Sugar," *Harvard Men's Health Watch* (blog), *Harvard Health Online*, May 2017, https://www.health.harvard.edu/heart-health/the-sweet-danger-of-sugar.

30. UNICEF and WHO, *Breastfeeding Advocacy Initiative* (UNICEF, February 2015), https://www.unicef.org/nutrition/files/Breastfeeding_Advocacy_Strategy-2015.pdf.

31. American Academy of Pediatrics, "Breastfeeding and the Use of Human Milk," *Pediatrics* 129, no. 3 (March 2012): e827–41; and ACOG, "ACOG Committee Opinion: Optimizing Support for Breastfeeding as Part of Obstetric Practice," American College of Obstetricians and Gynecologists, February 2015, https://www.acog.org/Clinical-Guidance-and-Publications/Committee-Opinions/Committee-on-Obstetric-Practice/Optimizing-Support-for-Breastfeeding-as-Part-of-Obstetric-Practice.

32. *Breastfeeding* (Centers for Disease Control and Prevention, last modified

October 3, 2018), https://www.cdc.gov/breastfeeding/index.htm; *The Surgeon General's Call to Action to Support Breastfeeding* (United States Surgeon General, last modified August 12, 2014), https://www.surgeongeneral.gov/library /calls/breastfeeding/index.html; and "Breastfeeding," Office on Women's Health, US Department of Health and Human Services, last modified August 27, 2018, https://www.womenshealth.gov/Breastfeeding/.

33. UNICEF, "Improving Breastfeeding, Complementary Foods and Feeding Practices," Nutrition, UNICEF, last modified March 6, 2017, https://www .unicef.org/nutrition/index_breastfeeding.html.

34. Jody Heymann, Amy Raub, and Alison Earle, "Breastfeeding Policy: A Globally Comparative Analysis," World Health Organization, April 18, 2013, http://www.who.int/bulletin/volumes/91/6/12-109363/en/; and Gashaw Andargie Biks et al., "Exclusive Breastfeeding Is the Strongest Predictor of Infant Survival in Northwest Ethiopia: A Longitudinal Study," *Journal of Health, Population, and Nutrition* 34 (May 2015): 9, https://doi.org/10.1186 /s41043-015-0007-z.

35. Alice Chen, Emily Oster, and Heidi Williams, "Why Is Infant Mortality Higher in the United States than in Europe?" *American Economic Journal* 8, no. 2 (May 2016): 89–124, https://doi.org/10.1257/pol.20140224; and Marian F. MacDorman et al., "International Comparisons of Infant Mortality and Related Factors: United States and Europe, 2010," *National Vital Statistics Reports* 63, no. 5 (September 2014): 1–6.

36. T. J. Matthews, Marian F. MacDorman, and Marie E. Thoma, "Infant Mortality Statistics from the 2013 Period Linked Birth/Infant Death Data Set," *National Vital Statistics Reports* 64, no. 9 (August 2015): 1–4.

37. Anna Marie Smith, *Welfare Reform and Sexual Regulation* (New York: Cambridge University Press, 2007), 262.

38. Bob Curley, "How to Combat 'Food Deserts' and 'Food Swamps,'" *Time: Healthline*, January 18, 2018, https://www.healthline.com/health-news /combat-food-deserts-and-food-swamps#1; and Olga Khazan, "Food Swamps Are the New Food Deserts," *Atlantic*, December 28, 2017, https://www.the atlantic.com/health/archive/2017/12/food-swamps/549275/.

39. Rita Henley Jensen, "'Baby Friendly' Hospitals Bypass Black Communities," *Women's eNews*, August 29, 2013, http://womensenews.org/2013/08 /baby-friendly-hospitals-bypass-black-communities; Kenneth D. Rosenberg et al., "Marketing Infant Formula through Hospitals: The Impact of Commercial Hospital Discharge Packs on Breastfeeding," *American Journal of Public Health* 98, no. 2 (February 2008): 290, https://doi.org/10.2105/AJPH.2006.103218; and Public Citizen, "Fact Sheet: Infant Formula Marketing in Healthcare Facilities," Public Citizen, accessed April 3, 2018, https://www.citizen.org/our-work /health-and-safety/infant-formula-marketing-healthcare-facilities#_edn4.

40. Steven J. Haider, Alison Jacknowitz, and Robert F. Schoeni, "Welfare

Work Requirements and Child Well-Being: Evidence from the Effects on Breast-Feeding," *Demography* 40, no. 3 (August 2003): 491–95.

41. Dorothy Roberts, *Killing the Black Body: Race, Reproduction, and the Meaning of Liberty* (New York: Pantheon Books, 1997), 14.

42. Wilma A. Dunaway, *The African-American Family in Slavery & Emancipation* (Cambridge, UK: Cambridge University Press, 2003), 139.

43. Ange-Marie Hancock, *The Politics of Disgust: The Public Identity of the Welfare Queen* (New York: New York University Press, 2004), 1–22.

44. Michele Estrin Gilman, "The Return of the Welfare Queen," *American University Journal of Gender, Social Policy & the Law* 22, no. 2 (Spring 2014): 258–61.

45. Kimberly Seals Allers, "Breastfeeding: Some Slavery Crap?," *Ebony*, August 31, 2012, http://www.ebony.com/wellness-empowerment/breastfeeding -some-slavery-crap; and LaSha, "Choosing Not to Breastfeed Was My Revolutionary Act," *Blogging while Black* (blog), *Kinfolk Kollective*, January 21, 2016, http://kinfolkkollective.com/2016/01/21/choosing-not-to-breastfeed-was-my -revolutionary-act/.

46. Margaret E. Bentley, Deborah L. Dee, and Joan L. Jensen, "Breastfeeding among Low Income, African-American Women: Power, Beliefs and Decision Making," *Journal of Nutrition* 133, no. 1 (January 2003): 308S, https://doi .org/10.1093/jn/133.1.305S.

47. Bentley, Dee, and Jensen, "Power, Beliefs and Decision Making," 305S.

48. Andrea Freeman, "'First Food' Justice: Racial Disparities in Infant Feeding as Food Oppression," *Fordham Law Review* 83, no. 6 (May 2015): 3053–87.

49. Freeman, "'First Food' Justice," 3053–87.

50. Jacobs, "Opposition to Breast-Feeding Resolution."

51. Jacobs; and Julia Belluz, "The Next Frontier of Trump's Defense of Baby Formula," *Vox*, July 10, 2018, https://www.vox.com/science-and -health/2018/7/10/17548028/trump-baby-formula-breastfeeding-mothers -health.

52. Andrea Freeman, "Fast Food: Oppression through Poor Nutrition," *California Law Review* 95, no. 6 (December 2007): 2221–393.

53. Jennifer L. Harris, Marlene B. Schwartz, and Kelly D. Brownell, *Fast Food Facts: Evaluating Fast Food Nutrition and Marketing to Youth* (Yale Rudd Center for Food Policy & Obesity, University of Connecticut, accessed April 16, 2018), https://www.issuelab.org/resources/9267/9267.pdf.

54. Simone French and Mary Story, "Food Advertising and Marketing Directed at Children and Adolescents in the US," *International Journal of Behavioral Nutrition and Physical Activity* 1, no. 1 (February 2004): 3, https://doi .org/10.1186/1479-5868-1-3.

55. Razib Khan, "Lactose Tolerance/Intolerance," *Gene Expression* (blog),

January 19, 2004, http://www.gnxp.com/new/2004/01/19/lactose-tolerance
-intolerance/.

56. "Health Concerns about Dairy Products," Physicians Committee for
Responsible Medicine, accessed April 16, 2018, http://www.pcrm.org/health
/diets/vegdiets/health-concerns-about-dairy-products; Li-Qiang Qin et al.,
"Milk Consumption Is a Risk Factor for Prostate Cancer in Western Countries:
Evidence from Cohort Studies," *Asia Pacific Journal of Clinical Nutrition* 16,
no. 3 (2007): 467–76; Susanna C. Larsson, Leif Bergkvist, and Alicja Wolk,
"Milk and Lactose Intakes and Ovarian Cancer Risk in the Swedish Mammog-
raphy Cohort," *American Journal of Clinical Nutrition* 80, no. 5 (2004): 1353–
57, https://doi.org/10.1093/ajcn/80.5.1353; and June M. Chan et al., "Dairy
Products, Calcium, and Prostate Cancer Risk in the Physicians' Health Study,"
American Journal of Clinical Nutrition 74, no. 4 (October 2001): 549, https://
doi.org/10.1093/ajcn/74.4.549.

57. Jack Smith, "Milk Is the New, Creamy Symbol of White Racial Purity
in Donald Trump's America," *Mic*, February 10, 2017, https://mic.com/articles
/168188/milk-nazis-white-supremacists-creamy-pseudo-science-trump-shia
-labeouf#.gSVETZiHe; Alex Swerdloff, "Got Milk? Neo-Nazi Trolls Sure as
Hell Do," *Vice: Munchies*, February 21, 2017, https://munchies.vice.com/en
_us/article/kbka39/got-milk-neo-nazi-trolls-sure-as-hell-do; and Andrea Free-
man, "Milk, a Symbol of Neo-Nazi Hate," *Conversation*, August 30, 2017,
http://theconversation.com/milk-a-symbol-of-neo-nazi-hate-83292.

58. Swerdloff, "Got Milk?"; and Sean O'Neal, "Milk-Chugging 'Alt-Right'
Trolls Shut Down Shia LaBeouf's Art Project," *A.V. Club*, February 13, 2017,
https://news.avclub.com/milk-chugging-alt-right-trolls-shut-down-shia-labeou
-1798257745.

59. Onusic, "Scandal of Infant Formula."

60. J. W. Anderson, B. M. Johnstone, and D. T. Remley, "Breast-Feeding
and Cognitive Development: A Meta-Analysis," *American Journal of Clinical
Nutrition* 70, no. 4 (October 1999): 525–35, https://doi.org/10.1093/ajcn
/70.4.525; and Nobuyoshi Kosaka et al., "microRNA as a New Immune-
Regulatory Agent in Breast Milk," *Silence* 1, no. 1 (March 2010): 7.

61. Anderson, Johnstone, and Remley, "Breast-Feeding and Cognitive Development," 525–35; and Ginna Wall, *Outcomes of Breastfeeding versus Formula
Feeding* (Bellevue, WA: Evergreen Perinatal Education, 2013), https://www
.evergreenperinataleducation.com/upload/OutcomesofBreastfeeding_Nov2013
.pdf.

62. WHO, "Infant and Young Child Feeding," World Health Organization,
updated July 2017, http://www.who.int/mediacentre/factsheets/fs342/en/.

63. UNICEF, "Improving Breastfeeding."

64. Freeman, "'First Food' Justice," 3062.

65. Emma Gray, "Natalie Hegedus, Mom, Kicked Out of Courtroom for
Breastfeeding," *Huffington Post*, November 14, 2011, https://www.huffington

post.com/entry/natalie-hegedus-courtroom-breastfeeding_n_1089271
.html; Meghan Holohan, "Victoria's Secret Store Bans Mom from Breastfeeding," *Today*, January 21, 2014, https://www.today.com/parents/victorias-secret
-store-bans-mom-breastfeeding-2D11968546; Scott Keyes, "Shelter Allegedly
Threatened to Kick Out Homeless Mother for Breastfeeding in Public," *Think-
Progress*, June 30, 2014, https://thinkprogress.org/shelter-allegedly-threatened
-to-kick-out-homeless-mother-for-breastfeeding-in-public-d26701078f3b/;
Julie Mazziotta, "Mom Helps Organize a Protest after Being Kicked Out
of Church for Breastfeeding," *People*, August 11, 2017, http://people.com
/bodies/mom-kicked-out-church-breastfeeding/; Carolyn Pesce, "Mom Says
Cops Kicked Her Out of Concert for Breastfeeding," *USA Today*, July 12, 2014,
https://www.usatoday.com/story/news/nation/2014/07/12/police-boot
-breastfeeding-mom/12567443/; and Monica Beyer, "Breastfeeding Mother
Told to Leave Restaurant after 'Offending' Customers," *She Knows*, July 13,
2015, http://www.sheknows.com/parenting/articles/1089239/breastfeeding
-mother-told-to-leave-restaurant-after-offending-customers.

66. Chelsea O. McKinney et al., "Racial and Ethnic Differences in Breastfeeding," *Pediatrics* 138, no. 2 (August 2016): 2, https://doi.org/10.1016/j
.apnr.2017.07.009.

67. Laura Harrison, "Milk Money: Race, Gender, and Breast Milk 'Donation,'" *Signs: Journal of Women in Culture and Society* 44, no. 2 (Winter 2019):
293.

68. McKinney et al., "Racial and Ethnic Differences in Breastfeeding," 2.

69. Kimberly Seals Allers, "Too Many U.S. Communities Are 'First Food
Deserts,'" *Women's eNews*, February 19, 2013, https://womensenews.org/2013
/02/too-many-us-communities-are-first-food-deserts/.

70. Kristen Cooksey-Stowers, Marlene B. Schwartz, and Kelly D. Brownell,
"Food Swamps Predict Obesity Rates Better than Food Deserts in the United
States," *International Journal of Environmental Research and Public Health* 14,
no. 11 (November 2017): 1366, https://doi.org/10.3390/ijerph14111366.

71. Donna L. Hoyert and Jiaquan Xu, "Deaths: Preliminary Data for 2011,"
National Vital Statistics Report 61, no. 6 (October 2012): 9–15.

72. Hoyert and Xu, 9–15.

73. Wall, *Outcomes of Breastfeeding*.

74. Melissa Healy, "Breastfeeding Counteracts Risk for a Type of Cancer, Study Says," *Los Angeles Times*, August 16, 2011, http://www.latimes.com
/health/la-heb-breastfeeding-cancer-black-women-20110816-story.html.

75. Dorothy Roberts, *Fatal Invention: How Science, Politics and Business
Re-Create Race in the Twenty-First Century* (New York: The New Press, 2011),
64–66; Lundy Braun et al., "Racial Categories in Medical Practice: How Useful
Are They?" *PLoS Medicine* 4, no. 9 (September 2007): 1423–28; Ian F. Haney
López, "The Social Construction of Race: Some Observations on Illusion, Fab-
rication, and Choice," *Harvard Civil Rights–Civil Liberties Law Review* 29,

no. 1 (Winter 1994): 1–62; and Sharona Hoffman, "'Racially-Tailored' Medicine Unraveled," *American University Law Review* 55, no. 2 (December 2005): 395–456.

76. Derrick Bell, *Faces at the Bottom of the Well: The Permanence of Racism* (New York: Basic Books, 1992).

77. Richard Delgado, "Storytelling for Oppositionists and Others: A Plea for Narrative," *Michigan Law Review* 87, no. 8 (August 1989): 2411–41; Mari J. Matsuda, "Looking to the Bottom: Critical Legal Studies and Reparations," *Harvard Civil Rights–Civil Liberties Law Review* 22, no. 2 (Spring 1987): 323–99; and Mario L. Barnes, "Reflection on a Dream World: Race, Post-Race and the Question of Making It Over," *Berkeley Journal of African-American Law & Policy* 11, no. 1 (January 2009): 6–18.

78. Kimani Paul-Emile, "Foreword: Critical Race Theory and Empirical Methods Conference," *Fordham Law Review* 83, no. 6 (May 2015): 2953–60; Osagie K. Obasogie, "Foreword: Critical Race Theory and Empirical Methods," *U.C. Irvine Law Review* 3, no. 2 (2013): 183–86; Laura E. Gómez, "Understanding Law and Race as Mutually Constitutive: An Invitation to Explore an Emerging Field," *Annual Review of Law and Social Science* 6 (December 2010): 487–505; and Tonya L. Brito, "Introduction to Symposium in New Directions in the Empirical Study of Access to Justice," *Law & Social Inquiry* 42, no. 4 (Fall 2017): 960–62.

79. Kimberlé Crenshaw, "Mapping the Margins: Intersectionality, Identity Politics, and Violence against Women of Color," *Stanford Law Review* 43, no. 6 (July 1991): 1241–300; and Angela P. Harris, "Race and Essentialism in Feminist Legal Theory," *Stanford Law Review* 42, no. 3 (February 1990): 581–616, https://doi.org/10.2307/1228886.

Chapter 1

1. Some reported Annie Mae as thirty-six or thirty-seven. "Quadruplets Born to N.C. Negress," *Anniston (AL) Star*, May 23, 1946, 1.

2. Jerry Bledsoe, *Bitter Blood* (New York: E. P. Dutton, 1988), 179.

3. Jerry Bledsoe, "Fritz Klenner, His Father's Son," *News & Record* (Greensboro, NC), August 26, 1985, http://www.greensboro.com/bitter-blood-fritz -klenner-his-father-s-son/pdf_38317586-0617-11e5-ac22-f7f8ec7b9153.html.

4. Bledsoe, *Bitter Blood*, 178–79; and Jim Schlosser, "Memories of Murder," *News & Record* (Greensboro, NC), June 3, 1995, http://www.greensboro.com /memories-of-murder/article_981baf03-4f07-5413-b29e-3d3461b6b71f.html.

5. Bledsoe, *Bitter Blood*, 183.

6. "Quads Born to Negro," *Waco News-Tribune*, May 24, 1946, 11; and Melba Newsome, "I Think It Was the Shots," *O, The Oprah Magazine*, April 1, 2005, 232.

7. Newsome, "I Think It Was the Shots"; and "Quadruplet Girls Born to N.C. Negro Couple," *Asheville (NC) Citizen-Times*, May 24, 1946, 11.

8. "Negro Quads 'Doing Fine,'" *Index-Journal* (Greenwood, SC), May 24, 1946, 8.

9. Frances M. Ward, "Seeing Double Times Two Famous Foursome Make Their Mark as World's First Black Quadruplets," *News & Record* (Greensboro, NC), May 22, 1990, http://www.greensboro.com/seeing-double-times-two-fa mous-foursome-make-their-mark-as/article_80d5c093-598c-55e1-8d39 -32d59b090368.html.

10. Ward, "Seeing Double Times Two"; and Newsome, "I Think It Was the Shots."

11. Lorraine Ahearn, "And Then There Was One," *News & Record* (Greens-boro, NC), August 3, 2002, http://www.greensboro.com/and-then-there-was -one-they-were-four-of-the/article_7d5869a7-3b2b-5b7d-b5d0-044464d8aba3 .html.

12. "Quadruplet Girls Are Born," *St. Louis Dispatch*, May 23, 1946, 24; and Ahearn, "And Then There Was One."

13. Ahearn, "And Then There Was One."

14. "Quadruplets Born to Mute at Reidsville," *Daily Times-News* (Burling-ton, NC), May 23, 1946, 14.

15. Newsome, "I Think It Was the Shots."

16. "Fultz Quads 'More Amazing' than Dionne Quintuplets," *Pittsburgh Courier*, August 3, 1946, 22.

17. "Reidsville Quads to Have First Santa Visit," *Bee* (Danville, VA), De-cember 24, 1946, 5; and Ahearn, "And Then There Was One."

18. "Pa of 4 Negroes Nearly Faints at Stork's Generosity," *Bee* (Danville, VA), May 24, 1946, 4; and "Quadruplets Born to Mute at Reidsville."

19. "Fultz Quads 'More Amazing' than Dionne Quintuplets."

20. "Quadruplets Born to N.C. Negress."

21. "Mother Deaf Mute: Carolina Tenant Farm Pair Parents of Quads," *Pittsburgh Courier*, June 1, 1946, 2.

22. "Quadruplets' First Birthday," *Ebony*, May 1947, 18.

23. "Quadruplet Girls Are Born in South; Condition Good," *Tipton (IN) Daily Tribune*, May 24, 1946, 8; and "Quadruplets' First Birthday."

24. "Pet Milk Company's 'New Pets,'" *Pittsburgh Courier*, June 29, 1946, 3.

25. "Quads Bring Joy to N.C. Family of Eight," *Baltimore Afro-American*, August 24, 1946, 20.

26. "Quadruplet Girls Born to N.C. Negro Couple."

27. Newsome, "I Think It Was the Shots."

28. Steve Hickey and Andrew W. Saul, *Vitamin C: The Real Story* (Laguna Beach, CA: Basic Health, 2008), 25.

29. Bledsoe, *Bitter Blood*, 178–79.

30. Bledsoe, 182–83.

31. Bledsoe, 86.

32. Bledsoe, 183.

33. Bledsoe, 184–85.

34. Hickey and Saul, *Vitamin C*, 25; and "Girl Quadruplets Born," *New York Times*, May 24, 1946.

35. Bledsoe, *Bitter Blood*, 77.

36. Ahearn, "And Then There Was One."

37. "Girl Quadruplets Born."

38. "Negro Quads 'Doing Fine.'"

39. "Names for Quads Posing Problem," *Statesville (NC) Daily Record*, May 25, 1946, 9.

40. "Mother Deaf Mute."

41. "Fultz Quads 'More Amazing' than Dionne Quintuplets"; and Ahearn, "And Then There Was One."

42. "N.C. Quads Named Mary," *Index-Journal* (Greenwood, SC), May 28, 1946, 6; "New Quadruplets All Named 'Mary,'" *Statesville (NC) Record and Landmark*, May 30, 1946, 5; "Just Call One and All Respond," *Akron (OH) Beacon Journal*, June 27, 1946, 10; "Fultz Quads 'More Amazing' than Dionne Quintuplets"; and "Couple Decide Mary Is Grand Old Name," *Waynesville (NC) Mountaineer*, July 9, 1946, 2.

43. "The Four Marys of Reidsville All Doing Well," *Bee* (Danville, VA), May 28, 1946, 1.

44. "Negro Quadruplets Asleep in One Bed," *Decatur (IL) Daily Review*, May 28, 1946, 10.

45. "Couple Decide Mary Is Grand Old Name"; and Bledsoe, *Bitter Blood*, 184.

46. "Fultz Quads 'More Amazing' than Dionne Quintuplets."

47. "Fultz Quads 'More Amazing' than Dionne Quintuplets."

48. Ahearn, "And Then There Was One."

49. Chinwe, "The Fultz Sisters: The Fascinating and Tragic Story of America's First Identical Black Quadruplets," *Black Girl Long Hair* (blog), September 18, 2015, https://bglh-marketplace.com/2015/09/the-fultz-sisters-the-fascinating-and-tragic-story-of-americas-first-identical-black-quadruplets/comment-page-3/.

50. Anna R. Hayes, *Without Precedent: The Life of Susie Marshall Sharp* (Chapel Hill: University of North Carolina Press, 2008), 89.

51. Lorraine Ahearn, "A Birthday Party with the Governor," *News & Record* (Greensboro, NC), August 4, 2002, http://www.greensboro.com/a-birthday-party-with-the-governor/article_c4aa1058-b794-5db1-b2e9-7ca5c53a6043.html; and Bledsoe, *Bitter Blood*, 184.

52. "Pride of North Carolina," *Endicott (NY) Daily Bulletin*, December 31, 1946, 2.

53. "Reidsville Quads to Have First Santa Visit"; and Bettye Cook, "Fultz Quads on Road to Long Life," *Baltimore Afro-American*, May 20, 1947, M-1.

54. Newsome, "I Think It Was the Shots."

55. Ahearn, "Birthday Party with the Governor."

56. Ahearn.

57. Charles L. Sanders, "The Fultz Quads: Grown-Up, Disappointed and Bitter," *Ebony*, November 1968, 216–17.

58. Although Elma was also Black, she saw herself as socially stationed far above the Fultz family. In the 1940s South, the class difference between a Black nurse and a Black tenant farmer and his wife was substantial. The profession of nursing began as a primarily White occupation. In 1925, of the 1,696 accredited nursing schools in the United States, only 108 of them accepted Black students. Jean C. Whelan, "Does American Nursing Have a Diversity Problem?," *Echoes & Evidence* (blog), February 26, 2015, https://historian.nursing .upenn.edu/2015/02/26/diversity_nursing/. The first professional organization for nurses, the American Nurses Association (ANA), did not include any Black nurses. Responding to this exclusion, Martha Minerva Franklin founded the National Association of Colored Graduate Nurses (NACGN) in 1908. Georgia Burnette, "Looking Back: Black Nurses Struggle for Admission to Professional Schools," *Afro-Americans in New York Life and History* 28, no. 2 (July 2004): 85. NACGN initially had very low membership, serving primarily as a registry of Black nurses, until Estelle Massey Riddle Osborne, the first Black nurse to receive a master's degree, became president. Gina M. Meyers, "Historical Leadership Figures," in *Nursing Leadership: A Concise Encyclopedia*, ed. Harriet R. Feldman (New York: Springer Publishing, 2012), 397. Together with her executive director, Mabel K. Staupers, Osborne began a twelve-year campaign to integrate the ANA. Meyers, 403. The campaign was a success, resulting in the voluntary dissolution of NACGN in 1951, when Black and White nurses united as equals in one organization. Burnette, "Looking Back."

59. Ahearn, "And Then There Was One."

60. Brent Swancer, "A Dark, Shameful History of Human Zoos," *Mysterious Universe*, April 4, 2016, http://mysteriousuniverse.org/2016/04/a-dark-shameful-history-of-human-zoos/.

61. Bernth Lindfors, *Early African Entertainments Abroad: From the Hottentot Venus to Africa's First Olympians* (Madison: University of Wisconsin Press, 2014), 13–15.

62. Nessy, "The Haunting 'Human Zoo' of Paris," *Messy Nessy Chic* (blog), March 2, 2012, http://www.messynessychic.com/2012/03/02/the-haunting -human-zoo-of-paris/.

63. Lindfors, *Early African Entertainments Abroad*, 31.

64. "History," Penn House, City of Reidsville, accessed November 13, 2018, http://www.ci.reidsville.nc.us/government/penn_house/government/history /index.php.

65. Ahearn, "Birthday Party with the Governor."

66. "Reidsville Quads to Have First Santa Visit."

67. "Famous Quads Make History," *Pittsburgh Courier*, October 22, 1949, 3; and "It's Happy Birthday!," *Ohio State News* (Columbus), May 17, 1950, 14.

68. "Nursemaid to the Quadruplets," *Ebony*, June 1948, 36.

69. Charles Stanbeck, "Fultz Quads Healthy, Noisy," *Baltimore Afro-American*, December 30, 1947, M-5.

70. Sanders, "Grown-Up, Disappointed and Bitter," 216–17.

71. "Quadruplets' First Birthday."

72. "Carolina Quads Plan Birthday," *Gastonia (NC) Gazette*, May 20, 1947, 3; and "It's 1st Birthday for NC Girls, Only Negro Quads," *Index-Journal* (Greenwood, SC), May 23, 1947, 4.

73. "It's 1st Birthday for NC Girls."

74. "It's 1st Birthday for NC Girls."

75. "Fultz Quads on Road to Long Life," M-1.

76. Alex M. Rivera Jr., "Mother of Fultz Quads Expecting Stork Next Fall," *Pittsburgh Courier*, May 8, 1948, 1.

77. Rivera, "Mother of Fultz Quads."

78. Jim Wise, "He Turned Lens on Push for Civil Rights," *Charlotte Observer*, October 26, 2008, http://www.charlotteobserver.com/news/local/article9019721.html.

79. "Renowned Photojournalist Alex Rivera Dies at 95," North Carolina Central University, October 24, 2008, http://www.nccu.edu/news/index.cfm?id=2FAC5CA5-19B9-B859-78D79468B9C1A9B2.

80. Wise, "He Turned Lens on Push for Civil Rights."

81. Courtney Nickle, "Let's Talk About: The Courier's Crusade for Civil Rights," *Pittsburgh Post-Gazette*, May 30, 2012, http://www.post-gazette.com/life/lifestyle/2012/05/31/Let-s-Talk-About-The-Courier-s-crusade-for-civil-rights/stories/201205310255.

82. Nickle, "Courier's Crusade for Civil Rights"; and Ashley Bianco, "A Fighting Press: Two Different Approaches from the Black and White Press," Georgia Civil Rights Cold Cases Project, Emory University, accessed April 8, 2018, https://coldcases.emory.edu/a-fighting-press-two-different-approaches-from-the-black-and-white-press/.

83. Alex M. Rivera Jr., "Four Famous Little Girls Celebrate 2nd Birthday," *Pittsburgh Courier*, May 22, 1948, 10.

84. Rivera, "Four Famous Little Girls."

85. Rivera.

86. Rivera.

87. Alex M. Rivera Jr., "Quads 3 Years Old Saturday," *Pittsburgh Courier*, April 23, 1949, 4.

88. Rivera, "Quads 3 Years Old Saturday."

89. Rivera.

90. "Fultz Quads Third Birthday," *Pittsburgh Courier*, April 23, 1949, 13.

91. Rivera, "Quads 3 Years Old Saturday."

92. Rivera.

93. Rivera.

94. Rivera.

95. "Quads Steal Show; Mother Faints," *Pittsburgh Courier*, May 28, 1949, 5.

96. "Quads Steal Show."

97. "Fultz Quads Make Public Appearance," *New York Age*, June 4, 1949, 19.

98. "Bet You Want to Hug Them, Don't You," *Pittsburgh Courier*, June 25, 1949, 1.

99. Black Past, s.v. "Palmer Memorial Institute (1902–1971)," by Allison Espiritu, accessed April 11, 2018, http://www.blackpast.org/aah/palmer -memorial-institute-1902-1971.

100. Black Past, "Palmer Memorial Institute."

101. Black Past.

102. Black Past.

103. "Bet You Want to Hug Them, Don't You."

104. "Fultz Quads in the News," *Pittsburgh Courier*, November 19, 1949, 16.

105. "President Greets Quads from South," *Pittsburgh Post-Gazette*, April 17, 1950, 2; and "President Greets Fultz Quadruplets," *Decatur Daily Review*, April 17, 1950, 16.

106. Leonard Lyons, "Lyons Den," *Des Moines Register*, April 29, 1950, 6.

107. Bill Pigott, "Odds and Ends," *Southern Illinoisan* (Carbondale), April 18, 1950, 3.

108. "It's 'Happy Birthday!,'" *Ohio State News* (Columbus), May 17, 1950, 14; and "Happy Birthday," *New York Age*, June 10, 1950, 16.

109. "Tot Quartet," *New York Age*, May 13, 1950, 14.

110. "Reidsville Honors Famous Quads," *Ohio State News* (Columbus), June 9, 1951, 5A.

111. Ahearn, "Birthday Party with the Governor."

112. Ahearn.

113. North Carolina History Project, s.v. "William Kerr Scott (1896–1958)," by Kellie Slappey, accessed April 11, 2018, http://northcarolinahistory .org/encyclopedia/william-kerr-scott-1896-1958/.

114. "About FPG," Frank Porter Graham Child Development Institute, accessed April 11, 2018, https://fpg.unc.edu/node/216.

115. Ahearn, "Birthday Party with the Governor."

116. Ahearn.

117. Ahearn.

118. Ahearn.

119. Ahearn.

120. Laura J. Thomson, "The Bennett Banner and Views on Disarmament," *Amistad Research Center* (blog), February 19, 2018, https://www.amistad researchcenter.org/single-post/2018/02/19/The-Bennett-Banner-and-Views -on-Disarmament.

121. Alex M. Rivera Jr., "Fultz Quads Take Over College on 5th Birthday," *Pittsburgh Courier*, May 26, 1951, 5.

122. Rivera, "Fultz Quads Take Over."

123. James Stewart, "Bennett College for Women: A Brief History to 1945," University of North Carolina at Greensboro, 2014, http://libcdm1.uncg.edu /cdm/ref/collection/ttt/id/37431.

124. Thomson, "Bennett Banner and Views on Disarmament."

125. Rivera, "Fultz Quads Take Over"; and Vivian Ferguson, "It's News to Me," *News-Journal* (Mansfield, OH), June 3, 1951, 2.

126. Rivera, "Fultz Quads Take Over"; and Ferguson, "It's News to Me."

127. Rivera, "Fultz Quads Take Over."

128. Alex M. Rivera Jr., "6-Year-Old Fultz Quads Face Big Problem," *Pittsburgh Courier*, May 31, 1952, 13.

129. Rivera, "Quads Face Big Problem."

130. Rivera.

131. "Fultz Quads Celebrate Sixth Birthday," *Pittsburgh Courier*, June 7, 1952, 13.

132. Rivera, "Quads Face Big Problem"; and "Fultz Quads Almost Ten Years Old!," *Pittsburgh Courier*, April 28, 1956, 7.

133. Rivera, "Fultz Quads Take Over."

134. Rivera, "Quads Face Big Problem."

135. Bledsoe, *Bitter Blood*, 216.

136. Ahearn, "Birthday Party with the Governor."

137. Ahearn.

138. Ahearn.

139. Hazel E. Rivera, "Their Big Desire Right Now Is a Piano," *Pittsburgh Courier*, September 27, 1952, 18.

140. Rivera, "Quads Face Big Problem."

141. Rivera.

142. Rivera, "Their Big Desire."

143. Rivera.

144. "Milton, N.C., Home of Quads," *Baltimore Afro-American*, January 3, 1953, 14.

145. "Negro Quads to Enter School in September," *Times-News* (Hendersonville, NC), July 19, 1952, 5; and Fultz Quads Near End of First School Term," *Jet*, March 5, 1953, 38.

146. Sanders, "Grown-Up, Disappointed and Bitter," 217.

147. Sanders, 216.

Chapter 2

1. Dorothy Roberts, *Killing the Black Body: Race, Reproduction, and the Meaning of Liberty* (New York: Pantheon Books, 1997), 22–25.

2. Jacquelyn S. Litt, *Medicalized Motherhood: Perspectives from the Lives of African-American and Jewish Women* (Piscataway, NJ: Rutgers University Press, 2002), 2.

3. Emily West and R. J. Knight, "Mother's Milk: Slavery, Wet-Nursing and Black and White Women in the Antebellum South," *Journal of Southern History* 83, no. 1 (February 2017): 41–42, https://doi.org/10.1353/soh.2017.0001; and Wilma A. Dunaway, *The African-American Family in Slavery & Emancipation* (Cambridge, UK: Cambridge University Press, 2003), 140.

4. Kimberley Mangun and Lisa M. Parcell, "The Pet Milk Company 'Happy Family' Advertising Campaign: A Groundbreaking Appeal to the Negro Market of the 1950s," *Journalism History* 40, no. 2 (Summer 2014): 72–74.

5. Marylynn Salmon, "The Cultural Significance of Breastfeeding and Infant Care in Early Modern England and America," *Journal of Social History* 28, no. 2 (Winter 1994): 249, https://doi.org/10.1353/jsh/28.2.247.

6. Valerie Fildes, *Wet Nursing: A History from Antiquity to the Present* (Oxford, UK: Basil Blackwell, 1988), 130–31.

7. Fildes, *Wet Nursing*, 130.

8. Fildes, 130–31; and Janet Golden, *A Social History of Wet Nursing in America: From Breast to Bottle* (Cambridge, UK: Cambridge University Press, 1996), 11–13.

9. Fildes, *Wet Nursing*, 130–31.

10. Alice Robb, "Bring Back the Wet Nurse," *New Republic*, July 22, 2014, https://newrepublic.com/article/118786/breastfeeding-wet-nurses-mommy-wars.

11. Diane Thulier, "Breastfeeding in America: A History of Influencing Factors," *Journal of Human Lactation* 25, no. 1 (February 2009): 86, https://doi.org/10.1177/0890334408324452.

12. Paula A. Treckel, "Breastfeeding and Maternal Sexuality in Colonial America," *Journal of Interdisciplinary History* 20, no. 1 (Summer 1989): 26, https://doi.org/10.2307/204048.

13. Treckel, "Breastfeeding and Maternal Sexuality," 30; and Robb, "Bring Back the Wet Nurse."

14. Jacqueline H. Wolf, *Don't Kill Your Baby: Public Health and the Decline of Breastfeeding in the 19th and 20th Centuries* (Columbus: Ohio State University Press, 2001), 137–38.

15. Erika Eisdorfer, *The Wet Nurse's Tale* (New York: Penguin Group, 2009).

16. Golden, *Social History of Wet Nursing*, 11–13; and Grace Peckham, "Infancy in the City," *The Popular Science Monthly* 28 (March 1886): 683–86.

17. Robb, "Bring Back the Wet Nurse."

18. Robb.

19. Vicki L. Lamb, "Historical and Epidemiological Trends in Mortality in the United States," in *Handbook of Death and Dying*, ed. Clifton D. Bryant (Thousand Oaks, CA: Sage Publications, 2003), 185–86.

20. Julie E. Artis, "Breastfeed at Your Own Risk," *Contexts* 8, no. 4 (Fall 2009): 29; and Golden, *Social History of Wet Nursing*, 9; Thulier, "Breastfeeding in America," 87.

21. Artis, "Breastfeed at Your Own Risk," 29; and Emily E. Stevens, Thelma E. Patrick, and Rita Pickler, "A History of Infant Feeding," *Journal of Perinatal Education* 18, no. 2 (Spring 2009): 34, https://doi.org/10.1624/105812409X4 26314.

22. Herbert S. Klein and Stanley L. Engerman, "Fertility Differentials between Slaves in the United States and the British West Indies: A Note on Lactation Practices and Their Possible Implications," *William & Mary Quarterly* 35, no. 2 (April 1978): 358, https://doi.org/10.2307/1921839; and Dunaway, *African-American Family*, 138.

23. Klein and Engerman, "Fertility Differentials," 358–59.

24. Dunaway, *African-American Family*, 135.

25. Dunaway, 136.

26. Dunaway, 139.

27. Justin Roberts, "Race and the Origins of Plantation Slavery," *Oxford Research Encyclopedia of American History* (March 2016): 12; and Philip Curtin, *The Rise and Fall of the Plantation Complex: Essays in Atlantic History* (New York: Cambridge University Press, 1990), 81.

28. Treckel, "Breastfeeding and Maternal Sexuality," 48.

29. "Human Factors and Malaria," Malaria, Centers for Disease Control and Prevention, last modified February 8, 2010, https://www.cdc.gov/malaria /about/biology/human_factors.html.

30. Treckel, "Breastfeeding and Maternal Sexuality," 50; West and Knight, "Mother's Milk," 39; and Thulier, "Breastfeeding in America," 86.

31. Fildes, *Wet Nursing*, 139.

32. Fildes, 139; and West and Knight, "Mother's Milk," 45.

33. Dunaway, *African-American Family*, 140.

34. "More Slavery at the South," *Independent*, January 25, 1912, 196–200.

35. Jennifer M. Spear, *Race, Sex, and Social Order in Early New Orleans* (Baltimore: Johns Hopkins University Press, 2009), 75–76.

36. Fildes, *Wet Nursing*, 141; and Treckel, "Breastfeeding and Maternal Sexuality," 47.

37. Dunaway, *African-American Family*, 136.

38. Dunaway, 139.

39. George P. Rawick, *The American Slave: A Complete Autobiography* (Westport, CT: Greenwood Press, 1979), 187–88.

40. West and Knight, "Mother's Milk," 52.

41. George P. Rawick, *The American Slave: Georgia Narratives* (Westport, CT: Greenwood Press, 1978), 96–97.

42. LaSha, "Choosing Not to Breastfeed Was My Revolutionary Act," *Blogging while Black* (blog), *Kinfolk Kollective*, January 21, 2016, http://kinfolkkollective.com/2016/01/21/choosing-not-to-breastfeed-was-my-revolutionary-act.

43. LaSha, "My Revolutionary Act."

44. Kimberly Seals Allers, "Breastfeeding: Some Slavery Crap?," *Ebony*, August 31, 2012, http://www.ebony.com/wellness-empowerment/breastfeeding-some-slavery-crap.

45. Toni Morrison, *Beloved* (New York: Vintage Books, 1987), 86.

46. Morrison, *Beloved*, 19–20.

47. Morrison, 19.

48. Morrison, 19.

49. Morrison, 19–20.

50. Robb, "Bring Back the Wet Nurse."

51. "More Slavery at the South," 196–200.

52. Dunaway, *African-American Family*, 136

53. Douglas A. Blackmon, *Slavery by Another Name: The Re-Enslavement of Black Americans from the Civil War to World War II* (London: Icon Books, 2012), 99.

54. U.S. Const. amend. XIII, § 1.

55. 5. Insightful analyses of how this loophole continues to oppress Blacks in the present can be found in Michelle Alexander, *The New Jim Crow: Mass Incarceration in the Age of Colorblindness* (New York: The New Press, 2012); and *13th*, directed by Ava DuVernay (2016; Los Gatos: Netflix).

56. "Black Code of Mississippi, 1865," in *Documents of American History: To 1898*, ed. Henry S. Commager (New York: Appleton-Century-Crofts, 1963), 442–47.

57. Eric Foner, *Reconstruction: America's Unfinished Revolution, 1863–1877* (New York: Harper Perennial, 2014), 203–4.

58. Foner, *Reconstruction*, 243–44.

59. Foner, 379, 396–98.

60. Foner, 524–63.

61. Jacqueline Jones, *Labor of Love, Labor of Sorrow: Black Women, Work, and the Family from Slavery to the Present* (New York: Basic Books, 2010), 61.

62. Foner, *Reconstruction*, 537; and David Oshinsky, *"Worse than Slavery": Parchman Farm and the Ordeal of Jim Crow Justice* (New York: Free Press Paperbacks, 1997), 223–27.

63. Plessy v. Ferguson, 163 U.S. 537 (1896).

64. L. P. McGehee, *Consolidated Statutes of North Carolina* (Raleigh, NC: Edwards & Broughton, 1920), 2:665.

65. "Jim Crow Laws," National Park Service, accessed April 7, 2018, https://www.nps.gov/malu/learn/education/jim_crow_laws.htm.

66. "The Black Code of St. Landry's Parish, 1865," Virginia Tech College of Liberal Arts & Human Sciences, accessed April 7, 2018, http://www.history.vt.edu/shifflet/blackcode.htm.

67. Isabel Wilkerson, *The Warmth of Other Suns: The Epic Story of America's Great Migration* (New York: Vintage Books, 2010), 161.

68. Roberts, *Killing the Black Body*, 15; and Jones, *Labor of Love*, 58–60.

69. Dunaway, *African-American Family*, 206; and Spencer R. Crew, "The Great Migration of Afro-Americans 1915–40," *Monthly Labor Review* 110, no. 3 (March 1987): 34–36.

70. West and Knight, "Mother's Milk," 39; Golden, *Social History of Wet Nursing*, 179; and Kate Dailey, "Who, What, Why: Why Do African-American Women Breastfeed Less?," *Magazine Monitor* (blog), *BBC*, June 10, 2014, https://www.bbc.com/news/blogs-magazine-monitor-27744391.

71. Harvey Levenstein, "'Best for Babies' or 'Preventable Infanticide'? The Controversy over Artificial Feeding of Infants in America, 1880–1920," *Journal of American History* 70, no. 1 (June 1983): 75–84, https://doi.org/10.2307/1890522.

72. Wolf, *Don't Kill Your Baby*, 104, 197.

73. Ruth Hill, "Towards a Constructionist Essentialism: Critical Race Studies and the Baroque," in *The Transatlantic Hispanic Baroque: Complex Identities in the Atlantic World*, ed. Harald E. Braun and Jesús Pérez-Magallón (Surrey, UK: Ashgate, 2014), 40.

74. Deborah J. Wilk, "Of Milk and Homeland: Breastfeeding, Immigrant Mothers, and Eugenics in the Nineteenth and Twenty-First Centuries," in *Reconciling Art and Mothering*, ed. Rachel Epp Buller (Surrey, UK: Ashgate, 2012), 31–41; and Hill, "Towards a Constructionist Essentialism," 40.

75. Fildes, *Wet Nursing*, 205, 250.

76. Viviana A. Zelizer, *Pricing the Priceless Child: The Changing Social Value of Children* (Princeton, NJ: Princeton University Press, 1994); and Thulier, "Breastfeeding in America," 87.

77. Andrea Freeman, "'First Food' Justice: Racial Disparities in Infant Feeding as Food Oppression," *Fordham Law Review* 83, no. 6 (May 2015): 3060.

78. Stevens, Patrick, and Pickler, "History of Infant Feeding," 36.

79. Wolf, *Don't Kill Your Baby*, 147–48.

80. Wolf, 159–60.

81. Wolf, 149–52.

82. Wolf, 133.

83. Golden, *Social History of Wet Nursing*, 179.

84. Wolf, *Don't Kill Your Baby*, 133.

85. Rima D. Apple, *Mothers and Medicine: A Social History of Infant Feeding, 1890–1950* (Madison: University of Wisconsin Press, 1987), 97.

86. Cathryn Britton, "Breastfeeding: A Natural Phenomenon or a Cultural

Construct?," in *The Social Context of Birth*, ed. Caroline Squire, 2nd ed. (London: Routledge, 2009), 305.

87. Wolf, *Don't Kill Your Baby*, 90.

88. Thulier, "Breastfeeding in America," 88–89.

89. Litt, *Medicalized Motherhood*, 22.

90. Apple, *Mothers and Medicine*, 143–46.

91. Litt, *Medicalized Motherhood*, 34; and Apple, *Mothers and Medicine*, 58.

92. Litt, *Medicalized Motherhood*, 24–25.

93. Litt, 31–35.

94. Marcia Berss, "Baby Milk Wars," *Forbes*, October 1992, 153; Kurt Andersen, Barbara Dolan, and Bruce Van Voorst, "The Battle of the Bottle," *Time*, June 1981, 36; Melody Petersen, "Pediatric Book on Breast-Feeding Stirs Controversy with Its Cover," *New York Times*, September 18, 2002, C1; Mary Catherine Bliss et al., "The Effect of Discharge Pack Formula and Breast Pumps on Breastfeeding Duration and Choice of Infant Feeding Method," *Birth: Issues in Perinatal Care & Education* 24, no. 2 (June 1997): 90, https://doi.org/10.1111/j.1523-536X.1997.tb00347.x; Claibourne I. Dungy et al., "Effect of Discharge Samples on Duration of Breast-Feeding," *Pediatrics* 90, no. 2 (August 1992): 233; and Cynthia J. Evans, Nancy B. Lyons, and G. Killien Marcia, "The Effect of Infant Formula Samples on Breastfeeding Practice," *Journal of Obstetric, Gynecologic, & Neonatal Nursing* 15, no. 5 (September 1986): 401, https://doi.org/10.1111/j.1552-6909.1986.tb01414.x.

95. Stevens, Patrick, and Pickler, "History of Infant Feeding," 36–37.

96. MattTheSaiyan, "1950s Carnation Evaporated Milk Commercial ('Babies')—Aired Live," YouTube, 1:40, April 25, 2010, https://www.youtube.com/watch?v=4Qn7fCikPsA.

97. Throwback, "Pet Evaporated Milk Commercial (1950s)," YouTube, 1:22, May 14, 2011, https://youtu.be/ZyzyzmuLvWQ.

98. Starr-Renee Corbin, "Raising Parents: Breastfeeding Trends from 1900 to Present Day" (master's thesis, University of Texas at Austin, 2010), 2, https://repositories.lib.utexas.edu/handle/2152/ETD-UT-2010-05-819.

99. American Academy of Pediatrics, "Breastfeeding and the Use of Human Milk," *Pediatrics* 115, no. 3 (March 2012): 496.

100. Anne L. Wright and Richard J. Schanler, "The Resurgence of Breast-feeding at the End of the Second Millennium," *Journal of Nutrition* 131, no. 2 (February 2001): 421S, https://doi.org/10.1093/jn/131.2.421S; and Nicoletta Iacovidou, "Breastfeeding in the Course of History," *Journal of Pediatrics and Neonatal Care* 2, no. 6 (2015): 7, https://doi.org/10.15406/jpnc.2015.02.00096.

101. Linda M. Blum, *At the Breast: Ideologies of Breastfeeding and Motherhood in the Contemporary United States* (Boston: Beacon Press, 1999), 63–108. La Leche was formed in Franklin Park, Illinois, by seven mothers. The "found-

ing mothers" of La Leche were Mary Ann Cahill, Edwina Froehlich, Mary Ann Kerwin, Viola Lennon, Marian Thompson, Betty Wagner, and Mary White. "A Brief History of La Leche League International," About, La Leche League International, accessed November 20, 2018, https://www.llli.org/about/history/.

102. Blum, *At the Breast*, 44–45; and Mike Muller, *The Baby Killer* (London: War on Want, 1974), 7–9.

103. American Academy of Pediatrics, *Pediatrics* 62, no. 4 (October 1978): 596–98.

104. Suzanne Macartney, Alemayehu Bishaw, and Kayla Fontenot, "Poverty Races for Selected Detailed Race and Hispanic Groups by State and Place: 2007–2011," US Census Bureau, February 2013, https://www2.census.gov/library/publications/2013/acs/acsbr11-17.pdf.

105. "Breastfeeding among Mothers 15–44 Years of Age, by Year of Baby's Birth and Selected Characteristics of Mother: United States, Average Annual 1986–1988 through 2002–2004," Centers for Disease Control and Prevention, 2010, https://www.cdc.gov/nchs/data/hus/2010/014.pdf.

106. Katherine M. Jones et al., "Racial and Ethnic Disparities in Breastfeeding," *Breastfeeding Medicine* 10, no. 4 (May 2015): 186, https://doi.org/10.1089/bfm.2014.0152.

107. Jessica A. Allen et al., "Progress in Increasing Breastfeeding and Reducing Racial/Ethnic Differences—United States, 2000–2008 Births," *Morbidity & Mortality Weekly Report* 62, no. 5 (February 8, 2013): 77–80.

108. Chelsea O. McKinney et al., "Racial and Ethnic Differences in Breastfeeding," *Pediatrics* 138, no. 2 (August 2016): 1, https://doi.org/10.1016/j.apnr.2017.07.009.

109. McKinney et al., "Racial and Ethnic Differences in Breastfeeding," 5.

110. McKinney et al., 5.

111. McKinney et al., 2.

112. Litt, *Medicalized Motherhood*, 6–7, 25–27.

113. Elizabeth Currid-Halkett, "The New, Subtle Ways the Rich Signal Their Wealth," *BBC*, June 14, 2017, http://www.bbc.com/capital/story/20170614-the-new-subtle-ways-the-rich-signal-their-wealth.

114. Elizabeth Currid-Halkett, "Conspicuous Consumption Is Over. It's All about Intangibles Now," *Aeon*, June 7, 2017, https://aeon.co/ideas/conspicuous-consumption-is-over-its-all-about-intangibles-now.

115. Esther Renfrew, "7% Growth for $50 Billion Global Infant Nutrition Market," *Zenith Global*, April 24, 2014, https://www.zenithglobal.com/articles/1355?7%25+growth+for+%2450+Billion+global+infant+nutrition+market; and Imogen Calderwood, "These 4 Baby Formula Brands Are Putting Profits before Science, Warns Report," *Global Citizen*, October 31, 2017, https://www.globalcitizen.org/en/content/breastfeeding-baby-formula-report/.

116. Dale D. Murphy, *The Structure of Regulatory Competition: Corpo-*

rations and Public Policies in a Global Economy (New York: Oxford University Press, 2004), 197.

117. Ken Goldman, "Food Producers and Retailers: The Bull/Bear Behemoth," North America Equity Research, January 27, 2017; and William Shurtleff and Akiko Aoyagi, *History of Soymilk and Other Non-Dairy Milks (1226–2013)* (Lafayette, CA: SoyInfo Center, 2013), 2116.

118. Josh Vander Plaats, *Infant Formula* (Iowa City, IA: Henry B. Tippie School of Management, University of Iowa, March 17, 2016), 2; and Sylvia Onusic, "The Scandal of Infant Formula," *Wise Traditions in Food, Farming and the Healing Arts*, Weston A. Price Foundation (December 9, 2015), https://www.westonaprice.org/health-topics/childrens-health/the-scandal-of-infant-formula/.

119. George Kent, "WIC's Promotion of Infant Formula in the United States," *International Breastfeeding Journal* 1, no. 1 (April 2006): 4, https://doi.org/10.1186/1746-4358-1-8.

120. "Enfamil Infant Formula Powder 12.5 oz. Canister," Walmart, accessed March 5, 2018, https://www.walmart.com/ip/Enfamil-trade-Infant-Formula-Powder-12-5-oz-Canister/16940594.

121. "Enfamil Infant Formula Powder"; Amber, "How Long Would 1 Tub of Formula Last a Baby!?," *Baby Center Community* (blog), February 12, 2012, https://community.babycenter.com/post/a31661809/%20how_long_would_1_tub_of_formula_last_a_baby.

122. *Milking It: How Milk Formula Companies Are Putting Profits Before Science* (n.p.: Changing Markets Foundation, 2017), 26–27.

123. Richard Eskow, "Death by Inequality: Poverty and Racism Are Killing America's Children," *Common Dreams*, January 23, 2018, https://www.commondreams.org/views/2018/01/23/death-inequality-poverty-and-racism-are-killing-americas-children; McKay Jenkins, "Flint's Water: Poisoned by Lead, and by Race," *Medium*, January 25, 2016, https://medium.com/galleys/race-and-lead-poisoning-in-flint-aedc635efc29; and Chauncey Devega, "Black America Is So Very Tired of Explaining and Debating," *Salon*, June 8, 2015, https://www.salon.com/2015/06/08/black_america_is_so_very_tired_of_explaining_and_debating/.

124. Dale D. Murphy, "Interjurisdictional Competition and Regulatory Advantage," *Journal of International Economic Law* 8, no. 4 (November 2005): 912, https://doi.org/10.1093/jiel/jgi050.

125. Linda C. Fentiman, "Marketing Mothers' Milk: The Commodification of Breastfeeding and the New Markets for Breast Milk and Infant Formula," *Nevada Law Journal* 10, no. 1 (Winter 2009): 70.

126. Fentiman, "Marketing Mothers' Milk," 70–71.

127. Fentiman, 70.

128. Murphy, "Interjurisdictional Competition," 915. An article by Barry

Meier stated that "between 1983 and 1991, the pediatric group received more than $8.3 million in donations from the major manufacturers, including $1.3 million for the construction of the group's Elk Grove, Ill., headquarters. The group also received indirect funds from manufacturers for parties and from advertising in its journals, according to court documents. Formula producers have also spent millions designing hospital pediatric clinics." "Battle for Baby Formula Market," *New York Times*, June 15, 1993, D1.

129. Murphy, 915.

130. Nestlé Food Co. v. Abbott Labs., No. 95-56273, 1997 WL 8578, at *1 (9th Cir. Jan. 9, 1997).

131. *Nestlé Food Co.*, 1997 WL 8578, at *1.

132. Murphy, "Interjurisdictional Competition," 915.

133. Murphy, *Structure of Regulatory Competition*, 203.

134. Fentiman, "Marketing Mothers' Milk," 71.

135. Matt Siegel, "Formula for Disaster," *American Lawyer* 16, no. 1 (January/February 1994): 63; and Michael Brick, "Formula Fight: A Generic vs. the Giants," *New York Times*, September 26, 1999, https://www.nytimes.com/1999/09/26/business/personal-business-formula-fight-a-generic-vs-the-giants.html.

136. Murphy, *Structure of Regulatory Competition*, 204.

137. Brick, "Formula Fight."

138. Olga Khazan, "The Epic Battle between Breast Milk and Formula Companies," *Atlantic*, July 10, 2018, https://www.theatlantic.com/health/archive/2018/07/the-epic-battle-between-breast-milk-and-infant-formula-companies/564782/.

139. Katie Allison Granju, "Milky Way of Doing Business," *Jay Gordon* (blog), February 23, 2010, http://drjaygordon.com/breastfeeding/milkyway.html.

140. Granju, "Milky Way of Doing Business."

141. Roni Rabin, "Breast-Feed or Else," *New York Times*, June 13, 2006, http://www.nytimes.com/2006/06/13/health/13brea.html.

142. Granju, "Milky Way of Doing Business."

143. Granju.

144. Kenneth D. Rosenberg et al., "Marketing Infant Formula through Hospitals: The Impact of Commercial Hospital Discharge Packs on Breastfeeding," *American Journal of Public Health* 98, no. 2 (2008): 290, https://doi.org/10.2105/AJPH.2006.103218; and Deborah L. Kaplan and Kristina M. Graff, "Marketing Breastfeeding—Reversing Corporate Influence on Infant Feeding Practices," *Journal of Urban Health* 85, no. 4 (2008): 489, https://doi.org/10.1007/s11524-008-9279-6.

145. "Guidelines and Evaluation Criteria for Facilities Seeking Baby-Friendly Designation," Baby Friendly USA, 2010, www.babyfriendlyusa.org/get-started/the-guidelines-evaluation-criteria.

146. Rita Henley Jensen, "'Baby Friendly' Hospitals Bypass Black Communities," *Women's eNews*, August 29, 2013, http://womensenews.org/2013/08/baby-friendly-hospitals-bypass-black-communities.

147. Barbara L. Philipp et al., "Baby-Friendly Hospital Initiative Improves Breastfeeding Initiation Rates in a US Hospital Setting," *Pediatrics* 108, no. 3 (September 2001): 677.

148. Philipp et al., "Baby-Friendly Hospital Initiative," 678.

149. Philipp et al., 678–80.

150. Center for Responsive Politics, "Employer Search: Abbott Laboratories," Open Secrets, accessed March 5, 2018, https://www.opensecrets.org/revolving/search_result.php?priv=Abbott+Laboratories.

151. Center for Responsive Politics, "Abbott Laboratories," Open Secrets, accessed March 5, 2018, http://www.opensecrets.org/orgs/summary.php?id=D000000383; "Abbott Laboratories," Follow the Money, accessed March 5, 2018, https://www.followthemoney.org/entity-details?eid=14.

152. Jim Edwards, "Pharma Election Money Backs Obama," *CBS News*, August 19, 2008, https://www.cbsnews.com/news/pharma-election-money-backs-obama/.

153. Center for Responsive Politics, "Employer Search."

154. Center for Responsive Politics, "Burnes, Austin," Open Secrets, accessed March 5, 2018, https://www.opensecrets.org/revolving/rev_summary.php?id=78108.

155. Center for Responsive Politics, "Lobbyists Representing Mead Johnson Nutritional, 2014," Open Secrets, accessed March 5, 2018, https://www.opensecrets.org/lobby/clientlbs.php?id=D000018653&year=2014.

156. Tennille Tracy, "Makers of Baby Formula Press Their Case on WIC Program," *Wall Street Journal*, April 27, 2015, https://www.wsj.com/articles/makers-of-baby-formula-press-their-case-on-wic-program-1430177799.

157. "Women, Infants, and Children (WIC)," Food and Nutrition Service, US Department of Agriculture, last modified October 17, 2018, https://www.fns.usda.gov/wic/women-infants-and-children-wic; and Fentiman, "Marketing Mothers' Milk," 72.

158. Center for Responsive Politics, "Lobbyists Representing Nestlé SA, 2013," Open Secrets, accessed March 5, 2018, https://www.opensecrets.org/lobby/clientlbs.php?id=D000042332&year=2013.

159. Kit O'Connell, "Nestlé Spent $11M Lobbying Congress to Control Water, Cocoa & Trade Since 2013," *Mint Press News*, September 27, 2016, https://www.mintpressnews.com/Nestlé-spent-11m-lobbying-congress-to-control-water-cocoa-trade-since-2013/220853/; and Center for Responsive Politics, "Annual Lobbying by Nestlé SA," Open Secrets, accessed March 5, 2018, https://www.opensecrets.org/lobby/clientsum.php?id=D000042332&year=2013.

160. "Supplemental Nutrition Assistance Program (SNAP)," Food and Nutri-

tion Service, US Department of Agriculture, last modified April 25, 2018, https://www.fns.usda.gov/snap/supplemental-nutrition-assistance-program-snap.

161. The dairy program is Subchapter III, Agricultural Act of 2014, 7 U.S.C. § 9051 (2015). Soy is a "covered commodity" eligible for subsidies. § 8702(4).

162. Freeman, "'First Food' Justice," 3068.

163. Kent, "WIC's Promotion," 5.

164. "Women, Infants, and Children (WIC) Participant and Program Characteristics 2012: Summary," Food and Nutrition Service, US Department of Agriculture, December 2013, http://www.fns.usda.gov/sites/default/files/WIC PC2012_Summary.pdf.

165. Jennifer Ludden, "Teaching Black Women to Embrace Breast-Feeding," *NPR*, December 23, 2009, http://www.npr.org/templates/story/story.php?story Id=121755349.

166. Murphy, "Interjurisdictional Competition," 913.

167. Cynthia Howard et al., "Office Prenatal Formula Advertising and Its Effect on Breast-Feeding Patterns," *Obstetrics and Gynecology* 95, no. 2 (March 2000): 296, https://doi.org/10.1016/S0029-7844(99)00555-4.

168. Hannah Ellis-Petersen, "How Formula Milk Firms Target Mothers Who Can Least Afford It," *Guardian*, February 26, 2018, https://www.theguardian.com/lifeandstyle/2018/feb/27/formula-milk-companies-target-poor-mothers-breastfeeding; and "National Implementation of the International Code of Marketing of Breastmilk Substitutes," Nutrition, UNICEF, April 2011, https://www.unicef.org/nutrition/files/State_of_the_Code_by_Country _April2011.pdf.

169. WHO, *International Code of Marketing of Breast-Milk Substitutes* (Geneva: World Health Organization, 1981), 10.

170. Alison Stuebe, "It's Time to Disarm the Formula Industry," *Breastfeeding Medicine*, May 20, 2016, https://bfmed.wordpress.com/2016/05/20 /its-time-to-disarm-the-formula-industry.

Chapter 3

1. Martin Bell, *A Portrait of Progress: A Business History of Pet Milk Company from 1885 to 1960* (St. Louis: Pet Milk, 1962), 103–4; and Kimberley Mangun and Lisa M. Parcell, "The Pet Milk Company 'Happy Family' Advertising Campaign," *Journalism History* 40, no. 2 (Summer 2014): 71.

2. Mangun and Parcell, "Pet Milk Company," 71.

3. Mangun and Parcell, 71; Robert E. Weems Jr., "African American Consumerism," in *The African American Experience: An Historical and Bibliographical Guide*, ed. Arvarh E. Strickland and Robert E. Weems Jr. (London: Greenwood Press, 2001).

4. Mangun and Parcell, "Pet Milk Company," 72; and Jason Chambers, *Madison Avenue and the Color Line: African Americans in the Advertising Industry* (Philadelphia: University of Pennsylvania Press, 2008), 86.

5. Samuel J. Fomon, "Infant Feeding in the 20th Century: Formula and Beikost," *Journal of Nutrition* 131, no. 2 (February 2001): 409S–20S, https://doi.org/10.1093/jn/131.2.409S.

6. Rima D. Apple, *Mothers and Medicine: A Social History of Infant Feeding 1890–1950* (Madison: University of Wisconsin Press, 1987), 78.

7. Apple, *Mothers and Medicine*, 78.

8. Kimberly Seals Allers, "Breastfeeding: Some Slavery Crap?," *Ebony*, August 31, 2012, http://www.ebony.com/wellness-empowerment/breastfeeding-some-slavery-crap.

9. Allers, "Some Slavery Crap?" In the 1960s, formula came to be viewed as a miraculous scientific advancement, similar to astronaut food.

10. Kimberly Seals Allers, *The Big Letdown: How Medicine, Big Business, and Feminism Undermine Breastfeeding* (New York: St. Martin's Press, 2017), 14–16.

11. H. A. Haring, "Selling to Harlem," *Advertising & Selling* (October 31, 1928): 17–18, 50–53; H. A. Haring, "The Negro as Consumer," *Advertising & Selling* (September 3, 1930): 20–21, 67–68; Mangun and Parcell, "Pet Milk Company," 72; and Chambers, *Madison Avenue and the Color Line*, 34–35.

12. Mangun and Parcell, "Pet Milk Company," 72; Lawrence Daniel Hogan, "Associated Negro Press," in *Encyclopedia of Chicago* (Chicago: Chicago Historical Society, n.d.) accessed April 4, 2018, http://www.encyclopedia.chicagohistory.org/pages/1734.html; and Chambers, *Madison Avenue and the Color Line*, 28–29.

13. Chambers, *Madison Avenue and the Color Line*, 36–37.

14. Mangun and Parcell, "Pet Milk Company," 72; and Marilyn Kern-Foxworth, *Aunt Jemima, Uncle Ben, and Rastus: Blacks in Advertising, Yesterday, Today, and Tomorrow* (Westport, CT: Greenwood Press, 1994), 155.

15. Mangun and Parcell, "Pet Milk Company," 72; Kern-Foxworth, *Aunt Jemima, Uncle Ben, and Rastus*, 116; and Deseriee A. Kennedy, "Marketing Goods, Marketing Images: The Impact of Advertising on Race," *Arizona State Law Journal* 32, no. 2 (Summer 2000): 622.

16. Katherine J. Parkin, *Food Is Love: Advertising and Gender Roles in Modern America* (Philadelphia: University of Pennsylvania Press, 2006), 81; and Chambers, *Madison Avenue and the Color Line*, 9.

17. Mangun and Parcell, "Pet Milk Company," 71.

18. Kern-Foxworth, *Aunt Jemima, Uncle Ben, and Rastus*, 116.

19. Raymond A. Bauer and Scott M. Cunningham, "The Negro Market," *Journal of Advertising Research* 10, no. 2 (April 1970): 7; Paul K. Edwards, *The Southern Urban Negro as a Consumer* (New York: Prentice-Hall, 1932); Skylar Harris, "Advertising," in *The Jim Crow Encyclopedia: Greenwood Milestones in African American History*, ed. Nikki L. M. Brown and Barry M. Stentiford (Westport, CT: Greenwood Press, 2008), 6; and Chambers, *Madison Avenue and the Color Line*, 35–36.

20. Edwards, *Southern Urban Negro*, 5.

21. Chambers, *Madison Avenue and the Color Line*, 35–36.

22. Chambers, 35–37.

23. Chambers, 36.

24. Andrew F. Smith, ed., *The Oxford Encyclopedia of Food and Drink in America* (New York: Oxford University Press, 2013), 96–98.

25. Chambers, *Madison Avenue and the Color Line*, 36–37.

26. Chambers, 36.

27. Bauer and Cunningham, "Negro Market," 7.

28. Bauer and Cunningham, 7.

29. Mangun and Parcell, "Pet Milk Company," 71.

30. Mangun and Parcell, 72.

31. Catherine Reef, *Working in America* (New York: Facts on File, 2007), 316–17.

32. Robert E. Weems Jr., *Desegregating the Dollar: African American Consumerism in the Twentieth Century* (New York: New York University Press, 1998), 31–55.

33. Chambers, *Madison Avenue and the Color Line*, 40; and Bauer and Cunningham, "Negro Market," 9–11.

34. Bauer and Cunningham, "Negro Market," 7–8.

35. Chambers, *Madison Avenue and the Color Line*, 68.

36. Weems Jr., *Desegregating the Dollar*, 32–33.

37. Parkin, *Food Is Love*, 13; and Mangun and Parcell, "Pet Milk Company," 71.

38. Mangun and Parcell, "Pet Milk Company," 72–73.

39. Chambers, *Madison Avenue and the Color Line*, 85–88.

40. Chambers, 85–86.

41. Chambers, 86.

42. US Department of Health and Human Services, *Tobacco Use among U.S. Racial/Ethnic Minority Groups* (Atlanta: US Department of Health and Human Services, Centers for Disease Control and Prevention, National Center for Chronic Disease Prevention and Health Promotion, Office on Smoking and Health, 1998), 12.

43. Mangun and Parcell, "Pet Milk Company," 72.

44. Lizabeth Cohen, *A Consumers' Republic: The Politics of Mass Consumption in Postwar America* (New York: Vintage Books, 2003), 323–25.

45. Andrew Wiese, *Places of Their Own: African American Suburbanization in the Twentieth Century* (Chicago: University of Chicago Press, 2010), 145.

46. Mangun and Parcell, "Pet Milk Company," 73.

47. Wiese, *Places of Their Own*, 145.

48. Charles E. Connerly, *"The Most Segregated City in America": City Planning and Civil Rights in Birmingham, 1920–1980* (Charlottesville: University of Virginia Press, 2005).

49. Mangun and Parcell, "Pet Milk Company," 73.

50. Mangun and Parcell, 74.

51. Wiese, *Places of Their Own*, 153; Reef, *Working in America*, 311.

52. Wiese, 153; and Reef, 318.

53. Mangun and Parcell, "Pet Milk Company," 71.

54. Mangun and Parcell, 71–72.

55. Allers, *Big Letdown*, 14–16.

56. Allers, "Some Slavery Crap?"

57. Mangun and Parcell, "Pet Milk Company," 71.

58. Allers, "Some Slavery Crap?"

59. Israel Feiler, "African Himba Women Breastfeeding," YouTube, 3:27, March 2, 2012, https://www.youtube.com/watch?v=ZC-r4xrESr0; and Heidi Akkers, "Mothers, Babies, Breastfeeding Worldwide," Pinterest, accessed November 20, 2018, https://www.pinterest.com/heidiakkers/mothers-babies-breast feeding-worldwide/.

60. Molly M. Ginty, "Industry, Feds Entice Black Mothers to Bottle Feed," *Women's eNews*, November 17, 2008, http://womensenews.org/2008/11 /industry-feds-entice-black-mothers-bottle-feed/.

61. Mangun and Parcell, "Pet Milk Company," 74–75.

62. "City's 1st Quads Thrive at Birth," *Oregonian* (Portland), August 23, 1946; and "Father of Quads Proud but Can't Avoid 'Shaking,'" *Times-News* (Twin Falls, ID), August 23, 1946, 5.

63. "Birth of Quadruplets Sets Father Looking for Work—In Earnest," *The Morning Call* (Allentown, PA), August 23, 1946, 1; and "Good Chance for Quads to Survive," *Santa Cruz Sentinel*, August 23, 1946, 2.

64. "Quadruplets Born to Oregon Negro," *Times-News* (Twin Falls, ID), August 22, 1946, 14.

65. "Tigner Quads Enter Teens as Healthy, Happy Children," *Oregonian* (Portland), January 6, 1960, 5.

66. "City's 1st Quads Thrive at Birth."

67. Polly Predmore, "Famous Alphabet Babies Are Doin' All Right," *Oregonian* (Portland), September 22, 1946, 5.

68. "Father of Quads Proud"; and "Quadruplets Doing Fine, Father Looks for Job," *Kenosha (WI) Evening News*, August 23, 1946, 1.

69. "City's 1st Quads Thrive at Birth."

70. "City's 1st Quads Thrive at Birth"; and "Four of a Kind, Bless 'Em!," *Oregonian* (Portland), August 24, 1946.

71. "Portland Quads Fine, but Father 'Just Can't Seem to Quit Shaking,'" *Bakersfield Californian*, August 23, 1946, 2; "Good Chance for Quads to Survive"; and "Quads to Couple in Portland, Ore.," *Neosho (MO) Daily News*, August 22, 1946, 4.

72. "Quads Get 'Nest Egg' of $25,000," *Oregonian* (Portland), August 28, 1946, 1; and "Father of Quads Proud."

73. "Wee Four Out of Incubator," *Oregonian* (Portland), August 24, 1946, 1.

74. "Wee Four"; and "'Quads' Thrive, Negress Worries about Washing," *News-Review* (Roseburg, OR), August 24, 1946, 6.

75. "Wee Four."

76. "Wee Four."

77. "Four of a Kind."

78. "A Real Fairy Godmother," *Oregonian* (Portland), August 29, 1946.

79. "Quads Get 'Nest Egg.'"

80. "Quads Get 'Nest Egg.'"

81. Anne Sullivan, "Tigner Quadruplets Healthy 1-Year-Olds but Doled-Out Legacy Gives Scant Living," *Oregonian* (Portland), August 22, 1947, 16.

82. "Quads Get 'Nest Egg.'"

83. Predmore, "Famous Alphabet Babies."

84. Predmore.

85. Predmore.

86. "Quads Get 'Nest Egg.'"

87. Predmore, "Famous Alphabet Babies."

88. Sullivan, "Healthy 1-Year-Olds"; and "Father 'Just Can't Seem to Quit Shaking.'"

89. "City Quads' Future Rosy as Portland Gifts Pour In," *Oregonian* (Portland), August 28, 1946, 7.

90. "Tigner Quadruplets Lined Up at Hospital for First Group Photo," *Oregonian* (Portland), September 1, 1946, 1.

91. "Real Fairy Godmother."

92. "Court Approves New Quad Names," *Oregonian* (Portland), September 24, 1946, 12.

93. "Tigner 'Big 4' Given Names," *Oregonian* (Portland), August 31, 1946, 1.

94. Predmore, "Famous Alphabet Babies."

95. Predmore.

96. Predmore.

97. Predmore.

98. "Spacious Home Awaiting Quads," *Oregonian* (Portland), October 23, 1946, 1; and Ann Sullivan, "Celebrated Tigner Quads Leave Hospital, Get Settled in Home," *Oregonian* (Portland), November 10, 1946, 20.

99. Predmore, "Famous Alphabet Babies."

100. "Court Okehs Quads' Home," *Oregonian* (Portland), November 1, 1946, 18.

101. "Court Okehs Quads' Home."

102. Sullivan, "Celebrated Tigner Quads Leave Hospital."

103. "Tigner Quads Triple Birth Weight at 6 Months," *Oregonian* (Portland), February 23, 1947, 15.

104. "Tigner Quads Go on View Sunday," *Oregonian* (Portland), February 22, 1947, 5.

105. "Tigner Quads Go on View Sunday."

106. Sullivan, "Celebrated Tigner Quads Leave Hospital."

107. Sullivan.

108. Sullivan, "Healthy 1-Year-Olds."

109. Sullivan.

110. Sullivan.

111. Sullivan.

112. Sullivan.

113. Sullivan.

114. S. E. Campian, "Quads' Dad Needs Job," *Oregonian* (Portland), February 4, 1948.

115. Campian, "Quads' Dad Needs Job."

116. Campian. Standardized tests are notoriously geared toward White cultural norms. Washington v. Davis, 426 U.S. 229 (1976); and Christopher Jencks and Meredith Phillips, "The Black-White Test Score Gap: Why It Persists and What Can Be Done," *Brookings* (March 1, 1998), https://www.brookings.edu /articles/the-black-white-test-score-gap-why-it-persists-and-what-can-be-done/.

117. Campian.

118. "Negro Father of Quadruplets Seeks Job to Earn Food for Many Hungry Mouths," *Oregonian* (Portland), February 5, 1948, 4.

119. "Many Hungry Mouths."

120. "Tigner Quadruplets to Celebrate 2d Birthday Sunday," *Oregonian* (Portland), August 22, 1948, 26.

121. "Tigner Quadruplets to Celebrate 2d Birthday Sunday."

122. "Quads' Father Faced by Suit," *Oregonian* (Portland), August 20, 1949, 4; "Tigner Quads, Portland's Only Set, to Celebrate Third Birthday," *Oregonian* (Portland), August 21, 1949; and "Father of Quads Bound to Jury," *Oregonian* (Portland), August 26, 1949, 10.

123. "Quads' Father Faced by Suit."

124. "Portland Tigner Quadruplets Don Neat Uniforms for First School Day," *Oregonian* (Portland), September 2, 1952, 11.

125. "First School Day."

126. "First School Day."

127. "First School Day."

128. "Tigner Quads Begin School in Portland," *Bend (OR) Bulletin*, September 2, 1952, 8.

129. "Quads Begin School."

130. "Tigner Quads Enter Teens as Healthy, Happy Children," *Oregonian* (Portland), January 6, 1960, 5.

131. "Tigner Quads to Hold Party," *Oregonian* (Portland), August 22, 1954, 31.

132. "Quads to Hold Party."

133. George Spagna, "Portland's Alphabet Quadruplets United for Day at Premature Birthday Party," *Oregonian* (Portland), August 5, 1955, 12.

134. Spagna, "Premature Birthday Party."

135. Spagna.

136. Spagna.

137. "Mother of Quads Held for Lye-Tossing Deed," *Oregonian* (Portland), July 6, 1956, 23.

138. "Mother of Quads Held"; "Assault Hearing Set for July 13," *Oregonian* (Portland), July 7, 1956, 7; "Victim's Condition Moves Back Lye-Throwing Case," *Oregonian* (Portland), July 14, 1956, 9; and "Lye Victim Signs Writ," *Oregonian* (Portland), July 28, 1956, 2.

139. "12 Convicted of Gambling," *Oregonian* (Portland), June 20, 1957, 13.

140. "Portland's First Quadruplets Now Normal, Happy-Go-Lucky 18-Year-Olds," *Oregonian* (Portland), November 19, 1964, 22

141. "Happy-Go-Lucky 18-Year-Olds."

142. "Happy-Go-Lucky 18-Year-Olds."

143. "Happy-Go-Lucky 18-Year-Olds."

144. Carnation, "Tigner Quads," advertisement, *Ebony*, May 1949, 8.

145. Carnation, "Tigner Quads."

146. Carnation.

147. Carnation.

148. Mangun and Parcell, "Pet Milk Company," 74.

149. Pet Milk, "Elzner Cave Family," advertisement, *Ebony*, September 1952, 89.

150. Pet Milk, "Elzner Cave Family,"; Pet Milk, "Griggs Family," advertisement, *Baltimore Afro-American*, April 14, 1953, 11; and Carnation, "Five Little Harringtons," advertisement, *Ebony*, April 1961, 115.

151. Enfamil, "Cow's Milk," advertisement, *Parents*, November 1976, 15.

152. Enfamil, "Cow's Milk." It is interesting that this ad acknowledges that cow's milk is for cows, not humans, but still uses it in its product.

153. Gerber, "What's Better than Formula?," advertisement, *Essence*, August 1984, 117.

154. Gerber, "We Hope You Breast-Feed," advertisement, *Ebony*, January 1991, 71.

155. Gerber, "We Hope You Breast-Feed."

156. Gerber, "She's Looking to You," advertisement, *Essence*, July 1993, 80.

157. Carnation, "After Graduation," advertisement, *Parents*, March 1995, 77.

158. Similac US, "She skipped a nap or two this weekend . . . and loved it. Don't judge me. (And I won't judge you.) How did you relax your own rules this week-

end? (We all do it, so we all get it.)," Facebook, November 2, 2015, https://www
.facebook.com/Similac/photos/a.980438458696210/1132894446783943.

159. Similac US, "Happy Mother's Day! Today and every day, Similac cele-
brates the strength of every mom," Facebook, May 14, 2017, https://www.face
book.com/Similac/photos/a.980438458696210/1697064013700314.

160. Enfamil, "The more belly badges the better, that's what we always say!
You can get a set when you join Enfamil Family Beginnings," Facebook, August 30, 2018, https://www.facebook.com/Enfamil/photos/a.4201203113881
94/1899881130078764.

161. Jennifer L. Harris et al., *Baby Food Facts: Nutrition and Marketing of
Baby and Toddler Food and Drinks* (Hartford: University of Connecticut Rudd
Center for Food Policy and Obesity, January 2017), 62–65, 70.

162. Similac (website), accessed November 28, 2018, https://similac.com/.

163. Enfamil (website), accessed November 28, 2018, https://www.enfamil
.com/.

164. Melissa Disney, "Similac Commercial the Mother 'Hood," YouTube,
2:38, October 4, 2016, https://www.youtube.com/watch?v=JUbGHeZCxe4.

165. Harris et al., *Baby Food Facts*, 83–84.

166. Corey H. Basch et al., "Prevalence of Infant Formula Advertisements
in Parenting Magazines Over a 5-Year Span," *Journal of Pediatric Nursing* 28
(July 31, 2013): e29, https://doi.org/10.1016/j.pedn.2013.07.001.

167. Kathleen Parry et al., "Understanding Women's Interpretations of Infant Formula Advertising," *Birth* 40, no. 2 (June 2013): 119–20, https://doi
.org/10.1111/birt.12044.

168. Ny MaGee, "Black History Forgotten: How the Fultz Quadruplets
Were Exploited by Pet Milk," *Inquisitr*, February 6, 2016, https://www.inquisitr
.com/2771496/black-history-forgotten-how-the-fultz-quadruplets-were
-exploited-by-pet-milk/.

169. "Four of a Kind, They're Healthy and Happy," *Plattsburgh (NY) Press-
Republican*, January 14, 1947; and Melba Newsome, "I Think It Was the Shots,"
O, The Oprah Magazine, April 1, 2005, 232.

170. Pet Milk, "Four Little Babies Become Four Little Ladies," advertisement, *Pittsburgh Courier*, October 22, 1949, 5.

171. "Fultz Quads Almost Ten Years Old!," *Pittsburgh Courier*, April 28,
1956, 7; and "Fultz Quads Celebrate 13th Birthday," *Ohio Sentinel* (Columbus),
June 20, 1959, 21.

172. "Fultz Quads in the News," *Pittsburgh Courier*, November 19,
1949, 16.

173. Pet Milk, "Good Milk for This Famous Four," advertisement, *Pittsburgh Courier*, August 5, 1950, 5.

174. Peters Park Music Festival, advertisement, *Bee* (Danville, VA), May 7,
1951, 11.

175. Chinwe, "The Fultz Sisters: The Fascinating and Tragic Story of America's First Identical Black Quadruplets," *Black Girl Long Hair* (blog), September 18, 2015, https://bglh-marketplace.com/2015/09/the-fultz-sisters-the-fascinating-and-tragic-story-of-americas-first-identical-black-quadruplets/comment-page-3/.

176. Hazel E. Rivera, "Their Big Desire Right Now Is a Piano," *Pittsburgh Courier*, September 27, 1952, 18; and Charles Stanback, "Fultz Quadruplets Enter N.C. School," *Baltimore Afro-American*, September 16, 1952, 1.

177. Rivera, "Their Big Desire Right Now."

178. Charles L. Sanders, "The Fultz Quads: Grown-Up, Disappointed and Bitter," *Ebony*, November 1968, 212–20.

179. Sanders, "Grown-Up, Disappointed and Bitter," 213.

180. Sanders, 217.

181. Newsome, "I Think It Was the Shots."

182. Newsome.

183. Frederick R. Klenner, "Observations on the Dose of Administration of Ascorbic Acid When Employed beyond the Range of a Vitamin in Human Pathology," *Journal of Applied Nutrition* 23 (1971): 61–88; and Newsome, "I Think It Was the Shots."

184. Lorraine Ahearn, "A Birthday Party with the Governor," *News & Record* (Greensboro, NC), August 4, 2002, http://www.greensboro.com/a-birthday-party-with-the-governor/article_c4aa1058-b794-5db1-b2e9-7ca5c53a6043.html.

185. Charles Stanback, "Fultz Quads Honored by Legislators," *Baltimore Afro-American*, April 18, 1953, 9; and "Quads All Named Mary Pay Visit to Legislature," *Statesville (NC) Record and Landmark*, April 13, 1953, 15.

186. Ahearn, "Birthday Party with the Governor."

187. Lorraine Ahearn, "Four Sisters, One Love," *News & Record* (Greensboro, NC), August 8, 2002, http://www.greensboro.com/four-sisters-one-love/article_cdccc43c-bd23-5e85-931f-2ad69c4a1f40.html.

188. Ahearn, "Four Sisters, One Love."

189. "World's Only Identical '4' Don Makeup, Sing for Pay," *Pittsburgh Courier*, May 1, 1954, 2.

190. "Quick Facts," About, National Mary Potter Club, accessed November 20, 2018, http://marypotter.org/about.htm.

191. Al Wheless, "Rev. Grover C. Hawley, Granville Educator, Leader, Dead at Age 82," *Daily Dispatch* (Henderson, NC), January 22, 1990, https://wakespace.lib.wfu.edu/bitstream/handle/10339/72859/MS615_Hawley_Grover_Cleveland_001.pdf.

192. "Don Makeup, Sing for Pay."

193. "Don Makeup, Sing for Pay."

194. "Don Makeup, Sing for Pay."

195. "Don Makeup, Sing for Pay."

196. "Don Makeup, Sing for Pay."

197. [Juanita Hall Visits Quads], *Pittsburgh Courier*, May 22, 1954, 18; and "Renown Foursome Reach Natal Milestone," *Ohio Sentinel* (Columbus), May 29, 1954.

198. "Juanita Hall," Masterworks Broadway, accessed November 20, 2018, http://www.masterworksbroadway.com/artist/juanita-hall/.

199. "Fultz Quads Fly," *Pittsburgh Courier*, August 13, 1955, 4; and Lorraine Ahearn, "From Madison, N.C., to Madison Ave.," *News & Record* (Greensboro, NC), August 4, 2002, http://www.greensboro.com/from-madison-n-c-to-madison-ave/article_e2389602-8fda-59c7-bc08-b99d73fd018c.html.

200. "History of the Chicago Defender Charities Bud Billiken Parade," Bud Billiken Parade, accessed November 20, 2018, http://www.budbillikenparade.org/about.

201. Peter Kendall and Terry Wilson, "Bud Billiken Day Not Just for Blacks," *Chicago Tribune*, August 12, 1990, http://articles.chicagotribune.com/1990-08-12/news/9003070701_1_first-parade-year-s-parade-duck-pond.

202. Ahearn, "From Madison, N.C., to Madison Ave."

203. "Owens Wins 4th Gold Medal," This Day in History, History.com, accessed November 20, 2018, https://www.history.com/this-day-in-history/owens-wins-4th-gold-medal.

204. "Fultz Quadruplets in Herbert Hope Bridal Party," *Pittsburgh Courier*, February 25, 1956, 16.

205. Ahearn, "From Madison, N.C., to Madison Ave."

206. Ahearn.

207. Ahearn.

208. Ahearn.

209. "Classic Officials Add Still Another 'Extra' to Dazzling Calendar," *St. Petersburg Times*, November 16, 1959, 14-B 1; "Famed Quads to Attend Orange Blossom Classic," *St. Petersburg Times*, November 18, 1959, 8-C; "Orange Blossom Classic Notable," *Ohio Sentinel* (Columbus), December 5, 1959, 30; and "Classic Quotes Show 'Best' Yet," *St. Petersburg Times*, December 25, 1959, 5-C.

210. Larry Schwartz, "Althea Gibson Broke Barriers," ESPN, accessed November 20, 2018, https://www.espn.com/sportscentury/features/00014035.html.

211. Frances M. Ward, "Seeing Double Times Two Famous Foursome Make Their Mark as World's First Black Quadruplets," *News & Record* (Greensboro, NC), May 22, 1990, http://www.greensboro.com/seeing-double-times-two-famous-foursome-make-their-mark-as/article_80d5c093-598c-55e1-8d39-32d59b090368.html.

212. Jae Jones, "Floyd Patterson: Youngest Heavyweight Champ Known as

the 'Gentleman of Boxing,'" *Black Then*, November 6, 2017, https://blackthen
.com/floyd-patterson-youngest-heavyweight-champ-known-as-the-gentleman
-of-boxing/.

213. Anna R. Hayes, *Without Precedent: The Life of Susie Marshall Sharp*
(Chapel Hill: University of North Carolina Press, 2008), 89.

214. Ahearn, "From Madison, N.C., to Madison Ave."

215. Newsome, "I Think It Was the Shots."

216. Sanders, "Grown-Up, Disappointed and Bitter," 216–17.

217. Lawrence Van Gelder, "Poppy Cannon White, 69, Dead; Writer Was
Authority on Food," *New York Times*, April 2, 1975, https://www.nytimes.com
/1975/04/02/archives/poppy-cannon-white-69-dead-writer-was-authority-on
-food.html; and "Walter Francis White and Poppy Cannon Papers," Beinecke
Rare Book & Manuscript Library, Yale University, June 2, 2009, http://beinecke
.library.yale.edu/about/blogs/african-american-studies-beinecke-library/2009
/06/02/walter-francis-white-and-poppy.

218. Van Gelder, "Poppy Cannon White"; and Kenneth Robert Janken,
Walter White: Mr. NAACP (Chapel Hill: University of North Carolina Press,
2003), 94.

219. "Walter White, 61, Dies in Home Here," *New York Times*, March 22,
1955, 30, https://www.nytimes.com/1955/03/22/archives/walteri1ite61-dies
-in-hoi-here-i-leader-in-civil-rights-fight-37.html.

220. Poppy Cannon, *The Can Opener Cookbook* (New York: Macfadden,
1952); and "Vintage Cookbook: Poppy Cannon's 'Can Opener Cookbook,'"
Huffington Post, February 5, 2013, https://www.huffingtonpost.com/2013/02
/05/vintage-cookbook-poppy-cannon_n_2616301.html.

221. Van Gelder, "Poppy Cannon White."

222. Lorraine Ahearn, "Corporate Adoptions, Golden Futures," *News
& Record* (Greensboro, NC), August 6, 2002, http://www.greensboro.com
/corporate-adoptions-golden-futures/article_2c63a2fb-0ab3-5ab7-860e
-f2adaa7a85b6.html.

223. "Here for a Few Days," *Pittsburgh Courier*, August 20, 1960, 15; and
Toki Schalk Johnson, "Mrs. Pinyon Cornish of D.C. Assumes President's Seat,"
Pittsburgh Courier, August 20, 1960, 18.

224. "Black History Fun Fact Friday—The Fultz Sisters," *The PBS Blog*, October 28, 2016, https://thepbsblog.com/tag/the-fultz-quadruplets/.

225. Ahearn, "Birthday Party with the Governor."

226. Ahearn, "Corporate Adoptions, Golden Futures."

227. Ahearn; and "Famous Fultz Quads, Now 16, Begin to Look Ahead for
Careers," *Baltimore Afro-American*, October 20, 1962, 6.

228. Lorraine Ahearn, "What Ever Happened to Alice's Baby?," *News &
Record* (Greensboro, NC), August 7, 2002, http://www.greensboro.com/what
-ever-happened-to-alice-s-baby/article_635ca64c-e1aa-585a-a6a6-c11871bff
bb0.html.

229. Ahearn, "What Ever Happened to Alice's Baby?"

230. Otis L. Hairston Jr., *Black America Series: Greensboro, North Carolina* (Charleston, SC: Arcadia, 2003), 8.

231. Ahearn, "What Ever Happened to Alice's Baby?"

232. Ahearn, "Corporate Adoptions, Golden Futures."

233. Ahearn, "What Ever Happened to Alice's Baby?"

234. Newsome, "I Think It Was the Shots."

235. Newsome.

236. Ahearn, "What Ever Happened to Alice's Baby?"

237. Ahearn.

238. Ahearn.

239. Newsome, "I Think It Was the Shots."

240. Ahearn, "Corporate Adoptions, Golden Futures."

241. "Quads Pay Visit Here," *Asheville (NC) Citizen-Times*, July 20, 1963, 3; and Ahearn, "Corporate Adoptions, Golden Futures."

242. Hayes, *Without Precedent*, 212; and Ahearn, "Corporate Adoptions, Golden Futures."

243. Ahearn.

244. Newsome, "I Think It Was the Shots."

245. Ahearn, "Corporate Adoptions, Golden Futures."

246. "Quads at White House," *Alton (IL) Evening Telegraph*, August 2, 1962, 2; "Identical Quads Visit President," *Daily Herald* (Chicago), August 2, 1962, 1; and "Quads at White House," *Pittsburgh Post-Gazette*, August 3, 1962, 23.

247. [Louise Prothro], *Pittsburgh Courier*, August 18, 1962, 8.

Chapter 4

1. Holly Yan, "'Hero' Security Guard Killed by Police Was Working Extra Shifts for His Son's Christmas," CNN, November 15, 2018, https://www.cnn.com/2018/11/15/us/chicago-area-security-guard-police-shooting/index.html.

2. Laura Westbrook, "Tamir Rice Shot 'within Two Seconds' of Police Arrival," November 27, 2014, BBC video, 1:44, https://www.bbc.com/news/av/world-us-canada-30220700/tamir-rice-shot-within-two-seconds-of-police-arrival.

3. Kimberly Wallace-Sanders, *Mammy: A Century of Race, Gender, and Southern Memory* (Ann Arbor: University of Michigan Press, 2008), 8.

4. Wallace-Sanders, *Mammy*, 2.

5. Shauna Weides, "Mammy, Jezebel, Sapphire, or Queen? Stereotypes of the African-American Female," *Skeptic Ink*, April 28, 2015, https://www.skepticink.com/gps/2015/04/28/mammy-jezebel-sapphire-or-queen-stereotypes-of-the-african-american-female/.

6. Regina Austin, "Sapphire Bound," *Wisconsin Law Review* 1989, no. 3 (1989): 570.

7. Austin, "Sapphire Bound," 570.

8. Wallace-Sanders, *Mammy*, 8.

9. Wallace-Sanders.

10. Wallace-Sanders.

11. Wallace-Sanders, 68–72; and Carolyn M. West, "Mammy, Jezebel, Sapphire, and Their Homegirls," in *Lectures on the Psychology of Women*, ed. Joan C. Chrisler, Carla Golden, and Patricia D. Rozee (Long Grove, IL: Waveland Press, 2008), 289.

12. Angela Onwuachi-Willig, *According to Our Hearts:* Rhinelander v. Rhinelander *and the Law of the Multiracial Family* (New Haven, CT: Yale University Press, 2013), 179–80.

13. David Pilgrim, "The Jezebel Stereotype," Jim Crow Museum, Ferris State University, July 2002, https://ferris.edu/HTMLS/news/jimcrow/jezebel/index.htm.

14. K. Sue Jewell, *From Mammy to Miss America and Beyond: Cultural Images and the Shaping of US Social Policy* (London: Routledge, 1993), 46.

15. Austin, "Sapphire Bound," 570; and West, "Mammy, Jezebel, Sapphire, and Their Homegirls," 294.

16. bell hooks, *Ain't I a Woman: Black Women and Feminism* (New York: South End Press, 1981), 33; and Deborah Gray White, *Ar'n't I a Woman? Female Slaves in the Plantation South* (New York: Norton, 1985), 28–30.

17. Emily West and R. J. Knight, "Mother's Milk: Slavery, Wet-Nursing and Black and White Women in the Antebellum South," *Journal of Southern History* 83, no. 1 (February 2017): 43, https://doi.org/10.1353/soh.2017.0001.

18. West, "Mammy, Jezebel, Sapphire, and Their Homegirls," 294–95.

19. West, 295; and Weides, "Mammy, Jezebel, Sapphire, or Queen?"

20. Patricia Hill Collins, *Black Feminist Thought: Knowledge, Consciousness, and the Politics of Empowerment* (New York: Routledge, 1991), 69–96. According to Tressie McMillan Cottom, "Controlling images have fallen a bit out of favor in the feminist literature, sometimes thought to be a taken-for-granted relic of older theory. But that is only if we confine our analysis to popular culture, where negative stereotypes do seem pedestrian. . . . Controlling images were never just about the object of study—popular culture memes or characters from movies and television shows—but about the process of reproducing structural inequalities in our everyday lives." *Thick: And Other Essays* (New York: The New Press, 2019).

21. Margaret E. Bentley, Deborah L. Dee, and Joan L. Jensen, "Breastfeeding among Low Income, African-American Women: Power, Beliefs and Decision Making," *Journal of Nutrition* 133, no. 1 (January 2003): 305S–07S, https://doi.org/10.1093/jn/133.1.305S.

22. Eisa Nefertari Ulen, "Black Women Do Breastfeed, Despite Intense Systemic Barriers in the U.S.," *Truthout*, August 26, 2016, http://www.truth-out

.org/news/item/37385-black-women-do-breastfeed-despite-intense-systemic
-barriers-in-the-us.

23. Kate Boyer, "Affect, Corporeality and the Limits of Belonging: Breast-feeding in Public in the Contemporary UK," *Health & Place* 18, no. 3 (May 2012): 552–60, https://doi.org/10.1016/j.healthplace.2012.01.010.

24. Austin, "Sapphire Bound," 539–40.

25. West, "Mammy, Jezebel, Sapphire, and Their Homegirls," 296.

26. West, 295–97; and Teri A. McMurtry-Chubb, "#SayHerName #Black WomensLivesMatter: State Violence in Policing the Black Female Body," *Mercer Law Review* 67, no. 3 (Winter 2016): 658.

27. David Pilgrim, "The Sapphire Caricature," Jim Crow Museum, Ferris State University, August 2008, https://ferris.edu/HTMLS/news/jimcrow/anti black/sapphire.htm.

28. McMurtry-Chubb, "#SayHerName," 657; and West, "Mammy, Jezebel, Sapphire, and Their Homegirls," 295–96.

29. Trina Jones and Kimberly Jade Norwood, "Aggressive Encounters & White Fragility: Deconstructing the Trope of the Angry Black Woman," *Iowa Law Review* 102, no. 5 (July 2017): 2049.

30. Jones and Norwood, "Aggressive Encounters & White Fragility," 2045–51.

31. Pamela J. Smith, "Teaching the Retrenchment Generation: When Sapphire Meets Socrates at the Intersection of Race, Gender, and Authority," *William & Mary Journal of Women and the Law* 6, no. 1 (Fall 1999): 114, 118.

32. White, *Ar'n't I a Woman?*, 176.

33. Emilie M. Townes, "From Mammy to Welfare Queen: Images of Black Women in Public-Policy Formation," in *Beyond Slavery: Overcoming Its Religious and Sexual Legacies*, ed. Bernadette J. Brooten (New York: Palgrave MacMillan, 2010), 61–63.

34. Ange-Marie Hancock, *The Politics of Disgust: The Public Identity of the Welfare Queen* (New York: New York University Press, 2004), 6.

35. Michele Estrin Gilman, "The Return of the Welfare Queen," *American University Journal of Gender, Social Policy & the Law* 22, no. 2 (Spring 2014): 258–61; Vivyan Adair, *From Good Ma to Welfare Queen: A Genealogy of the Poor Woman in American Literature, Photography, and Culture* (New York: Garland Publishing, 2000), 1–3; and Carly Hayden Foster, "The Welfare Queen: Race, Gender, Class, and Public Opinion," *Race, Gender & Class* 15, no. 3/4 (January 2008): 162–63.

36. Hancock, *Politics of Disgust*, 1–22.

37. Camille Gear Rich, "Reclaiming the Welfare Queen: Feminist and Critical Race Theory Alternatives to Existing Anti-Poverty Discourse," *Southern California Interdisciplinary Law Journal* 25, no. 2 (Spring 2016): 260–61.

38. George Bliss, "'Welfare Queen' Jailed in Tucson," *Chicago Tribune*, October 12, 1974, 3.

39. Josh Levin, "The Welfare Queen," *Slate*, December 19, 2013, http://www.slate.com/articles/news_and_politics/history/2013/12/linda_taylor_welfare_queen_ronald_reagan_made_her_a_notorious_american_villain.html.

40. Tonya L. Brito, "From Madonna to Proletariat: Constructing a New Ideology of Motherhood in Welfare Discourse," *Villanova Law Review* 44, no. 3 (April 1999): 415.

41. R. A. Lenhardt, "Black Citizenship through Marriage—Reflections on the Moynihan Report at Fifty," *Southern California Interdisciplinary Law Journal* 25, no. 2 (Spring 2016): 348–49.

42. Brito, "From Madonna to Proletariat," 418.

43. Kaaryn S. Gustafson, *Cheating Welfare: Public Assistance and the Criminalization of Poverty* (New York: New York University Press, 2011).

44. Laurel Parker West, "Soccer Moms, Welfare Queens, Waitress Moms, and Super Moms: Myths of Motherhood in State Media Coverage of Child Care During the Welfare Reforms of the 1990s," *Southern California Interdisciplinary Law Journal* 25, no. 2 (Spring 2016): 325.

45. Ann Cammett, "Welfare Queens Redux: Criminalizing Black Mothers in the Age of Neoliberalism," *Southern California Interdisciplinary Law Journal* 25, no. 2 (Spring 2016): 376–77.

46. Cammett, "Welfare Queens Redux," 376–77.

47. Cammett, 377–78.

48. Nina Bernstein, "Placing the Blame in an Infant's Death; Mother Faces Trial after Baby Dies from Lack of Breast Milk," *New York Times*, March 15, 1999, B1.

49. Dorothy Roberts, "Race, Gender, and the Value of Mothers' Work," *Social Politics* 2, no. 2 (July 1995): 195–96.

50. Roberts, "Value of Mothers' Work," 195–96.

51. Roberts, *Killing the Black Body*, 14.

52. Micki McElya, *Clinging to Mammy: The Faithful Slave in Twentieth-Century America* (Cambridge, MA: Harvard University Press, 2007), 9.

53. Melissa Harris-Perry, "Bad Black Mothers," *Nation: The Notion*, November 25, 2009, https://www.thenation.com/article/bad-black-mothers/.

54. Harris-Perry, "Bad Black Mothers."

55. National Housing Act, 12 U.S.C. § 1701 (1934).

56. Social Security Act, 42 U.S.C. §§ 1395 et seq. (1935).

57. Servicemen's Readjustment Act, 38 U.S.C. §§ 101 et seq. (1944).

58. Daniel Patrick Moynihan, *The Negro Family: The Case for National Action* (Washington, DC: US Department of Labor, 1965).

59. Moynihan, *Negro Family*, 6–14.

60. Moynihan, 29.

61. Moynihan, 9–14.

62. Charles Murray, *Losing Ground: American Social Policy, 1950–1980* (New York: BasicBooks, 1984).

63. Murray, *Losing Ground*, 228–33.

64. Murray, 228–33; and "Dethroning the Welfare Queen: The Rhetoric of Reform," *Harvard Law Review* 107, no. 8 (June 1994): 2024.

65. Murray, *Losing Ground*, 228–33.

66. Richard J. Herrnstein and Charles Murray, *The Bell Curve: Intelligence and Class Structure in American Life* (New York: Free Press Paperbacks, 1996), 130–37.

67. Herrnstein and Murray, *Bell Curve*, 523–26.

68. Rickie Solinger, *Beggars and Choosers: How the Politics of Choice Shapes Adoption, Abortion, and Welfare in the United States* (New York: Hill and Wang, 2001), 210–14.

69. Ira J. Chasnoff et al., "Cocaine Use in Pregnancy," *New England Journal of Medicine* 313, no. 11 (September 1985): 666–69.

70. Michael Winerip, "Retro Report: Revisiting the 'Crack Babies' Epidemic That Was Not," *New York Times* video, 10:09, May 20, 2013, https://www .nytimes.com/2013/05/20/booming/revisiting-the-crack-babies-epidemic -that-was-not.html.

71. Laura E. Gómez, *Misconceiving Mothers: Legislators, Prosecutors, and the Politics of Prenatal Drug Exposure* (Philadelphia: Temple University Press, 1997), 12–18.

72. Susan J. Douglas and Meredith Michaels, *The Mommy Myth: The Idealization of Motherhood and How It Has Undermined All Women* (New York: Free Press, 2004), 139.

73. Douglas and Michaels, *Mommy Myth*, 139.

74. Gómez, *Misconceiving Mothers*, 21–22.

75. Sarah Jaffe, "GOP's Bad Black Mother Myth: Meet the Modern-Day Welfare Queens," *Salon*, August 6, 2014, http://www.salon.com/2014/08/06 /gops_bad_black_mother_myth_meet_the_modern_day_welfare_queens/.

76. Priscilla A. Ocen, "Punishing Pregnancy: Race, Incarceration, and the Shackling of Pregnant Prisoners," *California Law Review* 100, no. 5 (October 2012): 1250–55; and Khiara M. Bridges, *Reproducing Race: An Ethnography of Pregnancy as a Site of Racialization* (Berkeley: University of California Press, 2011).

77. *Incarcerated Women and Girls* (Washington, DC: The Sentencing Project, 2015), 2.

78. Ocen, "Punishing Pregnancy," 1257–58, 1310.

79. Ocen, "Punishing Pregnancy," 1257; and Kebby Warner, "Pregnancy, Motherhood, and Loss in Prison: A Personal Story," in *Interrupted Life: Experiences of Incarcerated Women in the United States*, ed. Rickie Solinger, Paula C. Johnson, Martha L. Raimon, Tina Reynolds, and Ruby C. Tapia (Berkeley: University of California Press, 2010), 90–93.

80. *Trends in U.S. Corrections* (Washington, DC: The Sentencing Project, June 2018), 4.

81. *Incarcerated Women and Girls, 1980–2016* (Washington, DC: The Sentencing Project, May 2018), 1.

82. E. Ann Carson and Elizabeth Anderson, *Prisoners in 2015* (Washington, DC: US Department of Justice, December 2016), 13, 30, https://www.bjs.gov /content/pub/pdf/p15.pdf.

83. Franklin D. Gilliam Jr., "The 'Welfare Queen' Experiment," *Nieman Reports*, June 15, 1999, http://niemanreports.org/articles/the-welfare-queen -experiment/.

84. Gilliam Jr., "'Welfare Queen' Experiment."

85. Gilliam Jr.

86. Gilliam Jr.

87. Roberts, *Killing the Black Body*, 208.

88. Office of Family Assistance, *Characteristics and Financial Circumstances of TANF Recipients, Fiscal Year 2017* (Washington, DC: US Department of Health and Human Services, Office of Family Assistance, 2018), 23.

89. Office of Family Assistance, *Characteristics and Financial Circumstances*, 38.

90. "Distribution of the Nonelderly with Medicaid by Race/Ethnicity," State Health Facts, Henry J. Kaiser Family Foundation, accessed November 13, 2018, https://www.kff.org/medicaid/state-indicator/distribution-by-raceethnicity-4 /?currentTimeframe=0&sortModel=%7B%22colId%22:%22Location%22,%22 sort%22:%22asc%22%7D.

91. Tope Fadiran Charlton, "The Impossibility of the Good Black Mother," in *The Good Mother Myth: Redefining Motherhood to Fit Reality*, ed. Avital Norman Nathman (Berkeley, CA: Seal Press, 2014), 177–84.

92. Gustafson, *Cheating Welfare*, 157–63.

93. Michael Martin, "Mother Jailed for School Fraud, Flares Controversy," *NPR*, January 28, 2011, https://www.npr.org/2011/01/28/133306180 /Mother-Jailed-For-School-Fraud-Flares-Controversy.

94. Peter Applebome, "In a Mother's Case, Reminders of Educational Inequalities," *New York Times*, April 27, 2011, http://www.nytimes.com/2011/04 /28/nyregion/some-see-educational-inequality-at-heart-of-connecticut-case .html.

95. Kaaryn Gustafson, "Degradation Ceremonies and the Criminalization of Low-Income Women," *UC Irvine Law Review* 3, no. 2 (April 2013): 323.

96. Harris-Perry, "Bad Black Mothers."

97. Andres Jauregui, "Shanesha Taylor, Homeless Single Mom, Arrested after Leaving Kids in Car while on Job Interview," *Huffington Post*, March 28, 2014, http://www.huffingtonpost.com/2014/03/28/shanesha-taylor-homeless -mom-arrested_n_5050356.html.

98. Noah Remnick, "Debra Harrell and the Mythology of Bad Black Mothers," *LA Times*, July 18, 2014, http://www.latimes.com/opinion/opinion-la/la -ol-debra-harrell-mythology-black-mothers-20140718-story.html.

99. Kelly Wallace, "Mom Arrested for Leaving 9-Year-Old Alone at Park," CNN, July 21, 2014, https://www.cnn.com/2014/07/21/living/mom-arrested-left-girl-park-parents/index.html.

100. Wallace, "Mom Arrested."

101. Conor Friedersdorf, "Working Mom Arrested for Letting Her 9-Year-Old Play Alone at Park," *Atlantic*, July 15, 2014, https://www.theatlantic.com/national/archive/2014/07/arrested-for-letting-a-9-year-old-play-at-the-park-alone/374436/.

102. Radley Balko, "Grieving Mother Faces 36 Months in Jail for Jaywalking after Son Is Killed by Hit-and-Run Driver," *Huffington Post*, September 20, 2011, http://www.huffingtonpost.com/radley-balko/raquel-nelson-jail-for-jaywalking_b_905925.html.

103. Balko, "36 Months in Jail."

104. Jim O'Brien, "Black Women Are to Blame for Black Crime and Poverty," *Bacon, Books & Bullets*, accessed March 6, 2018, http://baconbooksandbullets.com/black-women-are-to-blame-for-black-crime-and-poverty/; and Ian Schwartz, "CNN's Don Lemon: Bill O'Reilly's Criticism of Black Community 'Doesn't Go Far Enough,'" *Real Clear Politics*, July 27, 2013, http://www.realclearpolitics.com/video/2013/07/27/cnns_don_lemon_bill_oreillys_criticism_of_black_community_doesnt_go_far_enough.html.

105. Monica Davey and Julie Bosman, "Protests Flare after Ferguson Police Officer Is Not Indicted," *New York Times*, November 24, 2014, https://www.nytimes.com/2014/11/25/us/ferguson-darren-wilson-shooting-michael-brown-grand-jury.html.

106. Jesse Lee Peterson, "Michael Brown: Bad Apple Doesn't Fall Far from Tree," *World Net Daily*, November 30, 2014, http://www.wnd.com/2014/11/michael-brown-bad-apple-doesnt-fall-far-from-tree/.

107. Shaila Dewan and Richard A. Oppel Jr., "In Tamir Rice Case, Many Errors by Cleveland Police, Then a Fatal One," *New York Times*, January 22, 2015, https://www.nytimes.com/2015/01/23/us/in-tamir-rice-shooting-in-cleveland-many-errors-by-police-then-a-fatal-one.html.

108. Sean Flynn, "The Tamir Rice Story: How to Make a Police Shooting Disappear," *GQ*, July 14, 2016, http://www.gq.com/story/tamir-rice-story.

109. Charlie LeDuff, "What Killed Aiyana Stanley-Jones?," *Mother Jones*, November/December 2010, https://www.motherjones.com/politics/2010/09/aiyana-stanley-jones-detroit/.

110. Jonathan Oosting, "Detroit Officer, Grandma Offer Conflicting Tales of Shot That Killed 7-Year-Old Aiyana Jones," *Michigan Live*, May 19, 2010, https://www.mlive.com/news/detroit/index.ssf/2010/05/detroit_officer_grandma_tell_c.html.

111. Tom Cleary, "Michelle Gregg: 5 Fast Facts You Need to Know," *Heavy*, May 30, 2016, https://heavy.com/news/2016/05/michelle-gregg-cincinnati-zoo-mother-mom-name-gorilla-harambe-facebook-photos-son-petition/; and

Carol Hood, "Stop Blaming Black Parents for Harambe's Death—Blame Zoos," *Establishment*, June 1, 2016, https://theestablishment.co/stop-blaming-black -parents-for-harambes-death-blame-zoos-3cc574788bc8#.e82sqn1u3.

112. "Justice for Harambe," Change.org, accessed March 6, 2018, https:// www.change.org/p/cincinnati-zoo-justice-for-harambe.

113. Aja Romano, "The Harambe Meme Is Still Going Strong. And It's about a Lot More Than a Dead Gorilla," *Vox*, September 13, 2016, https://www.vox .com/2016/8/17/12457468/harambe-meme-social-commentary-explained; and Charles Pulliam-Moore, "Your Favorite Harambe Memes Are Racist. It's Time to Stop Using Them," *Splinter News*, September 14, 2016, https://splinternews .com/your-favorite-harambe-memes-are-racist-its-time-to-sto-1793861858.

114. Tonia Thompson, "In the Wake of Tragedy, Black Parents Face a Racist Double Standard," *Medium: The Establishment*, June 17, 2016, https://medium .com/the-establishment/in-the-wake-of-tragedy-black-parents-face-a-racist -double-standard-f62c82653abf.

115. Laura Stampler, "Toddler Falls into Cheetah Pit after Parents Reportedly Dangle Him Over Railing," *Time*, April 13, 2015, http://time.com /3819153/cheetah-pit-cleveland-metroparks-zoo-child/.

116. Stephanie Land, "Free-Range Parenting Is a Privilege for the Rich and White," *Establishment*, August 8, 2016, https://theestablishment.co/free-range -parenting-is-a-privilege-for-the-white-and-affluent-1ac7ce8a4b8c#.ukwcrcb5z; and Lenore Skenazy, *Free-Range Kids: How to Raise Safe, Self-Reliant Children (without Going Nuts with Worry)* (San Francisco: Jossey-Bass, 2009).

117. Robin M. Boylorn, "Moonlight Musings & Motherhood: On Paula, Teresa, and the Complicated Role of Bad Black Mamas in Film," *Crunk Feminist Collective*, October 28, 2016, http://www.crunkfeministcollective.com/2016 /10/28/moonlight-musings-motherhood-on-paula-teresa-and-the-complicated -role-of-bad-black-mamas-in-film/.

118. Donald Bogle, *Toms, Coons, Mulattoes, Mammies, and Bucks: An Interpretive History of Blacks in American Films* (n.p.: Bloomsbury Academic, 2001).

119. W. Burlette Carter, "Finding the Oscar," *Howard Law Journal* 55, no. 1 (Fall 2011): 108.

120. Carter, "Finding the Oscar," 115–16.

121. "The Oscar Winners," *New York Times*, March 26, 1991, http://www .nytimes.com/1991/03/26/movies/the-oscar-winners.html.

122. Cerise L. Glenn and Landra J. Cunningham, "The Power of Black Magic: The Magical Negro and White Salvation in Film," *Journal of Black Studies* 40, no. 2 (November 2009): 137–40.

123. Glenn and Cunningham, "Power of Black Magic," 138.

124. Cole Delbyck, "The Most Memorable Best Actress Acceptance Speeches in Oscars History," *Huffington Post*, February 25, 2016, http://www.huffington post.com/entry/best-actress-oscars-speeches_us_56cb7667e4b0ec6725e3810b.

125. Shaun James, "How Halle Berry Tarnished the Image of Black

Women," *Black Freelance Writer* (blog), September 29, 2013, http://shawnsjames
.blogspot.com/2013/09/how-halle-berry-tarnished-image-of.html.

126. "Actor Says Monster's Ball Stereotypes Black Women," *Guardian*,
June 24, 2002, https://www.theguardian.com/film/2002/jun/24/news1.

127. LeRhonda S. Manigault-Bryant, Tamura A. Lomax, and Carol B. Dun-
can, eds., *Womanist and Black Feminist Responses to Tyler Perry's Productions*
(New York: Palgrave Macmillan, 2014); Brian C. Johnson, ed., *The Problematic
Tyler Perry* (New York: Peter Lang, 2016); and Gina Masullo Chen et al.,
"Male Mammies: A Social-Comparison Perspective on How Exaggeratedly Over-
weight Media Portrayals of Madea, Rasputia, and Big Momma Affect How Black
Women Feel about Themselves," *Mass Communication and Society* 15, no. 1
(January 2012): 115–35.

128. LeRhonda S. Manigault-Bryant, "'Don't Make Me Hop after You. . . .':
Black Womanhood and the Dangerous Body in Popular Film," in *Black Women
and Popular Culture: The Conversation Continues*, eds. Adria Y. Goldman,
VaNatta S. Ford, Alexa A. Harris, and Natasha R. Howard (Lanham, MD: Lex-
ington Books, 2014), 71–89.

129. Aneeka A. Henderson, "The Rebirth of Queer: Exile, Kinship and
Metamorphosis in Dee Rees' *Pariah*," in *African American Culture and Society after Rodney King: Provocations and Protests, Progression and Post-Racialism*,
eds. Josephine Metcalf and Carina Spaulding (Surrey, UK: Ashgate, 2015), 151.

130. "Oscars 2012: Octavia Spencer Wins Best Supporting Actress," *Guardian*, February 26, 2012, https://www.theguardian.com/film/2012/feb/27
/octavia-spencer-best-supporting-actress-oscar.

131. Armond White, "*Precious* Is the Most Damaging Film to the Black Image since *Birth of a Nation*," *Hip Hop & Politics*, November 19, 2009, http://
hiphopandpolitics.com/2009/11/19/armond-white-precious-is-the-most
-damaging-film-to-the-black-image-since-birth-of-a-nation/.

132. White, "Most Damaging Film."

133. White.

134. Claudia Miller, "The Welfare Mother and the Fat Poor: Stereotypical Images and the Success Narrative in Sapphire's *Push*," *Current Objectives of
Postgraduate American Studies* 14, no. 1 (2013): 1–15, https://doi.org/10.5283
/copas.162.

135. Harris-Perry, "Bad Black Mothers."

136. Darryl Lorenzo Wellington, "Sex, Race and *Precious*," *Dissent*, March 8,
2010, https://www.dissentmagazine.org/online_articles/sex-race-and-precious.

137. Ian Haney López, *Dog Whistle Politics: How Coded Racial Appeals
Have Reinvented Racism & Wrecked the Middle Class* (Oxford, UK: Oxford University Press, 2014).

138. Wellington, "Sex, Race and *Precious*."

139. A. O. Scott, "'Moonlight': Is This the Year's Best Movie?" *New York
Times*, October 20, 2016, https://www.nytimes.com/2016/10/21/movies

/moonlight-review.html; Hilton Als, "Moonlight; Undoes Our Expectations," *New Yorker*, October 24, 2016, http://www.newyorker.com/magazine/2016 /10/24/moonlight-undoes-our-expectations; David Sims, "Moonlight Is a Film of Uncommon Grace," *Atlantic*, October 26, 2016, https://www.theatlantic .com/entertainment/archive/2016/10/moonlight-barry-jenkins-review /505409/; and Peter Travers, "'Moonlight' Review: Story of African American Boy Growing Up Is a Gamechanger," *Rolling Stone*, October 19, 2016, http:// www.rollingstone.com/movies/reviews/peter-travers-moonlight-movie-review -w444552.

140. James Reed, "Too Nervous to Watch the Oscars Announcement, Naomie Harris Ends Up with a Supporting Actress Nomination," *LA Times*, January 24, 2017, http://www.latimes.com/entertainment/la-et-oscar-nominations -2017-live-too-nervous-to-watch-the-oscars-1485273042-htmlstory.html.

141. Cara Buckley, "Naomie Harris Explains How 'Moonlight' Avoided Crack Addict Stereotypes," *New York Times*, December 16, 2016; and Paula Rogo, "Moonlight's Naomie Harris on Why She Was Hesitant to Take a Role in This Powerful Movie," *Essence*, February 5, 2017, http://www.essence.com /celebrity/naomie-harris-hesistant-moonlight-role.

142. Buckley, "How 'Moonlight' Avoided Crack Addict Stereotypes."

143. Boylorn, "Moonlight Musings & Motherhood."

144. Another example of the nurturing, childless mother figure is Rose in *Fences*, a role for which Viola Davis also received a Best Supporting Actress nomination in 2017. Another is Ms. Rain, the kind social worker played by Paula Patton in *Precious*. Of course, there are some examples of good Black mothers in popular culture, including Julia, Claire Huxtable, the mother from *Good Times*, and Bow on *Black-ish*.

145. Harris-Perry, "Bad Black Mothers."

146. "Mother Pleads Guilty in Shaniya Davis' Death," *WRAL*, October 18, 2013, http://www.wral.com/mother-pleads-guilty-in-shaniya-davis-death/130 11614/.

147. Sammy Saltzman, "Shaniya Davis Found Dead; Mother Turned Little Girl into Sex Slave, Say Police," *CBS News*, November 16, 2009, https://www .cbsnews.com/news/shaniya-davis-found-dead-mother-turned-little-girl-into -sex-slave-say-police/.

148. Harris-Perry, "Bad Black Mothers."

149. Denene Millner, "Beyoncé Is Not the Magical Negro Mammy," *NPR: Code Switch*, February 15, 2017, http://www.npr.org/sections /codeswitch/2017/02/15/515060729/beyonce-is-not-the-magical-negro -mammy.

150. Mary Sauer, "Liv Tyler, Chrissy Teigan and More Celeb Moms Who Aren't Afraid to Breastfeed in Front of a Camera," *SheKnows*, August 17, 2016, https://www.sheknows.com/parenting/slideshow/4661/celeb-breastfeeding -selfies.

151. Ross Mcdonagh, "'This Is What My Body Is Made For': Proud Thandie Newton Posts Breastfeeding Selfie while at Festival with Her Two-Year-Old Son Booker," *Daily Mail*, July 18, 2016, https://www.dailymail.co.uk/tvshowbiz /article-3696047/Thandie-Newton-proudly-posts-selfie-breastfeeding-two -year-old-son-Booker-festival.html; Jocelyn Vena, "Kandi Burruss Just Revealed Her Unique Breastfeeding Style," *BravoTV*, January 20, 2016, http://www .bravotv.com/the-daily-dish/kandi-burruss-breastfeeding-baby-ace-pic; and Korey Lane, "Serena Williams Opened Up about Why She Stopped Breastfeeding, Hopefully Crushing the Stigma," *Romper*, May 31, 2018, https://www.romper .com/p/serena-williams-opened-up-about-why-she-stopped-breastfeeding-hope fully-crushing-the-stigma-9260245.

152. Ann Pride, "Breast Milk Is Best for Beyoncé! Singer Spotted Feeding Newborn Blue Ivy in Public," *Daily Mail*, March 1, 2012, http://www.dailymail .co.uk/tvshowbiz/article-2108734/Beyonc-spotted-breastfeeding-baby-Blue -Ivy-Carter-public.html.

153. "Beyonce's Instagram Pregnancy Photo Sets Record with Millions of Likes," Fox News, February 2, 2017, http://www.foxnews.com/tech/2017/02 /02/beyonces-instagram-pregnancy-photo-sets-record-with-millions-likes.html.

154. Beyoncé Knowles (@beyonce), "We would like to share our love and happiness. We have been blessed two times over. We are incredibly grateful that our family will be growing by two, and we thank you for your well wishes. —The Carters," Instagram photo, February 1, 2017, https://www.instagram.com/p /BP-rXUGBPJa/.

155. Knowles, "The Carters"; and Maane Khatchatourian, "Beyonce Announces She's Pregnant with Twins," *Variety*, February 1, 2017, http://variety .com/2017/music/news/beyonce-pregnant-twins-photo-1201975568/.

156. Olivier Laurent, "A Portrait Expert Analyzes Beyoncé's Pregnancy Photos," *Time: Lightbox*, February 2, 2017, http://time.com/4657982/beyonce -pregnant-2017-photo-analysis/.

157. Beyoncé Knowles (@beyonce), "Sir Carter and Rumi 1 Month today," Instagram photo, July 13, 2017, https://www.instagram.com/p/BWg8ZW yghFy/.

158. Steph Harmon, "Beyoncé Publishes Photo of Her Twins on Instagram," *Guardian*, July 14, 2017, https://www.theguardian.com/music/2017 /jul/14/beyonce-photo-twins-instagram-sir-carter-rumi.

159. Jonny Harvey (@JonnyHarvey3), Twitter, July 14, 2017, 1:57 a.m., https://twitter.com/jonny_harvey3/status/885785240400211968; Haiden (@new yorkscripts), Twitter, July 14, 2017, 12:10 a.m., https://twitter.com/newyork scripts/status/885758271042330628; and Lisa (@LittleLisaUSA), Twitter, July 14, 2017, 12:48 a.m., https://twitter.com/LittleLisaUSA/status/88576795 5362926592.

160. Kellee Terrell, "The Beyoncé Twins Backlash Proves Black Mothers Can't Get a Break," *Harper's Bazaar*, July 19, 2017, https://www.harpers

bazaar.com/culture/features/a10329274/beyonce-twins-instagram-photo
-backlash/; and Danielle Kwateng-Clark, "The Beyoncé Pregnancy Backlash Is
Unwarranted," *Essence*, February 4, 2017, https://www.essence.com/culture
/beyonce-pregnancy-backlash.

161. Terrell, "Beyoncé Twins Backlash"; and Amy Roberts, "Beyoncé's Baby
Photoshoots Aren't the Problem, You Are," *Bustle*, July 14, 2017, https://www
.bustle.com/p/beyonces-baby-photoshoots-arent-the-problem-you-are-70309.

162. Millner, "Magical Negro Mammy."

163. Millner.

164. Bernstein, "Placing the Blame," B1.

165. Bernstein, B3. One writer suggests that the delay reflected the deliberate policy of Rudolph Giuliani, who was mayor of New York at that time, to
make Medicaid more difficult to access, thereby cutting down on costs to the
city. Allan Whyte, "Young Mother Convicted of Criminally Negligent Homicide
in Her Baby's Death: New York Authorities Victimize the Victim," *World Socialist Web Site*, May 22, 1999, www.wsws.org/en/articles/1999/05/walr-m22
.html.

166. Bernstein, "Placing the Blame," B3.

167. Bernstein.

168. Nina Bernstein, "Mother Charged with Starving Baby Tells of Frantic
Effort to Save Him," *New York Times*, May 19, 1999, B5.

169. Bernstein, "Mother Charged with Starving Baby."

170. Bernstein; Bernstein, "Placing the Blame," B1.

171. Bernstein, "Mother Charged with Starving Baby."

172. "Report on Baby's Death Prompts Delay in Trial," *New York Times*,
March 18, 1999, B8.

173. Bernstein, "Placing the Blame," B3.

174. Kevin Helliker, "Dying for Milk," *Wall Street Journal*, July 22, 1994,
A1; I. A. Laing and C. M Wong, "Hypernatraemia in the First Few Days: Is
the Incidence Rising?," *Archives of Disease in Childhood—Fetal and Neonatal
Edition* 87, no. 3 (November 2002): F158–62; and Michael L. Moritz et al.,
"Breastfeeding-Associated Hypernatremia: Are We Missing the Diagnosis?," *Pe-
diatrics* 116 no. 3 (September 2005): e343–47.

175. Bernstein, "Placing the Blame," B3; and Sandra G. Boodman, "Discharged Too Soon?," *Washington Post*, June 27, 1995, https://www.washington
post.com/archive/lifestyle/wellness/1995/06/27/discharged-too-soon/1cb66
9dc-947b-4af8-8c16-9e3eb0d52a1e/?utm_term=.7290f8122581.

176. Bernstein, "Placing the Blame," B3.

177. Bernstein, B3; and Karen Augé, "Town's Ills an Uphill Struggle for
Practitioner," *Denver Post*, June 18, 2006, http://www.denverpost.com/news
/ci_3950524.

178. Augé, "Town's Ills."

179. Augé.

180. New Jersey and Maryland increased their minimum postnatal hospital stays. Stacey Burling, "One Day and Out the Door," *Chicago Tribune*, November 2, 1994, http://articles.chicagotribune.com/1994-11-02/news/9411030185_1_breast-feeding-robin- carter-dehydration; Mike Dorning, "Insurers Rush Out New Moms," *Chicago Tribune*, June 18, 1995, http://articles.chicagotribune.com/1995-06-18/news/9506180351_1_hospital-door-cost-conscious-insurance-companies-hours-of-hospital-care; and Ellen Meara et al., "Impact of Early Newborn Discharge Legislation and Early Follow-Up Visits on Infant Outcomes in a State Medicaid Population," *Pediatrics* 113, no. 6 (June 2004): 1619.

181. Rob Stein, "Race Gap Persists in Health Care, Three Studies Say," *Washington Post*, August 18, 2005, http://www.washingtonpost.com/wp-dyn/content/article/2005/08/17/AR2005081701437.html; and Vanessa Ho, "Doctors Treated Black Patients Worse in UW Study," *Seattle PI*, March 19, 2012, http://www.seattlepi.com/local/article/Doctors-treated-black-patients-worse-in-UW-study-3419063.php.

182. Bernstein, "Mother Charged with Starving Baby."

183. Nina Bernstein, "Bronx Woman Convicted in Starving of Her Breast-Fed Son," *New York Times*, May 20, 1999, B1.

184. Bernstein, "Placing the Blame," B3.

185. Bernstein, B3.

186. Bernstein, B3; and Karen Houppert, "Nursed to Death," *Salon*, May 21, 1999, www.salon.com/1999/05/21/nursing/.

187. "Jury Convicts Mother in Starved Baby Trial," CNN, May 19, 1999, http://www.cnn.com/US/9905/19/breastfeeding.trial.02/.

188. Rafael A. Olmeda and Marty Rosen, "Tot's Slow Death Recounted at Trial," *New York Daily News*, April 28, 1999, http://www.nydailynews.com/archives/news/tot-slow-death- recounted-trial-article-1.835343.

189. Houppert, "Nursed to Death."

190. Nina Bernstein, "Mother Convicted in Infant's Starvation Death Gets 5 Years' Probation," *New York Times*, September 9, 1999, B3.

191. Merle English, "Breast-Fed Infant's Death Sparks Debate," *Newsday*, May 29, 1999, http://www.newsday.com/news/new-york/queens-diary-breast-fed-infant-s-death-sparks-debate-1.239935; Rafael A. Olmeda, "Jurors See Photos of Starved Infant," *New York Daily News*, May 1, 1999, http://www.nydailynews.com/archives/news/jurors-photos-starved-infant-article-1.836938; Ikimulisa Sockwell-Mason, "Breast-Feeding Mom Recalls Watching Underfed Baby Die," *New York Post*, May 19, 1999, http://nypost.com/1999/05/19/breast-feeding-mom-recalls-watching-underfed-baby-die/; and Ikimulisa Sockwell-Mason, "Jurors Shaken by Pix of Infant Who Starved," *New York Post*, April 29, 1999, http://nypost.com/1999/04/29/jurors-shaken-by-pix-of-infant-who-starved/.

192. Olmeda, "Jurors See Photos."

193. Olmeda and Rosen, "Tot's Slow Death."

194. Sockwell-Mason, "Breast-Feeding Mom Recalls."

195. Sockwell-Mason, "Jurors Shaken by Pix."

196. Sockwell-Mason.

197. "Mother Arraigned in Starved Baby's Death," *New York Times*, May 30, 1998, B3; and Jake Pearson and Kevin Deutsch, "Mother Wrongly Accused of Murder after Her Baby Starved, Wins $2M Payday," *New York Daily News*, April 22, 2011, http://www.nydailynews.com/new-york/tatiana-cheeks-mother -wrongly-accused-murder-baby-starved-wins-2m-payday-article-1.111744.

198. Cara Buckley, "13 Years Later, a $2 Million Award," *New York Times*, April 23, 2011, A14.

199. Rachel L. Swarns, "Baby Starves, and Mother Is Accused of Homicide," *New York Times*, May 29, 1998, B3.

200. Buckley, "13 Years Later."

201. Pearson and Deutsch, "$2M Payday."

202. Bernstein, "5 Years' Probation."

203. Bernstein, "Bronx Woman Convicted."

204. Pearson and Deutsch, "$2M Payday."

205. Liena Gurevich, "Patriarchy? Paternalism? Motherhood Discourses in Trials of Crimes against Children," *Sociological Perspectives* 51, no. 3 (August 2008): 515–19, https://doi.org/10.1525/sop.2008.51.3.515; and Sandra Chung, "Mama Mia! How Gender Stereotyping May Play a Role in the Prosecution of Child Fatality Cases," *Whittier Journal of Child and Family Advocacy* 9, no. 1 (Fall 2009): 205–19.

206. For an excellent discussion of how narrative can serve to illuminate the experiences of Black women with the law, see Mario L. Barnes, "Race, Sex, and Working Identities: Black Women's Stories and the Criminal Law: Restating the Power of Narrative," *U.C. Davis Law Review* 39 (March 2006): 941.

207. Tabitha's story is also about the criminalization of Black mothers. This criminalization begins in pregnancy and continues throughout motherhood, justifying the prosecution and punishment of Black mothers. Kimberlé W. Crenshaw, "From Private Violence to Mass Incarceration: Thinking Intersectionally about Women, Race, and Social Control," *UCLA Law Review* 59, no. 6 (August 2012): 1418; Paula C. Johnson, "At the Intersection of Injustice: Experiences of African American Women in Crime and Sentencing," *American University Journal of Gender and the Law* 4, no. 1 (Fall 1995): 1; Ocen, "Punishing Pregnancy," 1239; Dorothy E. Roberts, "Prison, Foster Care, and the Systemic Punishment of Black Mothers," *UCLA Law Review* 59, no. 6 (August 2012): 1474; and Dorothy E. Roberts, "Punishing Drug Addicts Who Have Babies: Women of Color, Equality, and the Right of Privacy," *Harvard Law Review* 104, no. 7 (May 1991): 1419.

208. Katie Allison Granju, "Formula for Disaster," *Salon*, July 20, 1999, http://www.salon.com/1999/07/20/formula2/.

209. Jane D. Brown and Sheila Rose Pechaud, "Media and Breastfeeding: Friend or Foe," *International Breastfeeding Journal* 3, no. 1 (August 2008): 2.

210. This phenomenon operates in a variety of social contexts and across many racial lines. For example, when terrorists perpetrated the attacks on the United States on September 11, 2001, some individuals and government authorities began to view all people who fit their perception of someone who is "Muslim" as terrorists. Muneer I. Ahmad, "A Rage Shared by Law: Post September 11 Racial Violence as Crimes of Passion," *California Law Review* 92, no. 5 (October 2004): 1259; Jon Tehranian, "Compulsory Whiteness: Towards a Middle Eastern Legal Scholarship," *Indiana Law Journal* 82, no. 1 (Winter 2007): 1; and Leti Volpp, "The Citizen and the Terrorist," *UCLA Law Review* 49, no. 5 (June 2002): 1575. This classification, based on appearance alone, swept in a wide range of people of Middle Eastern and South Asian descent. It made them vulnerable to violent racist attacks, broad discrimination, and covert surveillance. In contrast, when Whites perpetrate terrorist attacks, such as mass shootings or the 1995 bombing of the Oklahoma City federal building, the media portrays them as sick, sometimes even sympathetic, individuals. They do not become representatives of their race. When Timothy McVeigh, a White man, detonated a bomb in front of the Oklahoma City federal building, society viewed him as an anomaly. He was not representative of his race, and people did not begin to perceive all Whites, by extension, as murderous terrorists. Melanie E. L. Bush, *Everyday Forms of Whiteness: Understanding Race in a Post-Racial World* (Lanham: Rowman & Littlefield, 2011), 92–93.

211. Annalisa Merelli, "'Lone Wolf' vs 'Terrorist': The Vocabulary of Mass Shootings," *Quartz*, October 2, 2017, https://qz.com/1092042/las-vegas-shooting-terrorist-vs-lone-wolf/.

212. *Chicago Hope*, season 5, episode 4, "The Breast and the Brightest," directed by Martha Mitchell, written by David E. Kelley, aired October 21, 1998, on CBS.

213. Bentley, Dee, and Jensen, "Power, Beliefs, and Decision Making," 305S–6S; and Granju, "Formula for Disaster."

214. Susan Gonzalez, "Director Spike Lee Slams 'Same Old' Black Stereotypes in Today's Films," *Yale Bulletin & Calendar* 29, no. 21 (2001); and Cesar G. Victora et al., "Breastfeeding in the 21st Century: Epidemiology, Mechanisms, and Lifelong Effect," *Lancet* 387, no. 10017 (January 2016): 485.

215. Editorial, "Breastfeeding: Achieving the New Normal," *The Lancet* 387, no. 10017 (January 30, 2016).

Chapter 5

1. CVS (website), accessed November 29, 2018, https://www.cvs.com/shop/cvs-health-advantage-infant-formula-with-iron-milk-based-powder-stage-2-35-oz-prodid-992225?skuId=992225.

2. CVS (website).

3. Tara Swenson, "Insuring a Healthier Society: The Need for Breastfeeding Promotion and Support through Private Insurance and Government Initiatives," *Kansas Journal of Law & Public Policy* 16, no. 1 (Fall 2006): 20, 25, 35, 39–40.

4. "Guide to UK Formula Marketing Rules—Product Labelling," Baby Milk Action, accessed April 3, 2018, http://www.babymilkaction.org/ukrules-pt4.

5. Jenny Hope, "Baby Formula Milk Should Have Cigarette-Style Health Warnings Telling Mothers Breast Is Best, Says Top Charity," *Daily Mail*, February 17, 2013, http://www.dailymail.co.uk/health/article-2280270/Baby -formula-milk-cigarette-style-health-warnings-telling-mothers-breast-best-says -charity.html; and Valerie Delp, "Should Formula Cans Contain Warning Labels?" *Families* (blog), accessed April 3, 2018, https://www.families.com/should -formula-cans-contain-warning-labels.

6. Ruth Marcus, "Lobbying Fight over Infant Formula Highlights Budget Gridlock," *Washington Post*, July 14, 2010, http://www.washingtonpost.com /wp-dyn/content/article/2010/07/13/AR2010071304634.html.

7. "Women, Infants, and Children," Food and Nutrition Service, US Department of Agriculture, last modified October 17, 2018, https://www.fns.usda .gov/wic/women-infants-and-children-wic.

8. George Kent, "WIC's Promotion of Infant Formula in the United States," *International Breastfeeding Journal* 1, no. 1 (April 2006): 8–9, https://doi.org /10.1186/1746-4358-1-8.

9. "WIC Participant and Program Characteristics 2014 (Summary)," Food and Nutrition Service, US Department of Agriculture, November 2015, https:// fns-prod.azureedge.net/sites/default/files/ops/WICPC2014-Summary.pdf.

10. "Frequently Asked Questions about WIC," Food and Nutrition Service, US Department of Agriculture, accessed April 20, 2018, https://www.fns.usda .gov/wic/frequently-asked-questions-about-wic.

11. "WIC Participant and Program Characteristics."

12. "WIC Participant and Program Characteristics."

13. "Quick Facts: United States," US Census Bureau, accessed November 23, 2018, https://www.census.gov/quickfacts/fact/table/US/PST045217 #PST045217.

14. "Quick Facts: United States."

15. "About WIC—WIC at a Glance," Food and Nutrition Service, US Department of Agriculture, last modified February 27, 2015, https://www.fns.usda .gov/wic/about-wic-wic-glance.

16. Katherine M. Jones et al., "Racial and Ethnic Disparities in Breastfeeding," *Breastfeeding Medicine* 10, no. 4 (May 2015): 189–90, https://doi.org /10.1089/bfm.2014.0152.

17. Alan S. Ryan and Wenjun Zhou, "Lower Breastfeeding Rates Persist among the Special Supplemental Nutrition Program for Women, Infants, and

Children Participants, 1978–2003," *Pediatrics* 117, no. 4 (April 2006): 1140–43, https://doi.org/10.1542/peds.2005-1555.

18. Steven J. Haider, Alison Jacknowitz, and Robert F. Schoeni, "Welfare Work Requirements and Child Well-Being: Evidence from the Effects on Breastfeeding," *Demography* 40, no. 3 (August 2003): 491–92, https://doi.org/10.1353/dem.2003.0023.

19. "Breastfeeding Report Card," Centers for Disease Control and Prevention, 2016, https://www.cdc.gov/breastfeeding/pdf/2016breastfeedingreportcard.pdf.

20. Cecilia E. Barbosa et al., "Factors Distinguishing Positive Deviance among Low-Income African American Women: A Qualitative Study on Infant Feeding," *Journal of Human Lactation* 33, no. 2 (May 2017): 375, https://doi.org/10.1177/0890334416673048.

21. Barbosa et al., "Positive Deviance," 375.

22. "WIC at a Glance."

23. Kent, "WIC's Promotion," 13.

24. Steven Carlson, Robert Greenstein, and Zoë Neuberger, "WIC's Competitive Bidding Process for Infant Formula Is Highly Cost-Effective," Food Assistance, Center on Budget and Policy Priorities, February 17, 2017, https://www.cbpp.org/research/food-assistance/wics-competitive-bidding-process-for-infant-formula-is-highly-cost.

25. Carlson, Greenstein, and Neuberger, "Competitive Bidding."

26. Carlson, Greenstein, and Neuberger.

27. Carlson, Greenstein, and Neuberger.

28. George Kent, "The High Price of Infant Formula in the United States," *AgroFOOD Industry Hi-Tech* 17, no. 5 (September/October 2006): 1.

29. Carlson, Greenstein, and Neuberger, "Competitive Bidding."

30. "Frequently Asked Questions about WIC."

31. Kent, "High Price," 1.

32. Kent, 2.

33. Kent, "WIC's Promotion," 12.

34. Kent, "High Price," 1–2; and Carlson, Greenstein, and Neuberger, "Competitive Bidding."

35. Victor Oliveira and Mark Prell, "Sharing the Economic Burden: Who Pays for WIC's Infant Formula," Economic Research Service, US Department of Agriculture, September 1, 2004, https://www.ers.usda.gov/amber-waves/2004/september/sharing-the-economic-burden-who-pays-for-wics-infant-formula/.

36. "Enfamil Infant Formula Powder 12.5 oz. Canister," Walmart, accessed March 5, 2018, https://www.walmart.com/ip/Enfamil-trade-Infant-Formula-Powder-12-5-oz-Canister/16940594.

37. Amber, "How Long Would 1 Tub of Formula Last a Baby!?," *Baby Center Community* (blog), February 12, 2012, https://community.babycenter.com/post/a31661809/%20how_long_would_1_tub_of_formula_last_a_baby.

38. Andrea Freeman, "'First Food' Justice: Racial Disparities in Infant Feeding as Food Oppression," *Fordham Law Review* 83, no. 6 (May 2015): 3062.

39. Freeman, "'First Food' Justice," 3062.

40. Adam Burtle and Stephen Bezruchka, "Population Health and Paid Parental Leave: What the United States Can Learn from Two Decades of Research," *Healthcare* 4, no. 2 (June 2016): 30, 37–40, https://doi.org/10.3390/healthcare4020030.

41. Haider, Jacknowitz, and Schoeni, "Welfare Work Requirements," 495.

42. Haider, Jacknowitz, and Schoeni, 495; and Pamela A. Morris, "The Effects of Welfare Reform Policies on Children," *Social Policy Report* 16, no. 1 (March 2002): 1–4.

43. "Frequently Asked Questions about WIC."

44. Loving Support, US Department of Agriculture, accessed April 3, 2018, https://wicbreastfeeding.fns.usda.gov/.

45. Elizabeth Brand, Catherine Kothari, and Mary Ann Stark, "Factors Related to Breastfeeding Discontinuation between Hospital Discharge and 2 Weeks Postpartum," *Journal of Perinatal Education* 20, no. 1 (Winter 2011): 36–44, https://doi.org/10.1891/1058-1243.20.1.36.

46. Ginna Wall, *Outcomes of Breastfeeding versus Formula Feeding* (Bellevue, WA: Evergreen Perinatal Education, 2013), https://www.evergreenperinatal education.com/upload/OutcomesofBreastfeeding_Nov2013.pdf.

47. Agricultural Act of 2014, 7 U.S.C. § 9051 (2015).

48. Michael Pollan, "You Are What You Grow," *New York Times Magazine*, April 22, 2007, http://michaelpollan.com/articles-archive/you-are-what-you-grow/.

49. David Lawder and Ben Blanchard, "Trump Sets Tariffs on $50 Billion in Chinese Goods; Beijing Strikes Back," *Reuters*, June 14, 2018, https://www.reuters.com/article/us-usa-trade-china-ministry/trump-sets-tariffs-on-50-billion-in-chinese-goods-beijing-strikes-back-idUSKBN1JB0KC.

50. Shuping Niu, "China Targets U.S. Farm Imports with Tariffs on Soy, Corn," *Bloomberg*, June 15, 2018, https://www.bloomberg.com/news/articles/2018-06-15/china-targets-u-s-farm-imports-with-tariffs-on-soybeans-corn.

51. Jeff Daniels, "Fear of 'Disastrous Situation' in Farm Economy as China Targets Huge US Soybean Business," *CNBC*, April 4, 2018, https://www.cnbc.com/2018/04/04/uneasiness-spreads-in-farm-economy-with-china-targeting-us-soybeans.html.

52. Niu, "China Targets U.S."

53. Andrea Freeman, "The Unbearable Whiteness of Milk: Food Oppression and the USDA," *UC Irvine Law Review* 3, no. 4 (December 2013): 1266–68.

54. Freeman, "'First Food' Justice," 3068.

55. Jessica Hopper, "Formula for Theft Success: Steal Food for a Baby," *ABC News*, April 13, 2011, http://abcnews.go.com/US/baby-formula-targeted-organized-retail-theft-rings/story?id=13293485.

56. M. Claire Donnelly, "Baby Formula: How Theft-Rings Impact an Entire Generation," *Civil Rights Clinic* (blog), Charlotte School of Law, October 2, 2014, https://cslcivilrights.com/2014/10/02/baby-formula-how-theft-rings-impact -an-entire-generation/ (site discontinued).

57. Kaaryn S. Gustafson, *Cheating Welfare: Public Assistance and the Criminalization of Poverty* (New York: New York University Press, 2011).

58. "There's a Thriving Black Market for Baby Formula," *New York Post*, January 7, 2016, https://nypost.com/2016/01/07/theres-a-thriving-black-market -for-baby-formula/.

59. Marcus, "Lobbying Fight."

60. Marcus.

61. Steven Abrams, "FDA Proposes Guidelines for Infant Formula Product Claims," *Dell Medical School* (blog), University of Texas, December 6, 2016, http://blog.dellmedschool.utexas.edu/2016/12/06/fda-proposes-guidelines -for-infant-formula-product-claims/.

62. Personal Responsibility and Work Opportunity Reconciliation Act, Pub. L. No. 104-193, 110 Stat. 2105 (1996).

63. Aid to Families with Dependent Children, 42 U.S.C. §§ 601 et seq. (1935); and Temporary Assistance for Needy Families, 42 U.S.C. §§ 601 et seq. (1996).

64. 42 U.S.C. § 601(a).

65. According to a study published in 2015, 78 percent of White children are living in a nuclear family (that is, a two-parent household), a stark contrast to the 43 percent of Latinx children and 38 percent of Black children who live in a nuclear family. "Parenting in America," Pew Research Center, December 17, 2015, http://www.pewsocialtrends.org/2015/12/17/1-the-american-family-today/.

66. "Parenting in America."

67. Paula Goodwin, Brittany McGill, and Anjani Chandra, "Who Marries and When? Age at First Marriage in the United States: 2002," National Center for Health Statistics, June 2009, https://www.cdc.gov/nchs/data/databriefs /db19.pdf.

68. Angela Onwuachi-Willig, *According to Our Hearts:* Rhinelander v. Rhinelander *and the Law of the Multiracial Family* (New Haven, CT: Yale University Press, 2013), 128.

69. Gretchen Livingston and Anna Brown, *Intermarriage in the U.S. 50 Years after* Loving v. Virginia (Washington, DC: Pew Research Center, May 18, 2017), 6.

70. Gretchen Livingston and Anna Brown, *Intermarriage in the U.S. 50 Years after Loving v. Virginia* (Washington, DC: Pew Research Center, 2017), 22. For earlier statistics and insightful analysis of this phenomenon, see Onwuachi-Willig, *According to Our Hearts*, 126; Renee C. Romano, *Race Mixing: Black-White Marriage in Postwar America* (Cambridge, MA: Harvard University Press, 2003), 218.

71. Goodwin, McGill, and Chandra, "Who Marries and When?"

72. *An Introduction to TANF* (Washington, DC: Center on Budget and Policy Priorities, 2015), 4, https://www.cbpp.org/research/policy-basics-an-intro duction-to-tanf.

73. *Introduction to TANF*, 4.

74. 42 U.S.C. § 607(b)(5).

75. *Background Material and Data on the Programs within the Jurisdiction of the Committee on Ways and Means (Green Book): Section 8. Aid to Families with Dependent Children and Related Programs* (Washington, DC: Government Publishing Office, 2000), 383, 411.

76. "Work Rules and Penalties," Michigan Department of Health and Human Services, accessed February 9, 2018, http://www.michigan.gov/mdhhs /0,5885,7-339-71547_5526_7028_7064-280420—,00.html.

77. Chris M. Herbst, "Are Parental Welfare Work Requirements Good for Disadvantaged Children? Evidence from Age-of-Youngest-Child Exemptions," *Journal of Policy Analysis and Management* 36, no. 2 (March 2017): 330.

78. Herbst, "Parental Welfare," 330–32.

79. Haider, Jacknowitz, and Schoeni, "Welfare Work Requirements," 479–97.

80. Haider, Jacknowitz, and Schoeni, 480; and Jacqueline H. Wolf, "Low Breastfeeding Rates and Public Health in the United States," *American Journal of Public Health* 93, no. 12 (December 2003): 2000–2007, https://doi.org /10.2105/AJPH.93.12.2000.

81. Debbie L. Montgomery and Patricia L. Splett, "Economic Benefit of Breast-Feeding Infants Enrolled in WIC," *Journal of the American Dietetic Association* 97, no. 4 (Summer 1997): 379–85, https://doi.org/10.1016/S0002 -8223(97)00094-1; Cynthia Reeves Tuttle and Kathryn G. Dewey, "Potential Cost Savings for Medi-Cal, AFDC, Food Stamps, and WIC Programs Associated with Increasing Breast-Feeding among Low-Income Hmong Women in California," *Journal of the Academy of Nutrition and Dietetics* 96, no. 9 (September 1996): 885–89, https://doi.org/10.1016/S0002-8223(96)00241-6; and Haider, Jacknowitz, and Schoeni, "Welfare Work Requirements," 495.

82. Haider, Jacknowitz, and Schoeni, "Welfare Work Requirements," 495.

83. Haider, Jacknowitz, and Schoeni, 494–95.

84. Burtle and Bezruchka, "Population Health," 30, 37–40.

85. Burtle and Bezruchka, 37–38. Analyzing data from an infant-feeding-practices study from before and after California implemented its paid family leave law, researchers found a 3 to 5 percent increase in exclusive breastfeeding at three and six months, and a 10 to 20 percent increase for some breastfeeding at the three-, six-, and nine-month marks. Burtle and Bezruchka, 37–38. Researchers also found that welfare-reform work requirements "substantially and statistically significantly reduce breastfeeding." Haider, Jacknowitz, and Schoeni, "Welfare Work Requirements," 494.

86. These results provide support for modeling US policies after ones in place in Canada and other countries where employers must provide a full year of maternity leave. Morris, "Welfare Reform Policies," 1–4.

87. Morris, 1–4.

88. Haider, Jacknowitz, and Schoeni, "Welfare Work Requirements," 481; and *Chart Book: Temporary Assistance for Needy Families* (Washington, DC: Center on Budget and Policy Priorities, August 21, 2018), https://www.cbpp.org/sites/default/files/atoms/files/8-22-12tanf_0.pdf.

89. Haider, Jacknowitz, and Schoeni, "Welfare Work Requirements," 481; and *Chart Book*, 2.

90. *Chart Book*, 11; and Jeffrey Grogger et al., "Consequences of Welfare Reform: A Research Synthesis," US Department of Health and Human Services, July 2002, https://www.acf.hhs.gov/sites/default/files/opre/consequences_of_welfare_reform.pdf.

91. Haider, Jacknowitz, and Schoeni, "Welfare Work Requirements," 495.

92. Ann Cammett, "Deadbeat Dads & Welfare Queens: How Metaphor Shapes Poverty Law," *Boston College Journal of Law and Social Justice* 34, no. 2 (Spring 2014): 233–66.

93. Cammett, "Deadbeat Dads & Welfare Queens," 261; Nathan J. Robinson, "It Didn't Pay Off," *Jacobin*, October 1, 2016, https://www.jacobinmag.com/2016/10/clinton-welfare-reform-prwora-tanf-lillie-harden/; and Francis X. Clines, "Clinton Signs Bill Cutting Welfare," *New York Times*, August 23, 1996, http://www.nytimes.com/1996/08/23/us/clinton-signs-bill-cutting-welfare-states-in-new-role.html.

94. Josh Levin, "The Welfare Queen," *Slate*, December 19, 2013, http://www.slate.com/articles/news_and_politics/history/2013/12/linda_taylor_welfare_queen_ronald_reagan_made_her_a_notorious_american_villain.html; Sarah Jaffe, "GOP's Bad Black Mother Myth: Meet the Modern-Day Welfare Queens," *Salon*, August 6, 2014, http://www.salon.com/2014/08/06/gops_bad_black_mother_myth_meet_the_modern_day_welfare_queens/; Melissa Harris-Perry, "Bad Black Mothers," *Nation: The Notion*, November 25, 2009, https://www.thenation.com/article/bad-black-mothers/; Cammett, "Deadbeat Dads & Welfare Queens," 255–56; Michele Estrin Gilman, "The Return of the Welfare Queen," *American University Journal of Gender, Social Policy & the Law* 22, no. 2 (Spring 2014): 247; Vivyan Adair, *From Good Ma to Welfare Queen: A Genealogy of the Poor Woman in American Literature, Photography, and Culture* (New York: Garland Publishing, 2000); Ange-Marie Hancock, "Contemporary Welfare Reform and the Public Identity of the 'Welfare Queen,'" *Race, Gender & Class* 10, no. 1 (January 2003): 31–59; and Franklin D. Gilliam Jr., "The 'Welfare Queen' Experiment," *Nieman Reports*, June 15, 1999, http://niemanreports.org/articles/the-welfare-queen-experiment/.

95. "When presented with the image of a Black mother on welfare, viewers commonly attributed her need for benefits to her own personal failings instead

of to public policy, historical discrimination, or any other structural factor." Andrea Freeman, "Racism in the Credit Card Industry," *North Carolina Law Review* 95, no. 4 (May 2017): 1112–13; and Hancock, "Contemporary Welfare Reform," 31–59.

96. Franklin D. Gilliam Jr., *The Architecture of a New Racial Discourse* (Washington, DC: Frameworks Institute, 2006), 11–13.

97. WHO, *International Code of Marketing of Breast-Milk Substitutes* (Geneva: World Health Organization, 1981); and Dale D. Murphy, "Interjurisdictional Competition and Regulatory Advantage," *Journal of International Economic Law* 8, no. 4 (2005): 913, https://doi.org/10.1093/jiel/jgi050.

98. Murphy, "Interjurisdictional Competition," 913.

99. Murphy, 914–15.

100. Murphy, 914–15.

101. Cynthia Howard et al., "Office Prenatal Formula Advertising and Its Effect on Breast-Feeding Patterns," *Obstetrics & Gynecology* 95, no. 2 (2000): 296.

102. Howard et al., "Prenatal Formula Advertising," 297.

103. *International Code*, 10.

104. *International Code*, 10.

105. *International Code*, 10–12.

106. Kent, "WIC's Promotion," 14.

107. Kent, 14.

108. 08. Anuradha Rao-Patel, "The Truth about Drug Companies' Influence on Your Doctor's Prescriptions," *Industry Perspectives* (blog), Blue Cross Blue Shield of North Carolina, May 15, 2018, http://blog.bcbsnc.com/2018/05/truth-drug-companies-influence-doctors-prescriptions/.

109. Deborah Kaplan and Kristina Graff, "Marketing Breastfeeding—Reversing Corporate Influence on Infant Feeding Practices," *Journal of Urban Health* 85, no. 4 (July 2008): 486–89, https://doi.org/10.1007/s11524-008-9279-6.

110. Kimberly Seals Allers, *The Big Letdown: How Medicine, Big Business, and Feminism Undermine Breastfeeding* (New York: St. Martin's Press, 2017).

111. Allers, *Big Letdown*, 14–16.

112. Kelly Winder, "9 Sneaky Ways Formula Companies Try to Sell Formula to You," *Belly Belly*, December 19, 2015, https://www.bellybelly.com.au/baby/sneaky-ways-formula-companies-try-to-win-you-over/.

113. Rebecca Schuman, "This Viral Formula Ad Absolves You for Using Formula," *Slate*, June 4, 2015, http://www.slate.com/articles/double_x/doublex/2015/06/a_century_of_formula_advertising_it_s_always_gone_straight_for_the_new_mother.html.

114. Kenneth D. Rosenberg et al., "Marketing Infant Formula through Hospitals: The Impact of Commercial Hospital Discharge Packs on Breastfeeding," *American Journal of Public Health* 98, no. 2 (February 2008): 290,

https://doi.org/10.2105/AJPH.2006.103218; and Kaplan and Graff, "Marketing Breastfeeding," 489.

115. Rosenberg et al., "Marketing Infant Formula," 290.

116. Rosenberg et al., 290.

117. "Fact Sheet: Infant Formula Marketing in Healthcare Facilities," Public Citizen, accessed April 3, 2018, https://www.citizen.org/our-work/health-and -safety/infant-formula-marketing-healthcare-facilities#_edn4.

118. Katherine R. Shealy et al., *The CDC Guide to Breastfeeding Interventions* (Atlanta: US Department of Health and Human Services, Centers for Disease Control and Prevention, 2005).

119. Mike Dorning, "Insurers Rush Out New Moms," *Chicago Tribune*, June 18, 1995, http://articles.chicagotribune.com/1995-06-18/news/9506180 351_1_hospital-door-cost-conscious-insurance-companies-hours-of-hospital -care; and Sharon Begley, "Deliver, Then Depart," *Sharon L. Begley* (blog), accessed April 3, 2018, http://www.sharonlbegley.com/deliver-then-depart.

120. "Guidelines and Evaluation Criteria for Facilities Seeking Baby-Friendly Designation," Baby Friendly USA, 2016, https://www.babyfriendlyusa .org/get-started/the-guidelines-evaluation-criteria.

121. Jami Dellifraine et al., "Cost Comparison of Baby Friendly and Non-Baby Friendly Hospitals in the United States," *Pediatrics* 127, no. 4 (April 2011): 989, 993, https://doi.org/10.1542/peds.2010-1591.

122. Jim Langabeer, Jami Dellifraine, and Rigoberto Delgado, *An Economic Cost Analysis of Becoming a Baby Friendly Hospital* (San Antonio: University of Texas Health Sciences Center, 2009).

123. Judith L. Gutowski, Marsha Walker, and Ellen Chetwynd, *Containing Health Care Costs Help in Plain Sight* (Washington, DC: United States Lactation Consultant Association, 2014), 5.

124. Langabeer, Dellifraine, and Delgado, *Economic Cost*.

125. "Baby-Friendly Hospital Laws," LawAtlas, last modified October 1, 2016, http://lawatlas.org/datasets/baby-friendly-hospital.

126. Bonnie Rochman, "Fewer Hospitals Hand Out Free Formula to New Moms," *Time: Healthland*, September 26, 2011, http://healthland.time.com /2011/09/26/are-mothers-being-manipulated-fewer-hospitals-hand-out -formula-freebies-to-new-moms/; and Jen Rini, "Decision Ignites Breastfeeding Debate," *Delaware Online*, July 23, 2015, https://www.delawareonline.com /story/news/health/2015/07/24/states-decision-end-formula-gifts-causes -heated-debate/30576961/.

127. In 2012, Massachusetts hospitals implemented a statewide ban through their Public Health Council, after first having the ban overturned when in 2005, then-governor Romney replaced council members in favor of the ban. Jessica Samakow, "Massachusetts Hospitals Ban Free Baby Formula Bags 7 Years after Mitt Romney Said No," *Huffington Post*, July 18, 2012, http://www.huffing tonpost.com/2012/07/18/massachusetts-formula-ban_n_1684259.html.

128. Bonnie Rochman, "What Mitt Romney Has to Do with Breast-Feeding and Infant Formula," *Time: Healthland*, July 17, 2012, http://healthland .time.com/2012/07/17/what-mitt-romney-has-to-do-with-breast-feeding-and -infant-formula/.

129. Rochman, "Romney Has to Do."

130. Rochman, "Romney Has to Do"; and Samakow, "7 Years."

131. Rochman, "Romney Has to Do."

132. "Hospitals Drop Formula-Marketing Bags Given to New Moms Upon Discharge," Maryland Department of Health, October 29, 2015, https://health .maryland.gov/newsroom/Pages/Md—hospitals-end-bag-marketing-to-new -mothers.aspx.

133. Meredith Cohn, "Maryland Hospitals Stop Giving Away Free Samples of Formula to New Mothers," *Baltimore Sun*, October 29, 2015, http://www .baltimoresun.com/health/blog/bal-new-mothers-no-longer-given-free -formula-story.html.

134. Inae Oh, "Bloomberg's Breastfeeding Program, 'Latch on NYC,' Wants Hospitals to Change Baby Formula Protocol," *Huffington Post*, August 18, 2012, http://www.huffingtonpost.com/2012/07/30/bloombergs-breast-feeding -latch-on-nyc- hospitals-hide-baby-formula_n_1718664.html.

135. Oh, "Latch on NYC."

136. Lenore Skenazy, "Sucking the Choice Out of Parenting," *New York Daily News*, August 1, 2012, http://www.nydailynews.com/opinion/sucking -choice-parenting-article-1.1125979.

137. "NYS Birthing Hospitals Will Provide Additional Breastfeeding Support Starting at Birth," New York State Department of Health, October 19, 2016, https://www.health.ny.gov/press/releases/2016/2016-10-19_additional _breastfeeding_support.htm.

138. "What We Do," About FDA, US Food and Drug Administration, last modified March 28, 2018, https://www.fda.gov/aboutfda/whatwedo/default .htm#mission.

139. Carrie J. Lawlor, "Nestlé Infant Nutrition—Close Out Letter 7/13/15," Warning Letters, Food and Drug Administration, July 13, 2015, https://www.fda.gov/ICECI/EnforcementActions/WarningLetters/2015 /ucm454778.htm.

140. Darren Yuvan, "Nestlé/Gerber Refute Allegations Despite Run of Lawsuits over Good Start Allergy Claims," *Legal NewsLine*, February 10, 2017, https://legalnewsline.com/stories/511080979-Nestlé-gerber-refute-allegations -despite-run-of-lawsuits-over-good-start-allergy-claims; and Paul Tassin, "Gerber Class Action Says Good Start Formula Can't Prevent Allergies," *Top Class Actions*, January 10, 2017, https://topclassactions.com/lawsuit-settlements /lawsuit-news/385256-gerber-class-action-says-good-start-formula-cant-pre vent-allergies/.

141. Greene v. Gerber Products Co., 262 F. Supp. 3d 38 (E.D.N.Y. 2017).

142. Peter F. Belamarich, Risa E. Bochner, and Andrew D. Racine, "A Critical Review of the Marketing Claims of Infant Formula Products in the United States," *Clinical Pediatrics* 55, no. 5 (May 2016): 437–42, https://doi.org /10.1177/0009922815589913.

143. Belamarich, Bochner, and Racine, "Critical Review of the Marketing Claims," 440.

144. Belamarich, Bochner, and Racine, 439–40.

145. "Draft Guidance for Industry: Substantiation for Structure/Function Claims Made in Infant Formula Labels and Labeling," Food and Drug Administration, September 2016, https://www.fda.gov/Food/GuidanceRegulation /GuidanceDocumentsRegulatoryInformation/ucm514640.htm.

146. *Busting the Myth of Science-Based Formula: An Investigation into Nestlé Infant Milk Products and Claims* (Utrecht, NL: Changing Markets Foundation, 2018), http://changingmarkets.org/wp-content/uploads/2018/02/BUSTING -THE-MYTH-OF-SCIENCE-BASED-FORMULA.pdf.

147. *Busting the Myth of Science-Based Formula*, 5.

148. "Gerber Good Start Soothe," Target (website), accessed April 3, 2018, https://www.target.com/p/gerber-good-start-soothe-non-gmo-powder-infant -formula-stage-1-22-2-oz/-/A-14138202?ref=tgt_adv_XS000000&AFID =google_pla_df&CPNG=PLA_Baby+Shopping&adgroup=SC_Baby&L ID=700000001170770pgs&network=g&device=c&location=9060110 &gclid=EAIaIQobChMIj8O9kauf2gIVFIh-Ch1THAl2EAkYASABEgJAd_D _BwE&gclsrc=aw.ds. Some bloggers have argued that formula-fed infants, and thus their mothers, sleep more. Amy Kiefer, "Let's Face It: Formula-Fed Babies Sleep Better," *Expecting Science* (blog), September 9, 2014, https://expect ingscience.com/2014/09/09/lets-face-it-formula-fed-babies-sleep-better-from -their-parents-perspective/.

149. Jennifer Graham, "The Formula Follies," *Wall Street Journal*, July 21, 2006, https://www.wsj.com/articles/SB115344851854613298.

150. Roni Rabin, "Breast-Feed or Else," *New York Times*, June 13, 2006, https://www.nytimes.com/2006/06/13/health/13brea.html.

151. HeLP America Act, S. 1074, 109th Cong. (2005); and "S. 1074— HeLP America Act," Legislation, US Congress, accessed November 15, 2018, https://www.congress.gov/bill/109th-congress/senate-bill/1074/.

152. Isolde Raftery, "This Mom's Choice: Nurse Her Baby or Quit the Postal Service," *KUOW*, November 18, 2016, https://kuow.org/stories/moms -choice-nurse-her-baby-or-quit-postal-service.

153. Raftery, "This Mom's Choice."

154. Lindsey Murtagh and Anthony D. Moulton, "Working Mothers, Breastfeeding, and the Law," *American Journal of Public Health* 101, no. 2 (February 2011): 217.

155. Fair Labor Standards Act, 29 U.S.C. §§ 201 et seq. (1938), as amended.

156. 29 U.S.C. § 207(r)(1)(A).

157. 29 U.S.C. § 207(r)(1)(B).

158. 29 U.S.C. § 207(r)(3).

159. Liz Morris, Jessica Lee, and Joan C. Williams, *Exposed: Discrimination against Breastfeeding Workers* (San Francisco, CA: Center for Worklife Law, UC Hastings College of the Law, 2019).

160. 29 U.S.C. § 213.

161. "Breastfeeding State Laws," National Conference of State Legislatures, July 9, 2018, http://www.ncsl.org/research/health/breastfeeding-state-laws.aspx.

162. Ind. Code § 22-2-14-2 (2008).

163. Colo. Rev. Stat. § 8-13.5-104 (2008).

164. Me. Rev. Stat. Ann. tit. 26, § 604 (2009); and Vt. Stat. Ann. tit. 21, § 305 (2008).

165. Or. Rev. Stat. §§ 653.077(7)–(8), (10) (2008).

166. Or. Rev. Stat. § 653.256(2).

167. Tenn. Code Ann. § 50-1-305(a) (1999).

168. Aja Goare, "New CA Law Requires Employers to Accommodate Breast Feeding Mothers with Special Room," *KSBY 6*, January 7, 2019, https://ksby.com/news/local-news/2019/01/07/new-ca-law-requires-employers-to-accommodate-breast-feeding-mothers-with-special-room.

169. Fla. Stat. § 383.016 (1994); N.D. Cent. Code § 23-12-17 (2009); and Wash. Rev. Code § 43.70.640 (2001).

170. "State Family and Medical Leave Laws," National Conference of State Legislatures, July 19, 2016, http://www.ncsl.org/research/labor-and-employment/state-family-and-medical-leave-laws.aspx.

171. Andrew Sheeler, "More Mothers Breastfeeding after California Passed Paid Leave Law, Study Finds," *Sacramento Bee*, October 26, 2018, https://www.sacbee.com/news/politics-government/capitol-alert/article220680020.html.

172. Claire Cain Miller, "Walmart and Now Starbucks: Why More Big Companies Are Offering Paid Family Leave," *New York Times*, January 24, 2018, https://www.nytimes.com/2018/01/24/upshot/parental-leave-company-policy-salaried-hourly-gap.html.

173. Miller, "Walmart and Now Starbucks."

174. Juliana Menasce Horowitz et al., "Americans Widely Support Paid Family and Medical Leave, but Differ over Specific Policies," Pew Research Center, March 23, 2017, http://www.pewsocialtrends.org/2017/03/23/americans-widely-support-paid-family-and-medical-leave-but-differ-over-specific-policies/.

175. "Characteristics of Minimum Wage Workers, 2016," Bureau of Labor Statistics, April 2017, https://www.bls.gov/opub/reports/minimum-wage/2016/home.htm.

176. Horowitz et al., "Americans Widely Support."

177. Maya Rossin-Slater, Christopher J. Ruhm, and Jane Waldfogel, "The Effects of California's Paid Family Leave Program on Mothers' Leave-Taking

and Subsequent Labor Market Outcomes" (working paper, National Bureau of Economic Research, 2011), 1–24.

178. "Rutgers Study Finds Paid Family Leave Leads to Positive Economic Outcomes," *Rutgers Today*, January 19, 2012, https://news.rutgers.edu/news-release/rutgers-study-finds-paid-family-leave-leads-positive-economic-outcomes/20120119#.WsQcXdPwaRs.

179. Sakiko Tanaka, "Parental Leave and Child Health across OECD Countries," *Economic Journal* 115, no. 501 (February 2005): 7–28.

180. Claire Cain Miller, "Paternity Leave: The Rewards and the Remaining Stigma," *New York Times*, November 7, 2014, https://www.nytimes.com/2014/11/09/upshot/paternity-leave-the-rewards-and-the-remaining-stigma.html.

181. Right to Breastfeed Act, H.R. 1848, 106th Cong. (1999).

182. "Breastfeeding State Laws."

183. Wyo. Stat. § 6-4-201 (2007); S.D. Codified Laws § 22-24A-2 (2002); Mich. Comp. Laws § 41.181(4)(a) (1994); Mich. Comp. Laws § 67.1(aa)(i) (1994); and Mich. Comp. Laws § 117.4i(e)(i) (1994).

184. P.R. Laws Ann. tit. 23, § 43-1 (2005).

185. P.R. Laws Ann. tit. 1, § 5165.

186. Ga. Code Ann. § 31-1-9 (2018).

187. Ga. Code Ann. § 31-1-9.

188. "Breastfeeding State Laws."

189. Becky Spencer, Karen Wambach, and Elaine Williams Domain, "African American Women's Breastfeeding Experiences: Cultural, Personal, and Political Voices," *Qualitative Health Research* 25, no. 7 (July 2015): 982, https://doi.org/10.1177/1049732314554097.

190. Cecilia S. Obeng, Roberta E. Emetu, and Terry J. Curtis, "African-American Women's Perceptions and Experiences about Breastfeeding," *Frontiers in Public Health* 3 (December 2015): 4, https://doi.org/10.3389/fpubh.2015.00273.

191. Angela Hanks, Danyelle Solomon, and Christian E. Weller, "Systematic Inequality: How America's Structural Racism Helped Create the Black-White Wealth Gap," Center for American Progress, February 21, 2018, https://www.americanprogress.org/issues/race/reports/2018/02/21/447051/systematic-inequality/.

192. Dorothy Roberts, *Shattered Bonds: The Color of Child Welfare* (New York: Basic Books, 2002), 25; and Jessica Dixon, "The African-American Child Welfare Act: A Legal Redress for African-American Disproportionality in Child Protection Cases," *Berkeley Journal of African-American Law & Policy* 10, no. 2 (June 2008): 109–45, https://doi.org/10.15779/Z385334.

193. "Racial Disproportionality and Disparity in Child Welfare," Children's Bureau, US Department of Health and Human Services, November 2016, https://www.childwelfare.gov/pubPDFs/racial_disproportionality.pdf.

194. Doug Schneider, "Wis. Woman Complains She Wasn't Allowed to

Breastfeed in Jail," *USA Today*, March 3, 2014, https://www.usatoday.com /story/news/nation/2014/03/03/breastfeeding-not-allowed-in-jail/5968445/; and Katy Huang, Farah M. Parvez, and Rebecca Atlas, "The Significance of Breast-feeding to Incarcerated Pregnant Women: An Exploratory Study," *Birth* 39, no. 2 (June 2012): 152–53, https://doi.org/10.1111/j.1523-536X.2012.00528.x.

195. Judith A. Seltzer and Suzanne M. Bianchi, "Demographic Change and Parent-Child Relationships in Adulthood," *Annual Review of Sociology* 39 (July 2013): 275–90, https://doi.org/10.1146/annurev-soc-071312-145602; and "The Decline of Marriage and Rise of New Families," Pew Research Center, November 18, 2010, http://www.pewsocialtrends.org/2010/11/18/iii-marriage/.

196. "Children in Single-Parent Families by Race," Kids Count Data Center, updated January 2018, http://datacenter.kidscount.org/data/tables/107-chil dren-in-single-parent-families-by#detailed/1/any/false/870,573,869,36,868 /10,11,9,12,1,185,13/432,431.

197. "Children in Single-Parent Families."

198. "Fact Sheets: African Americans," The State of Working America, accessed November 23, 2018, http://stateofworkingamerica.org/fact-sheets/afri can-americans/.

199. "Fact Sheets: African Americans."

200. Jennifer N. Lind et al., "Racial Disparities in Access to Maternity Care Practices That Support Breastfeeding—United States, 2011," *Morbidity and Mortality Weekly Report* 63, no. 33 (August 2014): 725–28.

201. Lind et al., "Racial Disparities in Access," 725–28.

202. Kimberly Seals Allers, "Too Many U.S. Communities are 'First Food Deserts,'" *Women's eNews*, February 19, 2013, http://womensenews.org/story /sisterspace/130219/too-many-us-communities-are-first-food-deserts#.Uu2N _BaD4lI.

203. Dayna Matthew, *Just Medicine: A Cure for Racial Inequality in American Medicine* (New York: New York University Press, 2015).

204. Cristina Novoa and Jamila Taylor, "Exploring African Americans' High Maternal and Infant Death Rates," *American Progress*, February 1, 2018, https://www.americanprogress.org/issues/early-childhood/reports/2018/02 /01/445576/exploring-african-americans-high-maternal-infant-death-rates/; and Marian F. Macdorman, Eugene Declercq, and Marie E. Thoma, "Trends in Maternal Mortality by Sociodemographic Characteristics and Cause of Death in 27 States and the District of Columbia," *Obstetrics and Gynecology* 129, no. 5 (May 2017): 811–18, https://doi.org/10.1097/AOG.0000000000001968. Data gathered by the CDC's Pregnancy Mortality Surveillance System showed that "considerable racial disparities in pregnancy-related mortality exist" and that Black women are three to four times as likely as White women are to be at risk of pregnancy-related death. "Pregnancy Mortality Surveillance System," Reproductive Health, Centers for Disease Control and Prevention, last updated August 7, 2018, https://www.cdc.gov/reproductivehealth/maternalinfanthealth

/pregnancy-mortality-surveillance-system.htm. Simply put, Black women are 243 percent more likely than White women to die of pregnancy- or childbirth-related causes, ProPublica reported. Nina Martin and Renee Montagne, "Nothing Protects Black Women from Dying in Pregnancy and Childbirth," *ProPublica*, December 7, 2017, https://www.propublica.org/article/nothing-protects-black-women-from-dying-in-pregnancy-and-childbirth.

205. P. R. Lockhart, "What Serena Williams's Scary Childbirth Story Says about Medical Treatment of Black Women," *Vox*, January 11, 2018, https://www.vox.com/identities/2018/1/11/16879984/serena-williams-childbirth-scare-black-women.

206. Shealy et al., *Breastfeeding Interventions*, 36.

207. Shealy et al., 35.

208. Margaret E. Bentley, Deborah L. Dee, and Joan L. Jensen, "Breastfeeding among Low Income, African-American Women: Power, Beliefs and Decision Making," *Journal of Nutrition* 133, no. 1 (January 2003): 305S, https://doi.org/10.1093/jn/133.1.305S.

209. Bentley, Dee, and Jensen, "Power, Beliefs and Decision Making," 307S; and Obeng, Emetu, and Curtis, "Perceptions and Experiences about Breastfeeding,"4–5.

210. Bentley, Dee, and Jensen, "Power, Beliefs and Decision Making," 307S.

211. Bentley, Dee, and Jensen, 307S.

212. Bentley, Dee, and Jensen, 308S.

213. Sojourner Marable Grimmett, "Support Establishing Lactation Rooms in Public Places: Would You Eat in the Bathroom?," *Married with Two Boys* (blog), September 2, 2011, http://sojournermarablegrimmett.blogspot.com/2011/09/support-establishing-lactation-rooms-in.html.

214. Grimmett, "Support Establishing Lactation Rooms"; and Sojourner Marable Grimmett, "Would You Eat in the Bathroom to Support This Campaign?," *Married with Two Boys* (blog), October 19, 2011, http://sojournermarablegrimmett.blogspot.com/2011/10/press-for-campaign-would-you-eat-in.html.

Chapter 6

1. A law in Ghana—Section 57 of the Labour Act of 2003—provides for "nursing pauses of one hour during the working hours for women to nurse her baby up to the baby's first year of age." Jane Hodges and Anthony Baah, "National Labour Law Profile: Ghana," International Labour Organization, accessed April 12, 2018, http://www.ilo.org/ifpdial/information-resources/national-labour-law-profiles/WCMS_158898/lang--en/index.htm.

2. For example, Brazil's constitution endows citizens with the right to health care; El Salvador's constitution grants the right to education; and South Africa's constitution includes the right to housing. Octavio L. M. Ferraz, "Harming the Poor through Social Rights Litigation: Lessons from Brazil," *Texas Law Review*

89, no. 7 (June 2011): 1643–68; Christopher Jeffords, "Constitutional Environmental Human Rights: A Descriptive Analysis of 142 National Constitutions" (unpublished manuscript, on file with author, 2013); and *Rethinking Poverty: Report on the World Social Situation 2010* (New York: United Nations, 2009), http://www.un.org/esa/socdev/rwss/docs/2010/fullreport.pdf.

3. U.S. Const. amend. XIV, § 1.

4. U.S. Const. amend. V.

5. *Dike*, 650 F.2d at 783; and Danielle M. Shelton, "When Private Goes Public: Legal Protection for Women Who Breastfeed in Public and at Work," *Law & Inequality* 14 (December 1995): 195.

6. Reno v. Flores, 507 U.S. 292, 302 (1993).

7. Griswold v. Connecticut, 381 U.S. 479 (1965) (Stewart, J., dissenting); Roe v. Wade, 410 U.S. 113 (1973) (White, J., dissenting); and Troxel v. Granville, 530 U.S. 57 (2000) (Scalia, J., dissenting).

8. *Roe*, 410 U.S. at 113.

9. Planned Parenthood v. Casey, 510 U.S. 1309 (1994). Strict scrutiny requires the government to demonstrate that a law or act is necessary to achieve a compelling government interest.

10. *Casey*, 510 U.S. at 1309.

11. Stephanie Russell-Kraft, "The Right to Abortion—and Religious Freedom," *Atlantic*, March 3, 2016, https://www.theatlantic.com/politics/archive/2016/03/abortion-rights-a-matter-of-religious-freedom/471891/.

12. *Griswold*, 381 U.S. at 479; Eisenstadt v. Baird, 405 U.S. 438 (1972); and Carey v. Population Services International, 431 U.S. 678 (1977).

13. *Views on Birth Control: Results from a National Survey of Voters on Federal Policy around Contraceptives* (Washington, DC: PerryUndem, 2017), 1, 9.

14. U.S. Const. amend. XIV, § 1.

15. Washington v. Davis, 426 U.S. 229 (1976); and McClesky v. Kemp, 481 U.S. 279 (1987).

16. *Davis*, 426 U.S. at 243.

17. Yick Wo v. Hopkins, 118 U.S. 356 (1886); and Gomillion v. Lightfoot, 364 U.S. 339 (1960).

18. *Yick Wo*, 118 U.S. at 356.

19. *Gomillion*, 364 U.S. at 339.

20. FCC v. Beach Communications, Inc., 508 U.S. 307, 313–14 (1993).

21. Williamson v. Lee Optical Co., 348 U.S. 483 (1955).

22. Intersectionality refers to oppression that occurs simultaneously on two or more axes. Kimberlé Williams Crenshaw, "Mapping the Margins: Intersectionality, Identity Politics, and Violence against Women of Color," *Stanford Law Review* 43, no. 6 (July 1991): 1241–99. In this case, race, sex, and wealth are implicated.

23. Craig v. Boren, 429 U.S. 90 (1975).

24. Personnel Administrator of Mass. v. Feeney, 442 U.S. 256 (1970).

25. Melissa Whitney, "The Statistical Evidence of Racial Profiling in Traffic Stops and Searches: Rethinking the Use of Statistics to Prove Discriminatory Intent," *Boston College Law Review* 49, no. 1 (January 2008): 263–99.

26. Whitney, "Statistical Evidence of Racial Profiling," 263–99.

27. Charles R. Lawrence III, "The Id, the Ego and Equal Protection: Reckoning with Unconscious Racism," *Stanford Law Review* 39, no. 2 (January 1987): 317–89; Robin A. Lenhardt, "Understanding the Mark: Race, Stigma, and Equality in Context," *New York University Law Review* 79, no. 3 (June 2004): 803–931; and Linda Hamilton Krieger, "The Content of Our Categories: A Cognitive Bias Approach to Discrimination and Equal Employment Opportunity," *Stanford Law Review* 47, no. 7 (July 1995): 1161–248.

28. U.S. Const. amend. XIII.

29. The Fourteenth Amendment begins "No state shall" and requires state action, but the Thirteenth Amendment simply prohibits slavery and involuntary servitude. U.S. Const. amend. XIV; and U.S. Const. amend. XIII.

30. In modern times, slavery includes sex trafficking, human trafficking, and other forms of forced labor. Shaheen P. Torgoley, "Trafficking and Forced Prostitution: A Manifestation of Modern Slavery," *Tulane Journal of International Law and Comparative Law* 14, no. 2 (Spring 2006): 553–78.

31. Civil Rights Cases, 109 U.S. 3 (1883); and Jones v. Alfred H. Mayer Co., 392 U.S. 409 (1968).

32. Andrea Freeman, "Unconstitutional Work Requirements," *UC Davis Law Review* (2020).

33. United States v. Kozminski, 487 U.S. 931, 944 (1988).

34. U.S. Const. amend. XIII, § 2. *Civil Rights Cases*, 109 U.S. at 20; and *Jones*, 392 U.S. at 439.

35. Atta v. Sun Co., 596 F. Supp. 103 (E.D. Pa. 1984); Alma Society v. Mellon, 601 F.2d 1225 (2d Cir. 1979); and William M. Carter Jr., "Race, Rights, and the Thirteenth Amendment: Defining the Badges and Incidents of Slavery," *UC Davis Law Review* 40, no. 4 (April 2007): 1311–80.

36. Alexander Tsesis, "Regulating Intimidating Speech," *Harvard Journal on Legislation* 41, no. 2 (Summer 2004): 389–406; Akhil Reed Amar, "The Case of the Missing Amendments: *R.A.V. v. City of St. Paul*," *Harvard Law Review* 106, no. 1 (November 1992): 124–61; Petal Nevella Modeste, "Race Hate Speech: The Pervasive Badge of Slavery That Mocks the Thirteenth Amendment," *Howard Law Journal* 44, no. 2 (Winter 2001): 311–48; and Alexander Tsesis, "The Problem of Confederate Symbols: A Thirteenth Amendment Approach," *Temple Law Review* 75, no. 3 (Fall 2002): 539–612.

37. Zoë Elizabeth Lees, "Payday Peonage: Thirteenth Amendment Implications in Payday Lending," *Scholar* 15 (2012): 63.

38. 45 C.F.R. § 261.14. This section provides that "(a) If an individual refuses to engage in work required under section 407 of *the Act*, the *State* must reduce or terminate the amount of assistance payable to the family, subject to any

good cause or other exceptions the *State* may establish. Such a reduction is governed by the provisions of *§ 261.16.* (b) (1) The *State* must, at a minimum, reduce the amount of *assistance* otherwise payable to the family pro rata with respect to any period during the month in which the individual refuses to work. (2) The *State* may impose a greater reduction, including terminating *assistance.* (c) A *State* that fails to impose penalties on individuals in accordance with the provisions of section 407(e) of *the Act* may be subject to the *State* penalty specified at *§ 261.54.*" Section 261.16 says, "A penalty imposed by a *State* against the family of an individual by reason of the failure of the individual to comply with a requirement under *TANF* shall not be construed to be a reduction in any wage paid to the individual." 45 C.F.R. § 261.16 (2002).

39. 45 C.F.R. § 261.56 (2012). Section 261.56 says, "What happens if a parent cannot obtain needed child care? (a) (1) If the individual is a single custodial parent caring for a child under age six, the State may not reduce or terminate assistance based on the parent's refusal to engage in required work if he or she demonstrates an inability to obtain needed child care for one or more of the following reasons: (i) Appropriate child care within a reasonable distance from the home or work site is unavailable; (ii) Informal child care by a relative or under other arrangements is unavailable or unsuitable; or (iii) Appropriate and affordable formal child care arrangements are unavailable. (2) Refusal to work when an acceptable form of child care is available is not protected from sanctioning."

40. "TANF recipients who are sanctioned are more likely to have characteristics that are associated with longer welfare stays and lower rates of employment. . . . African Americans are more likely to be sanctioned than other racial and ethnic groups." LaDonna Pavetti et al., *The Use of TANF Work-Oriented Sanctions in Illinois, New Jersey, and South Carolina* (Washington, DC: Department of Health and Human Services, 2004), 33, https://aspe.hhs.gov/report /use-tanf-work-oriented-sanctions-illinois-new-jersey-and-south-carolina.

41. Shannon M. Monnat, "The Color of Welfare Sanctioning: Exploring the Individual and Contextual Roles of Race on TANF Case Closures and Benefit Reductions," *Sociological Quarterly* 51, no. 4 (2010): 680, https://doi.org /10.1111/j.1533-8525.2010.01188.x.

42. Pavetti et al., *Use of TANF Work-Oriented Sanctions*, 33.

43. "Policies more stringent than required are found in the 36 states that impose full-family sanctions, which terminate cash assistance to the entire family, and in the 39 states that continue sanctions for fixed periods of time, even if the family has come into compliance with the requirements during the sanction period. Moreover, many states have curtailed or eliminated procedural protections for families facing a sanction." Heidi Goldberg and Liz Schott, *A Compliance Oriented Approach to Sanctions in State and County TANF Programs* (Washington, DC: Center on Budget and Policy Priorities, October 1, 2000), 1–2, https://www.cbpp.org/archiveSite/10-1-00sliip.pdf. "Sanctioned families are characterized by a high incidence of health problems and low education lev-

els as well as a lack of transportation and child care. In addition, there is evidence that sanctioned families often do not know or understand what actions they are required to take to be in compliance or the consequences of failing to take those actions." Goldberg and Schott, 2.

44. Taryn Lindhorst and Ronald J. Mancoske, "The Social and Economic Impact of Sanctions and Time Limits on Recipients of Temporary Assistance for Needy Families," *Journal of Sociology & Social Welfare* 33, no. 1 (March 2006): 93–109.

45. "Full family sanctions have contributed to a decline in program participation from 84% of eligible families in 1995 to 40% of eligible families in 2005. . . . Currently, only about two million families are receiving TANF although probably at least five million families are eligible." Timothy Casey, *The Sanction Epidemic in the Temporary Assistance for Needy Families Program* (New York, Legal Momentum, 2012), 1, https://www.legalmomentum.org/sites/default/files /reports/sanction-epidemic-in-tanf.pdf; and Ife Floyd, LaDonna Pavetti, and Liz Schott, *TANF Reaching Few Poor Families* (Washington, DC: Center on Budget and Policy Priorities, December 13, 2017), 1–21, https://www.cbpp .org/sites/default/files/atoms/files/6-16-15tanf.pdf.

46. Ife Floyd, "The Truth about 'Welfare Reform': TANF Is Disappearing," *Off the Charts* (blog), Family Income Support, Center on Budget and Policy Priorities, December 13, 2017, https://www.cbpp.org/blog/the-truth-about -welfare-reform-tanf-is-disappearing-0.

47. Casey, *Sanction Epidemic*, 2. Blacks are only 12.3 percent of the US population. Joseph Carroll, "Public Overestimates U.S. Black and Hispanic Populations," Gallup, June 4, 2001, http://news.gallup.com/poll/4435/public-over estimates-us-black-hispanic-populations.aspx.

48. Ife Floyd, "Despite Recent TANF Benefit Boosts, Black Families Left Behind," *Off the Charts* (blog), Family Income Support, Center on Budget and Policy Priorities, October 25, 2018, https://www.cbpp.org/blog/despite-recent -tanf-benefit-boosts-black-families-left-behind; and Ashley Burnside and Ife Floyd, *TANF Benefits Remain Low Despite Recent Increases in Some States* (Washington, DC: Center on Budget and Policy Priorities, October 25, 2018), 4–5, https://www.cbpp.org/sites/default/files/atoms/files/10-30-14tanf.pdf.

49. Burnside and Floyd, *TANF Benefits Remain Low*, 7.

50. Casey, *Sanction Epidemic*, 2. Of the 90 percent, over half have a child below age six and over a quarter have a child below age two. A third of parent recipients have a disability, and many experience domestic violence. One-quarter of TANF recipient families include a child who has at least one chronic health problem or disability. Casey, 2, 3; and Lindhorst and Mancoske, "Social and Economic Impact," 108.

51. Casey, *Sanction Epidemic*, 4. Approximately half of these states immediately impose full family sanctions for an initial violation, and about half begin with a partial sanction that escalates to full family if the violation continues

beyond a specified period or if there is a subsequent violation. "States continue a sanction at least until a parent demonstrates that she is willing to comply and may continue the sanction for a longer period. A majority of states impose minimum sanction periods generally ranging from 1 to 3 months for a first work requirement violation. Most states impose longer minimums generally ranging from 3 to 12 months for any subsequent work requirement violation. Four states authorize lifetime full family sanctions for repeated violations." Casey, 4.

52. Diane R. Pagen, "Breastfeeding Is a Must . . . for Moms Who Can Afford It," *City Limits*, February 25, 2011, https://citylimits.org/2011/02/25 /breastfeeding-is-a-must-for-moms-who-can-afford-it/.

53. Slaughter-House Cases, 83 U.S. 36, 72 (1872).

54. *Civil Rights Cases*, 109 U.S. at 20.

55. *Civil Rights Cases*, 109 U.S. at 22.

56. Jennifer Jason McAward, "Defining the Badges and Incidents of Slavery," *University of Pennsylvania Journal of Constitutional Law* 14, no. 3 (February 2012): 571.

57. McAward, "Defining the Badges and Incidents," 575; and *Jones*, 392 U.S. at 442–43.

58. *Civil Rights Cases*, 109 U.S. at 20.

59. *Jones*, 392 U.S. at 412.

60. *Jones*, 392 U.S. at 441–42. The opinion states: "For this Court recognized long ago that, whatever else they may have encompassed, the badges and incidents of slavery—its 'burdens and disabilities'—included restraints upon 'those fundamental rights which are the essence of civil freedom, namely, the same right . . . to inherit, purchase, lease, sell and convey property, as is enjoyed by white citizens.'" *Jones*, 392 U.S. at 441.

61. *Jones*, 392 U.S. at 441–43.

62. Palmer v. Thompson, 403 U.S. 217, 226–27 (1971).

63. *Palmer*, 403 U.S. at 218–20.

64. Michele Goodwin, "Policing America's Swimming Pools—an Old, Troubling Story," *Huffington Post*, June 11, 2015, https://www.huffingtonpost .com/michele-goodwin/policing-americas-swimmin_b_7547416.html.

65. Robbie Ann Darby, "Swimming in the Black Community: How Racism Is Drowning Us," *Root*, July 11, 2016, https://www.theroot.com/swimming-in -the-black-community-how-racism-is-drowning-1790855966.

66. Lee v. Mathews, 10 Ala. 682, 688–89 (1846).

67. Alexander Tsesis, "Furthering American Freedom: Civil Rights & the Thirteenth Amendment," *Boston College Law Review* 45, no. 2 (2004): 377–79.

68. George M. Stroud, *Sketch of the Laws Relating to Slavery in the Several States of the United States of America* (Philadelphia: Kimber and Sharpless, 1856).

69. Stroud, *Sketch of the Laws*, 46–55.

70. Emily West and R. J. Knight, "Mothers' Milk: Slavery, Wet-Nursing, and Black and White Women in the Antebellum South," *Journal of Southern*

History 83, no. 1 (February 2017): 37–68, https://doi.org/10.1353/soh.2017 .0001. "Slaveholders forced enslaved women to wean their own infants early (from around six months), so they could return to their labors; yet, ironically, wet nurses had to feed white children until they were about two years old." Wilma A. Dunaway, *The African-American Family in Slavery & Emancipation* (Cambridge, UK: Cambridge University Press, 2003), 134–41.

71. Cong. Globe, 38th Cong., 1st Sess. 1439–40 (1864); and Alexander Tsesis, "Interpreting the Thirteenth Amendment," *University of Pennsylvania Journal of Constitutional Law* 11, no. 5 (July 2009): 1339.

72. Carter, "Race, Rights, and the Thirteenth Amendment," 1323.

73. Cong. Globe, 1439–40.

74. Tsesis, "Interpreting the Thirteenth Amendment," 1340.

75. Meyer v. Nebraska, 262 U.S. 390 (1923); and Pierce v. Society of Sisters, 268 U.S. 510 (1925).

76. Wet nursing or cross-nursing were satisfactory alternatives to maternal nursing, but anything else came with a high risk. West and Knight, "Mother's Milk," 41; and Sally McMillen, "Mothers' Sacred Duty: Breast-Feeding Patterns among Middle- and Upper-Class Women in the Antebellum South," *Journal of Southern History* 51, no. 3 (August 1985): 348–49, https://doi.org/10.2307 /2209248.

77. Pat Thomas, "Suck on This," *Ecologist*, April 1, 2006, https://the ecologist.org/2006/apr/01/suck.

78. E. Melanie Dupuis, *Nature's Perfect Food: How Milk Became America's Drink* (New York: New York University Press, 2002), 19–20.

79. Dunaway, *African-American Family*, 141.

80. T. J. Matthews, Marian F. MacDorman, and Marie E. Thoma, "Infant Mortality Statistics from the 2013 Period Linked Birth/Infant Death Data Set," *National Vital Statistics Reports* 64, no. 9 (August 2015): 4; and Andrea Freeman, "'First Food' Justice: Racial Disparities in Infant Feeding as Food Oppression," *Fordham Law Review* 83, no. 6 (May 2015): 3064.

81. Centers for Disease Control and Prevention, "Progress in Increasing Breastfeeding and Reducing Racial/Ethnic Differences—United States, 2000– 2008 Births," *Morbidity and Mortality Weekly Report* 62, no. 5 (February 2013). This is also an issue in the context of maternal mortality. Nina Martin and Renee Montagne, "Nothing Protects Black Women from Dying in Pregnancy and Childbirth," *ProPublica*, December 7, 2017, https://www.propublica.org/article /nothing-protects-black-women-from-dying-in-pregnancy-and-childbirth.

82. Maria L. Ontiveros, "Immigrant Workers' Rights in a Post-Hoffman World—Organizing around the Thirteenth Amendment," *Georgetown Immigration Law Journal* 18, no. 4 (2004): 654–58; Bahar Azmy, "Unshackling the Thirteenth: Modern Slavery and a Reconstructed Civil Rights Agenda," *Fordham Law Review* 71, no. 3 (December 2002): 983–84; Tobias Barrington Wolff, "The Thirteenth Amendment and Slavery in the Global Economy," *Columbia*

Law Review 102, no. 4 (May 2002): 973–1050; Samantha C. Halem, "Slaves to Fashion: A Thirteenth Amendment Litigation Strategy to Abolish Sweatshops in the Garment Industry," *San Diego Law Review* 36, no. 2 (Spring 1999): 399–400; and Lea S. Vandervelde, "The Labor Vision of the Thirteenth Amendment," *University of Pennsylvania Law Review* 138, no. 2 (December 1989): 437–38.

83. United States v. Harris, 106 U.S. 629 (1883).

84. *Harris*, 106 U.S. at 641.

85. "United States v. Harris," Oyez, accessed February 13, 2018, https://www.oyez.org/cases/1850-1900/106us629.

86. *Harris*, 106 U.S. at 641.

87. *Harris*, 106 U.S. at 643–44. Ironically, here the defendant was a state actor.

88. Plessy v. Ferguson, 163 U.S. 537 (1896).

89. *Plessy*, 163 U.S. at 551.

90. *Plessy*, 163 U.S. at 542.

91. Hodges v. United States, 203 U.S. 1, 17 (1906). In the case, White sawmill workers and farmers in Arkansas threatened Black workers with violence if they did not immediately stop working at their jobs. The aggressors faced charges for this intimidation under a law prohibiting interference with the ability to make contracts. The Court struck down the law, declaring that Congress had no authority to enact it under the Thirteenth Amendment, because it did not involve forced labor. Instead of compelling the victims to labor, their attackers had forced them to stop working.

92. Pollock v. Williams, 322 U.S. 4 (1944).

93. *Pollock*, 322 U.S. at 5.

94. *Pollock*, 322 U.S. at 8–10.

95. Eric Foner, *Reconstruction: America's Unfinished Revolution, 1863–1877* (New York: Harper Perennial, 2014), 199–200.

96. *Pollock*, 322 U.S. at 5n1.

97. *Pollock*, 322 U.S. at 15.

98. *Pollock*, 322 U.S. at 11.

99. *Pollock*, 322 U.S. at 17.

100. *Pollock*, 322 U.S. at 18.

101. "Researchers found the growth of families living in extreme poverty occurred among the groups most affected by welfare reform. . . . The limited availability of TANF benefits has put poor families—and especially their children—at risk of much greater hardship, with the potential for long-term negative consequences." Floyd, Pavetti, and Schott, *TANF Reaching Few Poor Families*, 2.

102. Alejandra Marchevsky and Jeanne Theoharis, "Why It Matters That Hillary Clinton Championed Welfare Reform," *Nation*, March 1, 2016, https://

www.thenation.com/article/why-it-matters-that-hillary-clinton-championed
-welfare-reform/.

103. Lindhorst and Mancoske, "Social and Economic Impact," 96.

104. *Kozminski*, 487 U.S. at 931.

105. Catherine M. Page, "*United States v. Kozminski*: Involuntary Servitude—A Standard at Last," *University of Toledo Law Review* 20, no. 4 (Summer 1989): 1025–32; and Kenneth T. Koonce Jr., "*United States v. Kozminski*: On the Threshold of Involuntary Servitude," *Pepperdine Law Review* 16, no. 3 (April 1989): 690–97.

106. *Kozminski*, 487 U.S. at 934. The first, § 241, "prohibits conspiracy to interfere with an individual's Thirteenth Amendment right to be free from 'involuntary servitude.'" Conspiracy against Rights, 18 U.S.C. § 241 (1994). The second, § 1584, "makes it a crime knowingly and willfully to hold another person 'to involuntary servitude.'" 18 U.S.C. § 1584 (2008).

107. *Kozminski*, 487 U.S. at 934–35.

108. *Kozminski*, 487 U.S. at 935.

109. *Kozminski*, 487 U.S. at 956n3.

110. *Kozminski*, 487 U.S. at 935, 956n3.

111. *Kozminski*, 487 U.S. at 935.

112. *Kozminski*, 487 U.S. at 935.

113. *Kozminski*, 487 U.S. at 935.

114. *Kozminski*, 487 U.S. at 943. Lauren Kares, "The Unlucky Thirteenth: A Constitutional Amendment in Search of a Doctrine," *Cornell Law Review* 80, no. 2 (January 1995): 375. (Lauren Kares rues the Court's vague definition of involuntary servitude: "Nearly 130 years of judicial construction have failed to provide a uniform definition of involuntary servitude and thus have failed to afford the Thirteenth Amendment a clear role in the shaping of civil rights law.")

115. *Kozminski*, 487 U.S. at 944.

116. *Kozminski*, 487 U.S. at 952.

117. *Kozminski*, 487 U.S. at 952.

118. These types of work requirements also exist in other government assistance programs including food stamps and Medicaid. There are ten HUD housing authorities that are "MTW [Moving to Work] agencies" that have work requirement policies. Diane K. Levy, Leiha Edmons, and Jasmine Simington, *Work Requirements in Public Housing Authorities* (Washington, DC: Urban Institute, 2018), 3, https://www.urban.org/sites/default/files/publication/95821 /work-requirements-in-public-housing-authorities.pdf. Part-time work does not count as employment, and there is no exemption for mothers with infants. Rachel M. Cohen and Zaid Jilani, "Draft Legislation Suggests Trump Administration Weighing Work Requirements and Rent Increases for Subsidized Housing," *Intercept*, February 1, 2018, https://theintercept.com/2018/02/01/hud-subsi

dized-housing-rent-increase-work-requirement/. These programs raise the same constitutional issues as welfare to work.

119. *Kozminski*, 487 U.S. at 959 (Brennan, J., concurring).

120. Kathleen M. Sullivan, "Unconstitutional Conditions," *Harvard Law Review* 102, no. 7 (May 1989): 1415.

121. Sherbert v. Verner, 374 U.S. 398 (1963).

122. Speiser v. Randall, 357 U.S. 513 (1958).

123. Shapiro v. Thompson, 394 U.S. 618 (1969).

124. *Pierce*, 268 U.S. at 510.

125. *Meyer*, 262 U.S. at 390.

126. Alice Robb, "Bring Back the Wet Nurse," *New Republic*, July 22, 2014, https://newrepublic.com/article/118786/breastfeeding-wet-nurses-mommy-wars.

127. Robb, "Bring Back the Wet Nurse."

128. Robb.

129. Robb.

130. "Breastfeeding Is Now Required by Law in the United Arab Emirates," *Huffington Post*, January 30, 2014, https://www.huffingtonpost.com/2014/01/30/united-arab-emirates-breastfeeding-law_n_4689740.html.

131. Out of the Blues, "Mandatory Breastfeeding Law Could Be a Step Too Far," *National*, January 28, 2014, https://www.thenational.ae/mandatory-breastfeeding-law-could-be-a-step-too-far-1.250326.

132. "Why Breastfeeding Law Is Impractical," *National*, January 28, 2014, http://www.thenational.ae/thenationalconversation/comment/why-breastfeeding-law-is-impractical.

133. Hessa Al Ghazal, Shehnaz Rashid, and Evelyne Ruf, "The Sharjah Baby-Friendly Campaign: A Community-Based Model for Breastfeeding Promotion, Protection, and Support," *Breastfeeding Medicine* 10, no. 9 (November 2015): 437–41.

134. "Breastfeeding Is Now Required."

135. "Breastfeeding Is Now Required."

136. Cat Wise, "New Indonesia Law: Allow Breastfeeding, or Face Punishment," *PBS*, July 5, 2011, http://www.pbs.org/newshour/rundown/in-indonesia-allow-breast-feeding-or-face-punishment/.

137. Wise, "New Indonesia Law."

138. Nisha Susan, "Why a Madras High Court Judge Wants the Union Government to Declare Breastmilk a Fundamental Right This Year," *Ladies Finger*, January 9, 2018, http://theladiesfinger.com/fundamental-right-breastmilk-breastfeeding-madras-hc/.

139. "HC Poses 15 Questions to Centre, TN Govt on Maternity Leave," *Outlook India*, January 2, 2018, https://www.outlookindia.com/newsscroll/hc-poses-15-questions-to-centre-tn-govt-on-maternity-leave/1221543.

140. "HC Poses 15 Questions to Centre."

141. Catherine E. Choichet, "Breast-Feeding Is Best, So Ban Bottles, Venezuelan Lawmaker Proposes," CNN, June 18, 2013, https://www.cnn.com/2013/06/17/health/venezuela-baby-bottle-ban/index.html.

142. Sex Discrimination Act 1984, as amended (Cth.) (Austl.) (2014).

143. "Breastfeeding in Public," Breastfeeding Network, accessed November 3, 2018, https://www.breastfeedingnetwork.org.uk/breastfeeding-help/out-about/.

144. Discrimination includes refusing to provide a service, providing a lower standard of service, or providing a service on different terms. Breastfeeding women also receive some protection under the 1975 Sex Discrimination Act. "Breastfeeding in Public Places," Maternity Action, updated March 2016, http://www.maternityaction.org.uk/wp-content/uploads/2015/05/Breastfeeding-in-a-public-place-2016.pdf.

145. "Sao Paulo to Fine Entities That Ban Breastfeeding in Public," *TeleSUR*, March 20, 2015, http://www.telesurtv.net/english/news/Sao-Paulo-to-Fine-Entities-that-Ban-Breastfeeding-in-Public-20150320-0029.html. The fines imposed go up to $150 US dollars.

146. Sara Levine, "Sao Paolo Is Now Fining People for Shaming Breastfeeding Moms, Thank God Somebody Gets It," *Bustle*, March 21, 2015, https://www.bustle.com/articles/71167-sao-paulo-is-now-fining-people-for-shaming-breastfeeding-moms-thank-god-somebody-gets-it.

147. Thomas Roberts, Emily Carnahan, and Emmanuela Gakidou, "Burden Attributable to Suboptimal Breastfeeding: A Cross-Country Analysis of Country-Specific Trends and Their Relation to Child Health Inequalities," *Lancet* 381 (June 2013): 126, https://doi.org/10.1016/S0140-6736(13)61380-X.

148. WHO, *Country Implementation of the International Code of Marketing of Breast-Milk Substitutes: Status Report 2011* (Geneva: World Health Organization, 2013), 29.

149. Khyber Pakhtunkhwa Protection of Breastfeeding and Child Nutrition Act 2015, Khyber Pakhtunkhwa Assembly, http://www.pakp.gov.pk/2013/acts/the-khyber-pakhtunkhwa-protection-of-breast-feeding-and-child-nutrition-act2015/.

150. Khyber Pakhtunkhwa Protection of Breastfeeding and Child Nutrition Act.

151. Jessica Hester, "Sweden Considers Banning Babies in Formula Ads," *Parents Magazine*, November 9, 2012, http://www.parents.com/blogs/parents-news-now/2012/11/09/parents-news-now/sweden-considers-banning-babies-in-formula-ads/.

152. Jenny Ong, "More on the Legal Rights of Breastfeeding and Working Women," *Chronicles of a Nursing Mom* (blog), March 27, 2013, http://www.chroniclesofanursingmom.com/2013/03/more-on-legal-rights-of-breastfeeding.html; and Expanded Breastfeeding Promotion Act of 2009, Rep. Act No. 10028 (Mar. 16, 2010) (Phil.).

153. Yvette Manes, "What Are Breastfeeding Laws in Other Countries? A Breakdown of Nursing around the World," *Romper*, October 3, 2016, https://www.romper.com/p/what-are-breastfeeding-laws-in-other-countries-a-break down-of-nursing-around-the-world-19434.

154. Manes, "What Are Breastfeeding Laws?"

155. "Norway—The WHO Code and Breastfeeding: An International Comparative Overview," Australian Government Department of Health, May 3, 2012, http://www.health.gov.au/internet/publications/publishing.nsf/Content /int-comp-whocode-bf-init~int-comp-whocode-bf-init-ico~int-comp-whocode -bf-init-ico-norway.

156. Manes, "What Are Breastfeeding Laws?"

157. Lisette Alvarez, "Norway Leads Industrial Nations Back to Breastfeed- ing," *New York Times*, October 21, 2003, http://www.nytimes.com/2003/10 /21/world/norway-leads-industrial-nations-back-to-breast-feeding.html

158. "Norway—The WHO Code and Breastfeeding."

159. Alvarez, "Norway Leads Industrial Nations."

160. Alvarez, "Norway Leads Industrial Nations." Helsing went on to write several other manuals on the subject. Elisabet Helsing and Felicity Savage, *Breast-Feeding in Practice: A Manual for Health Workers* (Oxford, UK: Oxford University Press, 1982); Tine Vittner and Elisabet Helsing, *Breastfeeding: How to Support Success: A Practical Guide for Health Workers* (Copenhagen: World Health Organization, 1997); and Elisabet Helsing and Anna-Pia Haggkvist, *Understanding Breastfeeding and How to Succeed* (n.p., Praeclarus Press, 2012).

161. Alvarez, "Norway Leads Industrial Nations."

162. Alvarez, "Norway Leads Industrial Nations."

163. Manes, "What Are Breastfeeding Laws?"; and Charis Chairopoulos, "Employment and Employee Benefits in Greece: Overview," Practical Law, ac- cessed April 12, 2018, http://us.practicallaw.com/5-620-5757?source=related content.

164. Manes, "What Are Breastfeeding Laws?"

165. Adam Minter, "China's Growing Breastfeeding Problem," *Bloomberg View*, April 22, 2015, https://www.bloomberg.com/view/articles/2015-04-22 /china-s-growing-breastfeeding-problem.

166. Louisa Lim, "For Chinese Moms, Birth Means 30 Days in Pa- jamas," *NPR: All Things Considered*, July 20, 2011, https://www.npr .org/2011/07/20/138536998/for-chinese-moms-birth-means-30-days-in -pajamas.

167. Donald G. McNeil Jr., "Study Finds Lower, but Still High, Rate of C-Sections in China," *New York Times*, January 9, 2017, https://www.nytimes .com/2017/01/09/health/c-section-births-china.html.

168. Kerrie Armstrong, "Baby Formula Shortage: Why Do Chinese Women Shun Breastfeeding?" SBS, November 12, 2015, http://www.sbs.com.au/news

/article/2015/11/12/baby-formula-shortage-why-do-chinese-women-shun
-breastfeeding.

169. Minter, "China's Growing Breastfeeding Problem."

170. Minter, "China's Growing Breastfeeding Problem"; and Armstrong, "Baby Formula Shortage."

171. Armstrong, "Baby Formula Shortage."

172. Shu Pengqian, "No Room in Public for China's Breastfeeding Moms," *Beijing Today*, December 25, 2015, https://beijingtoday.com.cn/2015/12/no -room-in-public-for-chinas-breastfeeding-moms/.

173. Pengqian, "No Room in Public"; and Shen Lu and Katie Hunt, "Photo of Breastfeeding Mom in Public Ignites Online Storm in China," CNN, December 1, 2015, http://www.cnn.com/2015/12/01/asia/china-beijing-subway -breastfeeding/.

174. Lu and Hunt, "Online Storm in China."

175. Nicoletta Iacovidou, "Breastfeeding in Public: A Global Review of Different Attitudes Towards It," *Journal of Pediatrics & Neonatal Care* 1, no. 6 (November 2014): 40, https://doi.org/10.15406/jpnc.2014.01.00040. China. news.com reported about one mother in Chongqing who was rebuked by her father for breastfeeding in public. A man said she was "indecent" and "offended public morals." The *Nanfang Metropolis Daily* reported the case of a young mom in Jiangsu province who was verbally abused by a female passenger on the bus for the same reason. Pengqian, "No Room in Public."

176. Pengqian, "No Room in Public." With the exception of the Beijing Zoo.

177. Pengqian, "No Room in Public." According to China.news.com, only one in every eleven major bus stations in Zhengzhou, Henan province, has a room in which mothers can feed their children; the city's thirty-one parks, squares, and high-speed rail stations have no accommodations. Only one of the city's sixty-four shopping malls claimed to provide a feeding room, although that room remains out of service. Pengqian, "No Room in Public."

178. Pengqian.

179. For example, in Canada, although breastfeeding rates among different racial populations do not vary widely, there is a 10 percent disparity in breastfeeding rates between First Nations women and non-indigenous women. "Breastfeeding Initiation in Canada: Key Statistics and Graphics (2009–2010)," Health Canada, Government of Canada, accessed April 12, 2018, https:// www.canada.ca/en/health-canada/services/food-nutrition/food-nutrition -surveillance/health-nutrition-surveys/canadian-community-health-surve-cchs /breastfeeding-initiation-canada-key-statistics-graphics-2009-2010-food -nutrition-surveillance-health-canada.html. A study of Brazilian infant and maternal health reveals significant racial disparities but does not focus on breastfeeding rates. Kwame A. Nyarko et al., "Explaining Racial Disparities in Infant

Health in Brazil," *American Journal of Public Health* 103, no. 9 (September 2013): 1675–84, https://doi.org/10.2105/AJPH.2012.301021.

180. "Employment Insurance Maternity and Parental Benefits," Government of Canada, accessed April 10, 2019, https://www.canada.ca/en/employ ment-social-development/programs/ei/ei-list/reports/maternity-parental.html #h2.0.

181. For the data collection period 2009–2010, the rate for exclusive breast-feeding was 25.9 percent overall. Specifically, 30.2 percent of Asian mothers, 27 percent of Black mothers, and 25.8 percent of White mothers breastfed exclusively. "Duration of Exclusive Breastfeeding in Canada: Key Statistics and Graphics (2009–2010)," Canadian Community Health Survey, Health Canada, accessed November 23, 2018, https://www.canada.ca/en/health-canada /services/food-nutrition/food-nutrition-surveillance/health-nutrition-surveys /canadian-community-health-survey-cchs/duration-exclusive-breastfeeding -canada-key-statistics-graphics-2009-2010.html.

182. Formula feeding can lead to cancer; ear, respiratory and blood infections; asthma; gastroenteritis; diabetes; impaired speech, language, motor, and brain development; and eczema. Lawrence M. Gartner and Arthur I. Eidelman, "Breastfeeding and the Use of Human Milk," *Pediatrics* 115, no. 2 (February 2005): 496; and Ginna Wall, *Outcomes of Breastfeeding versus Formula Feeding* (Bellevue, WA: Evergreen Perinatal Education, 2013), https://www.evergreen perinataleducation.com/upload/OutcomesofBreastfeeding_Nov2013.pdf.

183. Gillian Weaver, "Cashing In on Breastmilk? From Wet Nursing to Milk Banks to Internet Distribution," *Breastfeeding Briefs* 52 (May 2012): 1–9.

184. Approximately $1,000 more a week is standard.

185. Maureen Munchin, *Food for Thought: A Parent's Guide to Food Intolerance* (Oxford, UK: Oxford University Press, 1986); and Robb, "Bring Back the Wet Nurse."

186. Robb, "Bring Back the Wet Nurse." Amy Graff, " 'Cross Nursing': A Small but Growing Trend," *SF Gate* (blog), July 29, 2009, https://blog .sfgate.com/sfmoms/2009/07/29/cross-nursing-a-small-but-growing-trend/. ("A 'Good Morning America' host can hardly keep the skepticism out of her voice as she reports on a pair of best friends who 'share everything—even what many people consider the most intimate act between a mother and child: breast-feeding.' 'The majority of moms,' she hastens to add, 'feel uncomfortable—even repulsed—by the idea.' ")

187. Kimberly Kaplan, "Salma Hayek on Why She Breastfed Another Woman's Baby," *ABC News*, February 11, 2009, https://abcnews.go.com/Enter tainment/story?id=6854285&page=1.

188. "Woman Charged with Nursing Stranger's Baby," *Smoking Gun*, June 3, 2003, http://www.thesmokinggun.com/documents/crime/woman -charged-nursing-strangers-baby.

189. Judy Minami, "Wet Nursing and Cross Nursing," *Leaven* 31, no. 4 (July–August 1995): 53–55.

190. Weaver, "Cashing In on Breastmilk?"

191. Weaver.

192. Prolacta Bioscience, accessed November 5, 2018, http://www.prolacta.com/home.

193. Ricardo Lopez, "Prolacta Develops Niche Delivering Breast Milk to Hospitals," *LA Times*, October 25, 2013.

194. "Milk Bank," *Ebony*, September 1949, 64–66.

195. "Milk Bank," 64–66.

196. Laura Harrison, "Milk Money: Race, Gender, and Breast Milk 'Donation,'" *Signs: Journal of Women in Culture and Society* 44, no. 2 (Winter 2019): 281–306.

197. "Co-op Campaign to Increase Breastfeeding in Urban Areas," Commitments, Clinton Global Initiative, Clinton Foundation, accessed November 30, 2018, https://www.clintonfoundation.org/clinton-global-initiative/commitments/co-op-campaign-increase-breastfeeding-urban-areas; and Harrison, "Milk Money," 288–89.

198. Harrison, 287, 295–96; and Megan Elizabeth Morrissey and Karen Y. Kimball, "#SpoiledMilk: Blacktavists, Visability, and the Exploitation of the Black Breast," *Women's Studies in Communication* 40, no. 1 (2017): 48–49, https://doi.org/10.1080/07491409.2015.1121945.

199. Harrison, "Milk Money," 289–90.

200. Harrison, 291–92; and Morrissey and Kimball, "#SpoiledMilk," 48–66. These activists included Kiddada Green of BMBFA, Afrykayn Moon of Breastfeeding Mothers Unite, Danielle Atkinson of Mothering Justice, Anayah Sangodele-Ayoka of momsrising.org, Kimberly Seals Allers of Mocha Manual, and State Representative Erika Geiss. "An Open Letter to Medolac Laboratories from Detroit Mothers," Black Mothers' Breastfeeding Association, January 12, 2015, http://blackmothersbreastfeeding.org/2015/01/open-letter-to-medolac-laboratories-from-detroit-mothers/; and Kimberly Seals Allers, "Inviting African-American Mothers to Sell Their Breast Milk, and Profiting," *Motherlode* (blog), *New York Times*, December 3, 2014, https://parenting.blogs.nytimes.com/2014/12/03/inviting-african-american-mothers-to-sell-their-breast-milk-and-profiting/.

201. Harrison, "Milk Money," 301–2; and Morrisey and Kimball, "#Spoiled Milk," 62–63.

Chapter 7

1. "Fultz Quads Debut at Zeta Cotillion," *Ebony*, April 1964, 56–61.

2. "Fultz Quads Debut," 56.

3. Lorraine Ahearn, "From Madison, N.C., to Madison Ave.," *News & Record* (Greensboro, NC), August 4, 2002, http://www.greensboro.com/from

-madison-n-c-to-madison-ave/article_e2389602-8fda-59c7-bc08-b99d73fd018c
.html.

4. Lorraine Ahearn, "Corporate Adoptions, Golden Futures," *News & Record* (Greensboro, NC), August 6, 2002, http://www.greensboro.com/corporate
-adoptions-golden-futures/article_2c63a2fb-0ab3-5ab7-860e-f2adaa7a85b6
.html; and Anna R. Hayes, *Without Precedent: The Life of Susie Marshall Sharp* (Chapel Hill: University of North Carolina Press, 2008), 89.

5. Lorraine Ahearn, "Four Sisters, One Love," *News & Record* (Greensboro, NC), August 6, 2002, http://www.greensboro.com/four-sisters-one-love/arti
cle_cdccc43c-bd23-5e85-931f-2ad69c4a1f40.html.

6. Ahearn, "Corporate Adoptions, Golden Futures."

7. Ahearn.

8. Ahearn.

9. Ahearn.

10. James Avery, "African-American Pioneers in the Corporate Sector," Black Economic Development, February 12, 2011, http://www.blackeconomic
development.com/african-american-pioneers-in-the-corporate-sector/33110/.

11. "Introducing: Mrs. Louise R. Prothro," *Pittsburgh Courier*, April 30, 1955, 9.

12. "Noted Home Economist Listed as Commentator for 'Best of Seven,'" *Indianapolis Recorder*, October 26, 1957, https://newspapers.library.in.gov/cgi
-bin/indiana?a=d&d=INR19571026-01.1.5; and "Krey Puts a Smile in Canned Cookery," *Pittsburgh Courier*, January 14, 1956, 8, http://fultonhistory.com
/Newspapers%2023/Pittsburgh%20PA%20Courier/Pittsburgh%20PA%20Cou
rier%201956/Pittsburgh%20PA%20Courier%201956%20%20-%200062.pdf.

13. "Mrs. Louise R. Prothro," 9; "Cooking Is Fun," *Washington Afro-American*, August 31, 1957, 10, https://news.google.com/newspapers?id=7rg9
AAAAIBAJ&sjid=5ysMAAAAIBAJ&pg=844%2C13081652; and "Krey Puts a Smile."

14. Ahearn, "Corporate Adoptions, Golden Futures."

15. Mary Frances Berry, *The Pig Farmer's Daughter and Other Tales of American Justice* (New York: Vintage Books, 1999).

16. "Matt Ingram Trial (1951–1953)," Caswell County Historical Association, December 5, 2005, http://nccha.blogspot.com/2005/12/mack-ingram
-trial-1951-1953.html; and Mary Frances Berry, "'Reckless Eyeballing': The Matt Ingram Case and the Denial of African American Sexual Freedom," *Journal of African-American History* 93, no. 2 (April 2008): 223–34, https://doi
.org/10.1086/JAAHv93n2p223.

17. Ahearn, "Four Sisters, One Love."

18. Melba Newsome, "I Think It Was the Shots," *O, The Oprah Magazine*, April 1, 2005, 232.

19. Charles L. Sanders, "The Fultz Quads: Grown-Up, Disappointed and Bitter," *Ebony*, November 1968, 218; "Quadruplet Girls Seek Music Careers at

Bethune-Cookman," *Daytona Beach Morning Journal*, June 17, 1965, 13; and "Fultz Quads Attend Bethune-Cookman for Summer Session," *Pittsburgh Courier*, July 17, 1965, 6.

20. Sanders, "Grown-Up, Disappointed and Bitter," 220.

21. Sanders, 213, 220.

22. Sanders, 212.

23. Sanders, 213–14.

24. Sanders, 214.

25. Sanders, 214.

26. Sanders, 214.

27. Sanders, 214.

28. Ahearn, "From Madison, N.C., to Madison Ave."

29. Sanders, "Grown-Up, Disappointed and Bitter," 217.

30. Sanders, 216.

31. Sanders, 216.

32. Newsome, "I Think It Was the Shots," 232.

33. Frances M. Ward, "Seeing Double Times Two," *News & Record* (Greensboro, NC), May 22, 1990, http://www.greensboro.com/seeing-double-times-two-famous-foursome-make-their-mark-as/article_80d5c093-598c-55e1-8d39-32d59b090368.html.

34. Gay Pauley, "Fultz Quadruplets Aim for Careers in Music, Fashions," *Washington Afro-American*, May 4, 1971.

35. Ahearn, "From Madison, N.C., to Madison Ave."

36. Sanders, "Grown-Up, Disappointed and Bitter," 216.

37. Ahearn, "Four Sisters, One Love."

38. Sanders, "Grown-Up, Disappointed and Bitter," 222.

39. Newsome, "I Think It Was the Shots," 232.

40. Ahearn, "What Ever Happened to Alice's Baby?"

41. Ahearn.

42. Ahearn.

43. Ahearn.

44. Ahearn, "Corporate Adoptions, Golden Futures."

45. Ahearn.

46. Jim Schlosser, "Memories of Murder," *News & Record* (Greensboro, NC), June 3, 1995, http://www.greensboro.com/memories-of-murder/article_981baf03-4f07-5413-b29e-3d3461b6b71f.html. Jerry Bledsoe provides a fascinating account of these murders and of Fred Klenner's life in *Bitter Blood: A True Story of Southern Family Pride, Madness, and Multiple Murder* (New York: Dutton, 1988).

47. Ahearn, "Corporate Adoptions, Golden Futures."

48. Ahearn, "Four Sisters, One Love."

49. Ahearn, "What Ever Happened to Alice's Baby?"

50. Ahearn.

51. Ward, "Seeing Double Times Two."

52. Ward.

53. Michelle Cater, "'Quad' Sister Dies at Age 55," *News & Record* (Greensboro, NC), October 9, 2001, http://www.greensboro.com/quad-sister-dies-at-age-reidsville-s-mary-alice-fultz/article_cd9cfc35-ca79-50f7-8504-408c9498da2d.html.

54. Ahearn, "What Ever Happened to Alice's Baby?"

55. Lorraine Ahearn, "And Then There Was One," *News & Record* (Greensboro, NC), August 3, 2002, http://www.greensboro.com/and-then-there-was-one-they-were-four-of-the/article_7d5869a7-3b2b-5b7d-b5d0-044464d8aba3.html; and Ahearn, "Four Sisters, One Love."

56. Newsome, "I Think It Was the Shots," 232.

57. Ahearn, "And Then There Was One."

58. Ahearn, "From Madison, N.C., to Madison Ave."

59. Ahearn, "Four Sisters, One Love."

60. Ahearn.

61. Ahearn, "Corporate Adoptions, Golden Futures."

62. Newsome, "I Think It Was the Shots," 232.

63. Ahearn, "What Ever Happened to Alice's Baby?"

64. Ahearn, "Four Sisters, One Love."

65. Ahearn.

66. Brown v. Board of Education, 347 U.S. 483 (1954).

67. This Facebook post, with the accompanying GoFundMe campaign, has since been removed. Other posts express a similar sentiment: "My mother and Aunts were used." The Fultz Quads My Family and Our Stories, Facebook, June 14, 2015, https://www.facebook.com/plugins/post.php?href=https%3A%2F%2Fwww.facebook.com%2FTFQds%2Fposts%2F667168103427016.

Conclusion

1. Wilaiporn Rojjanasrirat and Valmi D. Sousa, "Perceptions of Breastfeeding and Planned Return to Work or School among Low-Income Pregnant Women in the USA," *Journal of Clinical Nursing* 19, no. 13/14 (July 2010): 2019.

2. Linda Villarosa, "Why America's Black Mothers and Babies Are in a Life-or-Death Crisis," *New York Times*, April 11, 2018, https://www.nytimes.com/2018/04/11/magazine/black-mothers-babies-death-maternal-mortality.html.

3. Citizens United v. FEC, 558 U.S. 310 (2009).

4. Burwell v. Hobby Lobby Stores, Inc., 134 S. Ct. 2751 (2014).

5. *Black-ish*, season 4, episode 2, "Mother Nature," directed by Ken Whittingham, written by Corey Nickerson, featuring Anthony Anderson and Tracee Ellis Ross, aired October 10, 2017, on ABC.

6. Nicola Fumo, "Gap Applauded by Moms for Breastfeeding Post," *Forbes*, February 26, 2018, https://www.forbes.com/sites/nicolafumo/2018/02/26/gap-breastfeeding-instagram-ad/#b0a95a562c8c.

7. Alison Bowen, "Model for Gap Paused to Breastfeed Toddler during a Shoot. The Moment Became the Campaign," *Chicago Tribune*, February 26, 2018, https://www.chicagotribune.com/lifestyles/ct-life-gap-ad-model-breast feeding-baby-0226-story.html.

8. Angela Johnson, Rosalind Kirk, and Maria Muzik, "Overcoming Workplace Barriers: A Focus Group Study Exploring African American Mothers' Needs for Workplace Breastfeeding Support," *Journal of Human Lactation* 31, no. 3 (August 2015): 425–33, https://doi.org/10.1177/0890334415573001; Angela Johnson et al., "Enhancing Breastfeeding Rates among African American Women: A Systematic Review of Current Psychosocial Interventions," *Journal of the Academy of Breastfeeding Medicine* 10, no. 1 (January/February 2015): 45–62, https://doi.org/10.1089/bfm.2014.0023; Ifeyinwa V. Asiodu et al., "Infant Feeding Decision-Making and the Influences of Social Support Persons among First-Time African American Mothers," *Maternal and Child Health Journal* 21, no. 4 (April 2017): 863–72, https://doi.org/10.1007/s10995-016-2167-x; Ifeyinwa Asiodu and Jacquelyn H. Flaskerud, "Got Milk? A Look at Breastfeeding from an African American Perspective," *Issues in Mental Health Nursing* 32, no. 8 (July 2011): 544–46; and Chelsea O. McKinney et al., "Racial and Ethnic Differences in Breastfeeding," *Pediatrics* 138, no. 2 (August 2016): 1–11, https://doi.org/10.1016/j.apnr.2017.07.009.

9. Black Women Do Breastfeed, accessed November 30, 2018, https://black womendobreastfeed.org/.

10. Breanna Edwards, "Chocolate Milk Mommies Encourage Black Women to Breast-Feed in Stunning Photoshoot," *Root*, December 7, 2017, https://thegrapevine.theroot.com/chocolate-milk-mommies-encourage-black-women-to-breastf-1821080884.

11. Lakisha Cohill (@hc_incorporated), "I Make Chocolate Milk What's Your Super Power," Instagram photo, October 3, 2017, https://www.instagram.com/p/BZzsnA1gyIa.

INDEX